7.95

D0598988

Another Simply Delicious Cookbook

The

Love

of

Eating

by Renny Darling

Author of "The Joy of Eating"

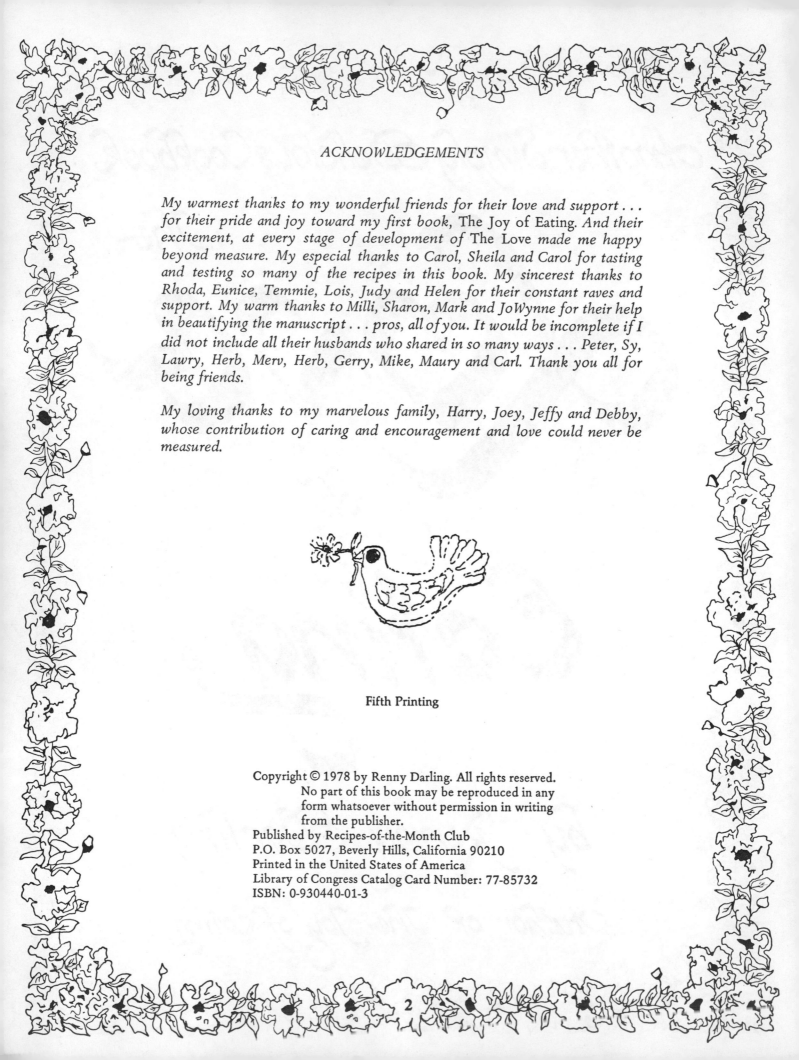

ACKNOWLEDGEMENTS

My warmest thanks to my wonderful friends for their love and support . . . for their pride and joy toward my first book, The Joy of Eating. *And their excitement, at every stage of development of* The Love *made me happy beyond measure. My especial thanks to Carol, Sheila and Carol for tasting and testing so many of the recipes in this book. My sincerest thanks to Rhoda, Eunice, Temmie, Lois, Judy and Helen for their constant raves and support. My warm thanks to Milli, Sharon, Mark and JoWynne for their help in beautifying the manuscript . . . pros, all of you. It would be incomplete if I did not include all their husbands who shared in so many ways . . . Peter, Sy, Lawry, Herb, Merv, Herb, Gerry, Mike, Maury and Carl. Thank you all for being friends.*

My loving thanks to my marvelous family, Harry, Joey, Jeffy and Debby, whose contribution of caring and encouragement and love could never be measured.

Fifth Printing

Copyright © 1978 by Renny Darling. All rights reserved.
No part of this book may be reproduced in any
form whatsoever without permission in writing
from the publisher.
Published by Recipes-of-the-Month Club
P.O. Box 5027, Beverly Hills, California 90210
Printed in the United States of America
Library of Congress Catalog Card Number: 77-85732
ISBN: 0-930440-01-3

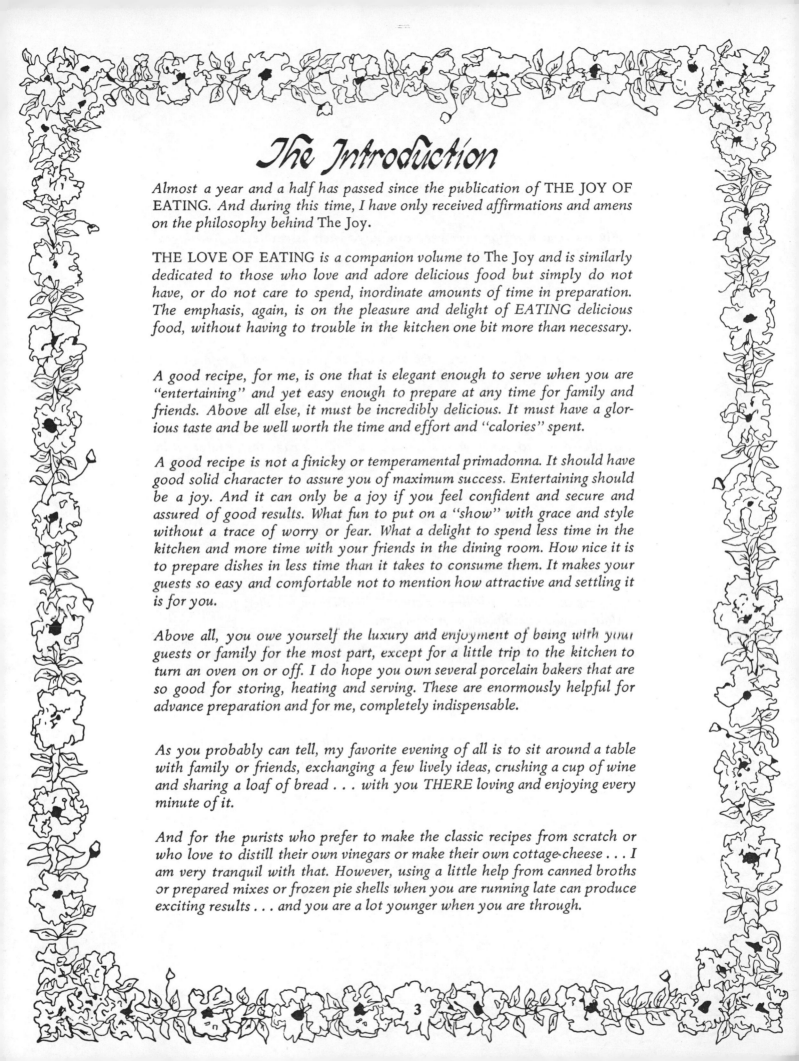

The Introduction

Almost a year and a half has passed since the publication of THE JOY OF EATING. And during this time, I have only received affirmations and amens on the philosophy behind The Joy.

THE LOVE OF EATING is a companion volume to The Joy and is similarly dedicated to those who love and adore delicious food but simply do not have, or do not care to spend, inordinate amounts of time in preparation. The emphasis, again, is on the pleasure and delight of EATING delicious food, without having to trouble in the kitchen one bit more than necessary.

A good recipe, for me, is one that is elegant enough to serve when you are "entertaining" and yet easy enough to prepare at any time for family and friends. Above all else, it must be incredibly delicious. It must have a glorious taste and be well worth the time and effort and "calories" spent.

A good recipe is not a finicky or temperamental primadonna. It should have good solid character to assure you of maximum success. Entertaining should be a joy. And it can only be a joy if you feel confident and secure and assured of good results. What fun to put on a "show" with grace and style without a trace of worry or fear. What a delight to spend less time in the kitchen and more time with your friends in the dining room. How nice it is to prepare dishes in less time than it takes to consume them. It makes your guests so easy and comfortable not to mention how attractive and settling it is for you.

Above all, you owe yourself the luxury and enjoyment of being with your guests or family for the most part, except for a little trip to the kitchen to turn an oven on or off. I do hope you own several porcelain bakers that are so good for storing, heating and serving. These are enormously helpful for advance preparation and for me, completely indispensable.

As you probably can tell, my favorite evening of all is to sit around a table with family or friends, exchanging a few lively ideas, crushing a cup of wine and sharing a loaf of bread . . . with you THERE loving and enjoying every minute of it.

And for the purists who prefer to make the classic recipes from scratch or who love to distill their own vinegars or make their own cottage-cheese . . . I am very tranquil with that. However, using a little help from canned broths or prepared mixes or frozen pie shells when you are running late can produce exciting results . . . and you are a lot younger when you are through.

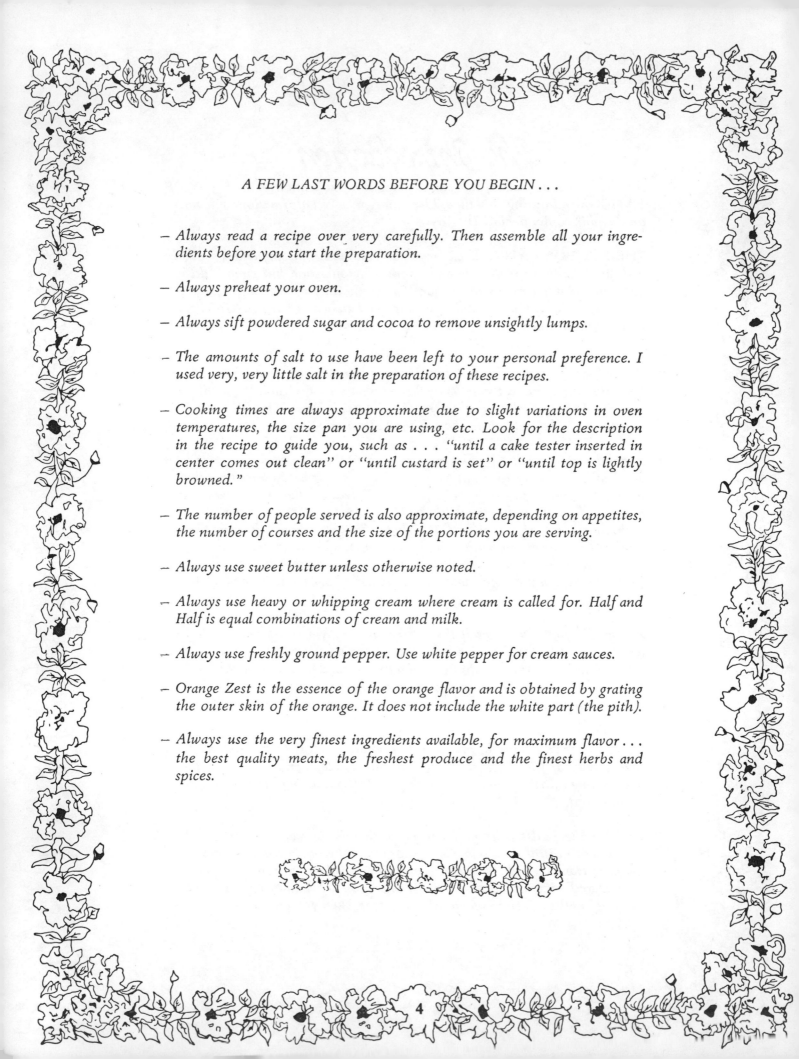

A FEW LAST WORDS BEFORE YOU BEGIN . . .

— *Always read a recipe over very carefully. Then assemble all your ingredients before you start the preparation.*

— *Always preheat your oven.*

— *Always sift powdered sugar and cocoa to remove unsightly lumps.*

— *The amounts of salt to use have been left to your personal preference. I used very, very little salt in the preparation of these recipes.*

— *Cooking times are always approximate due to slight variations in oven temperatures, the size pan you are using, etc. Look for the description in the recipe to guide you, such as . . . "until a cake tester inserted in center comes out clean" or "until custard is set" or "until top is lightly browned."*

— *The number of people served is also approximate, depending on appetites, the number of courses and the size of the portions you are serving.*

— *Always use sweet butter unless otherwise noted.*

— *Always use heavy or whipping cream where cream is called for. Half and Half is equal combinations of cream and milk.*

— *Always use freshly ground pepper. Use white pepper for cream sauces.*

— *Orange Zest is the essence of the orange flavor and is obtained by grating the outer skin of the orange. It does not include the white part (the pith).*

— *Always use the very finest ingredients available, for maximum flavor . . . the best quality meats, the freshest produce and the finest herbs and spices.*

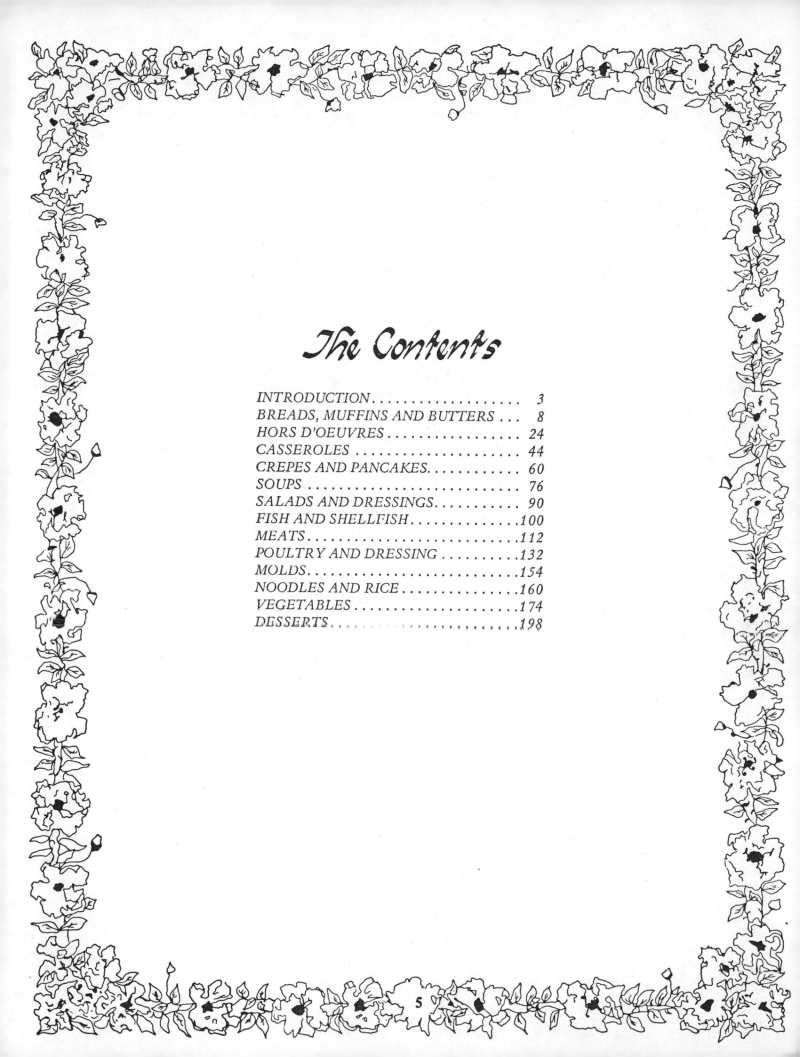

The Contents

This book
is dedicated to

all those beautiful people
from all over the country
and other parts of the world
for their affectionate letters and phone calls.

Breads, Muffins & Butters

Instant 2-Minute Onion Poppy Seed Bread

You will enjoy serving hot fresh bread some evening soon. This delectable bread requires no kneading, punching, rising. You will feel like a magician, just stirring and making bread.

3 cups self-rising flour
3 tablespoons sugar
1 can (12 ounces) beer at *room temperature*
2 tablespoons dried minced onions
1 tablespoon poppy seeds

2 teaspoons salad oil

In the large bowl of your electric mixer, place the first 5 ingredients. Beat at low speed for 1 minute or until the mixture is smooth. Pour batter into 2 4x8-inch greased loaf pans. Brush 1 teaspoon salad oil over each loaf.

Bake in a 350° oven for 45 minutes or until top is golden brown and a knife inserted in center comes out clean. Cool in pans for 5 minutes. Then remove from pans and finish cooling on a rack. Serve with sweet whipped butter. Makes 2 loaves.

Instant Cheese & Onion Croissants

3 ounces butter or margarine (3/4 stick)
1 cup cottage cheese (can use the lo-fat)
pinch of salt

1 teaspoon sugar
2 tablespoons grated Parmesan cheese
1 teaspoon dehydrated onion flakes

1 cup Wondra flour (quick mixing flour)

In the large bowl of your electric mixer, beat together the butter, cottage cheese and salt until the mixture is well blended. Add the remaining ingredients and beat for two minutes, at medium speed, until mixture is smooth.

Divide dough into thirds. Roll each third out on a floured pastry cloth (use a stocking on your rolling pin, too) until circle measures about 10 inches. Cut dough into 8 triangular wedges. Roll each triangle from the wide end toward the center and curve into a crescent.

Place croissants on a lightly buttered cookie sheet and bake them at 350° for about 30 or 35 minutes or until they are a deep golden brown. Remove from pan and allow to cool on a brown paper bag. Makes 24 croissants.

Swiss Puffs for Soups or Salads

1 package frozen patty shells (6), defrosted

1-1/4 cups grated Swiss cheese
3 teaspoons chopped chives

water
grated Parmesan cheese

Roll each patty shell out to measure a 6-inch square. Sprinkle about 3 table-spoons Swiss cheese over the top and sprinkle top with about 1/2 teaspoon chopped chives. Roll the shell up 3 times, jelly roll fashion, tuck in the ends, and place on a teflon-coated baking pan, seam-side down. Brush top with a little water and sprinkle generously with grated Parmesan cheese.

Bake in a 400° oven for about 25 minutes or until top is a deep golden brown. Cut the cheese puffs in half with a serrated knife and serve warm. Serves 6.

Note – Cheese puffs can be made earlier in the day and reheated at time of serving.

Swiss Puffs with Cheese & Currants

Substitute 6 teaspoons black currants for the chives in the above recipe. Prepare and bake in the same manner.

Note – This is such an exciting taste that I hope you don't overlook it, placed as it is, on the bottom of the page.

Beaten Biscuits

There has been a great deal of controversy lately on the whole subject of Beaten Biscuits. Traditionally, they are beaten with a rolling pin or a hammer for 30 minutes . . . which, of course, I would never ask anyone to do. However, I became intrigued with the whole commotion and I experimented with Thelma Linton's recipe. The results were a biscuit, crisp like a cracker, but with a taste and texture that I feel you might enjoy.

I had to make several changes in the recipe, so that the stiff dough could be handled in my mixer (Kitchen Aid). I used the paddle. I am telling you this because the dough is very stiff and a lightweight mixer might not be able to handle it.

In any case, the biscuits were delicious with sweet butter and jam . . . the kids loved them and so did their friends.

3 cups sifted flour
1/2 teaspoon salt
1/3 cup shortening
3/4 cup cold milk

Combine all the ingredients in your large mixer bowl and beat the dough at medium speed for 20 to 25 minutes. Dough will be smooth, but very stiff. Roll dough out on a floured pastry cloth until it is 1/3-inch thick. Cut biscuits with a 2-inch biscuit cutter. Pierce with the tines of a fork and bake on a greased cookie sheet at 400° for 20 minutes. Makes 24 biscuits. Serve warm or at room temperature . . . warm is better.

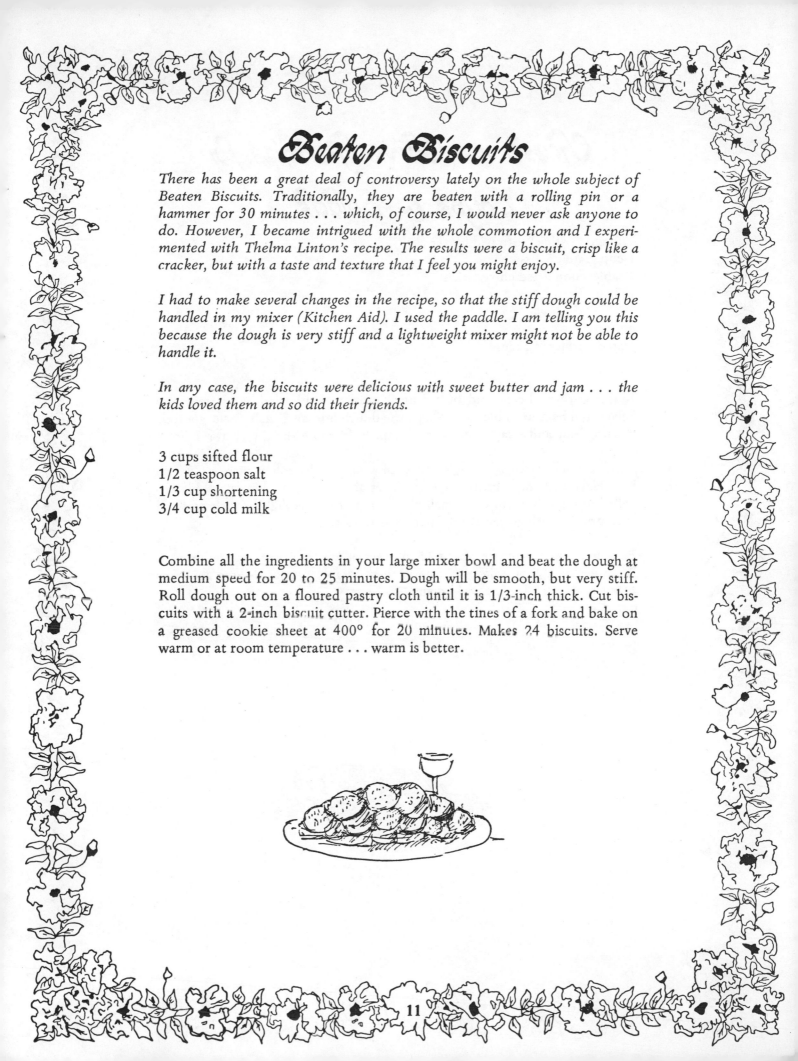

Cheese & Chive Pennies for Soups & Salads

1/2 cup (1 stick) softened butter
1 cup grated Swiss cheese
1 tablespoon dried chive flakes
2/3 cup flour

mustard
grated Parmesan cheese

Beat together cheese and butter until mixture is blended. Add flour and chives and beat until blended. Shape the dough into an 8-inch circle, sprinkle it with flour and wrap it in plastic wrap. Refrigerate the dough for 1 hour.

Pinch a small piece of dough and with your hands, roll it into a 1/2-inch ball. Place balls on a greased cookie sheet about 1-1/2 inches apart. Flatten balls with the bottom of a small glass. Brush the tops lightly with mustard and sprinkle with grated Parmesan cheese to taste.

Bake in a 350° oven for about 15 minutes or until tops are a golden brown. Serve with soups or salad for a never-to-be-forgotten treat. Makes about 20 pennies, about 1-1/2 inches in diameter.

Garlic & Herb French Bread

1 large French bread, cut in half lengthwise

1/2 pound butter (2 sticks), softened
4 tablespoons olive oil
2 cloves garlic, mashed
1/2 cup grated Parmesan cheese
1/2 teaspoon Italian Herb Seasoning

paprika

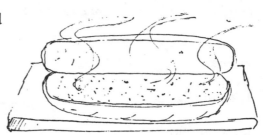

Slice French bread in half, lengthwise. Combine next five ingredients and beat to blend thoroughly. Spread half the butter mixture on each half of the French bread. Sprinkle with paprika generously. Cut slices into bread about 2/3 through. Wrap each half of the loaf in foil and heat in a 400° oven for 15 minutes. Serves 8.

French Bread with Garlic & Cheese

French bread slices
butter, at room temperature
garlic powder
grated Parmesan cheese
paprika

Cover bread slices generously with butter. Sprinkle with garlic powder. Dip the buttered side of the bread slice into the grated cheese. Sprinkle top lightly with paprika.

Place bread slices on a cookie sheet and broil until lightly browned.

Italian Bread with Garlic & Cheese

Substitute olive oil for the butter in the above recipe. Proceed in the same fashion on Italian bread slices.

Apple Bread with Toasted Walnuts

This is one of my preferred sweet breads. It is moist and delicious and so good with whipped cream cheese or sweet butter.

2 eggs
1 cup sugar
1/2 cup salad oil

1-1/4 cup flour
1 teaspoon baking powder
1/2 teaspoon baking soda
1/4 teaspoon salt
1 teaspoon cinnamon

1 cup grated apples (about 2 medium apples, peeled, cored and grated)
1 cup toasted walnuts, coarsely chopped
1 teaspoon vanilla

Beat together the eggs, sugar and salad oil for about 2 minutes at medium speed. Add the flour, baking powder, baking soda, salt and cinnamon all at once and beat until blended. Stir in the apples, walnuts and vanilla.

Pour mixture into 3 baby loaf pans that have been greased and lightly floured. Place pans on a cookie sheet and bake in a 350° oven for 40 to 45 minutes or until a cake tester inserted in center comes out clean. Yields 3 baby loafs 6x3-1/2x2 inches.

Walnut Raisin Butter

1/2 cup butter, softened
1/4 cup finely chopped toasted walnuts
1/4 cup golden raisins, plumped in orange juice and finely chopped
2 tablespoons cinnamon sugar

Cream butter until light and fluffy. Add remaining ingredients and blend. Serve with hot bread or muffins.

Banana Bread
with Chocolate Chips & Walnuts

For brunch or snacking this moist, delicious sweet bread will thrill your family and friends.

2 bananas, mashed
1-1/8 cups sugar
1/2 cup orange juice
2 eggs
1/4 cup (1/2 stick) butter, softened
1 teaspoon vanilla

2 cups flour
2 teaspoons baking powder
1/2 teaspoon baking soda
1/8 teaspoon salt

1 cup chocolate chips, semi-sweet
1 cup chopped walnuts

Beat together the first six ingredients until blended. Add the dry ingredients all at once and stir until mixture is moistened. Do not overmix. Stir in chocolate and nuts.

Divide mixture evenly between *two* greased and floured 4x8-inch foil loaf pans. Bake at 350° for about 45 to 50 minutes or until a cake tester inserted in center comes out clean. Cool in pan on a rack. Makes 2 heavenly loaves.

Note — Bread freezes beautifully. Wrap in double thickness of plastic wrap and foil. Remove wrappers to defrost.

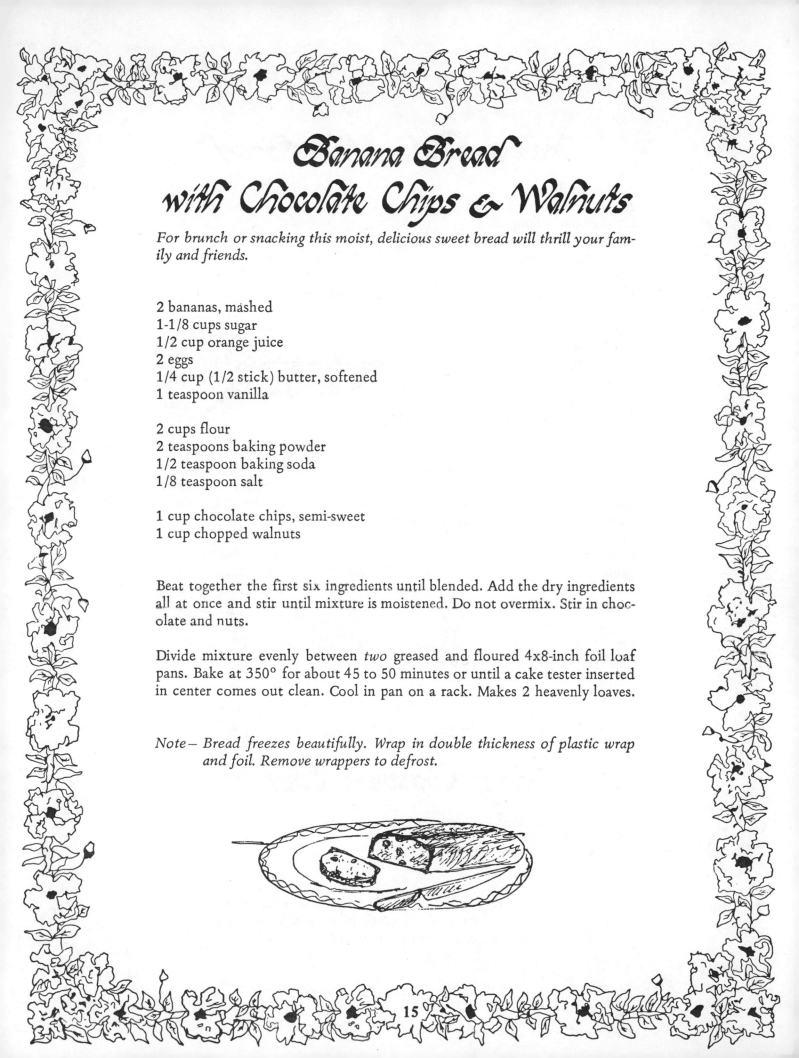

Orange Date Nut Bread

2-1/4 cups flour
2 teaspoons baking powder
1/2 teaspoon baking soda
1/4 teaspoon salt

2 eggs
1/2 orange, grated (remove any large pieces of membrane)
1 cup buttermilk
1 cup sugar
1/4 cup melted butter
1 teaspoon vanilla

1 cup chopped walnuts
1 cup moist, pitted dates, finely chopped

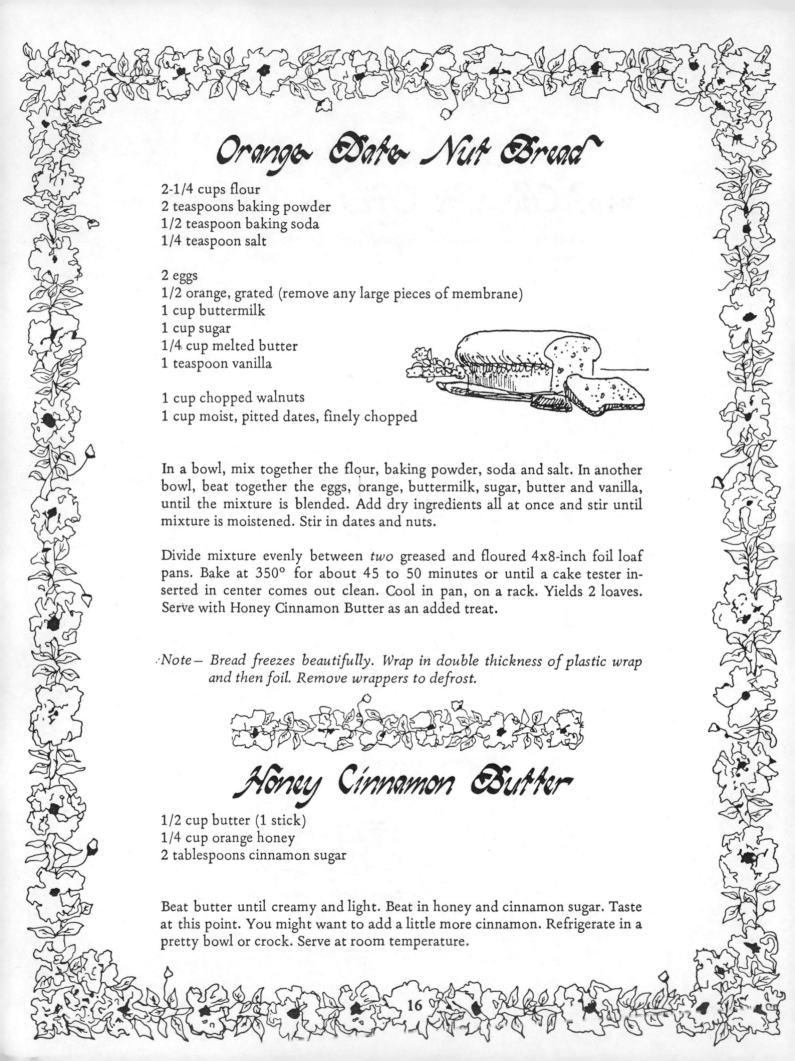

In a bowl, mix together the flour, baking powder, soda and salt. In another bowl, beat together the eggs, orange, buttermilk, sugar, butter and vanilla, until the mixture is blended. Add dry ingredients all at once and stir until mixture is moistened. Stir in dates and nuts.

Divide mixture evenly between *two* greased and floured 4x8-inch foil loaf pans. Bake at 350° for about 45 to 50 minutes or until a cake tester inserted in center comes out clean. Cool in pan, on a rack. Yields 2 loaves. Serve with Honey Cinnamon Butter as an added treat.

·Note— Bread freezes beautifully. Wrap in double thickness of plastic wrap and then foil. Remove wrappers to defrost.

Honey Cinnamon Butter

1/2 cup butter (1 stick)
1/4 cup orange honey
2 tablespoons cinnamon sugar

Beat butter until creamy and light. Beat in honey and cinnamon sugar. Taste at this point. You might want to add a little more cinnamon. Refrigerate in a pretty bowl or crock. Serve at room temperature.

Sour Cream Pumpkin Bread with Walnuts & Raisins

1 package (18-1/2 ounces) yellow cake mix
1-1/2 cups canned pumpkin
1/4 cup sour cream
2 eggs
2 teaspoons pumpkin pie spice
1 teaspoon baking soda
1 tablespoon grated orange peel

1 cup chopped walnuts
1 cup yellow raisins

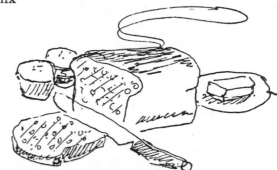

In your large mixer bowl, place first seven ingredients and beat for 3 minutes at medium speed. Stir in the walnuts and raisins. Pour batter into 4 little loaf pans, 5x2-1/2 inches, that have been greased and lightly floured.

Bake in a 350° oven for 35 minutes or until a cake tester inserted in center comes out clean. Allow to cool for 15 minutes and then invert on a rack. Makes 4 baby loaves.

Cherry Heering Butter

1/2 cup butter
1 cup sifted powdered sugar
2 tablespoons Cherry Heering Liqueur

Beat butter with sugar until it is light and fluffy. Add liqueur and beat until it is blended. Makes 1 cup of whipped butter.

Zucchini Bread with Raisins & Walnuts

1 cup flour
1 cup sugar
1 teaspoon baking powder
1/2 teaspoon baking soda
1/4 teaspoon salt
1 teaspooon cinnamon

2 eggs
1/2 cup salad oil
1 teaspoon vanilla

2 medium zucchini, peeled and grated (about 1 cup). If you do not mind
    green flecks in your bread (which I do) you need not peel the zucchini.
1 cup walnuts, chopped
1 cup golden raisins

Combine first 6 ingredients and set aside. Beat together the eggs, oil and
vanilla until blended. Add the dry ingredients, all at once, and beat until
thoroughly blended. Beat in the zucchini, walnuts and raisins.

Divide mixture into 3 baby loaf pans that have been greased and lightly
floured. Bake in a 350° oven for 40 to 45 minutes or until a cake tester,
inserted in center, comes out clean. Serve with cream cheese or whipped
butter.

Yields 3 baby loafs 6x3-1/2x2 inches.

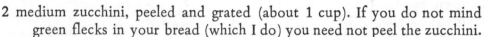

Orange Butter

1/2 cup butter, softened
1/2 cup orange marmalade

Cream butter until light and fluffy. Add orange marmalade and blend well.
Chill. Serve with toasted bread or muffins. Makes 1 cup.

Cherry Almond Muffins

2 cups flour
2 teaspoons baking powder
1/2 teaspoon salt

6 tablespoons sugar
3 tablespoons melted butter
2 eggs, beaten
1-1/2 cups sour cream

1 cup chopped toasted almonds
1/2 cup glazed cherries, finely chopped

Combine flour, baking powder and salt. Set aside. Beat together the sugar, butter, eggs and sour cream. Combine flour mixture and egg mixture all at once and mix together until the dry ingredients are just moistened. Do not overmix. Add almonds and cherries and mix them in quickly.

Line two muffin pans with 24 paper liners. Fill each muffin cup with 1 heaping tablespoon of batter. Bake at 400° for about 20 minutes or until a cake tester inserted in the center comes out clean. Makes 24 muffins.

Cream Cheese & Honey Butter

1/4 cup butter, softened
1/4 cup cream cheese, softened
1/3 cup orange honey
1 teaspoon grated orange peel

Cream butter with cream cheese until light and fluffy. Add honey and grated orange peel and blend well. Chill. Serve with toasted English muffins or raisin bread. Makes about 1 cup.

Dark & Fruity Bran Muffins

2 cups whole wheat flour
1-1/2 cups 100% All-Bran cereal
1-1/2 cups sugar
1/4 teaspoon salt
1 teaspoon baking soda

1 cup milk
1 cup sour cream
1 egg, beaten
1/2 cup honey
1/4 cup soft butter
1 orange, grated (remove any large pieces of membrane)
1 cup golden raisins (plumped overnight in orange juice)
1 teaspoon vanilla

Combine the dry ingredients in the first group. Combine the ingredients in the second group and mix together. Add the dry ingredients to the moist ingredients all at once and mix until even. Do not overmix. Divide mixture among 24 paper muffin cups; place in 2 muffin pans (12 each) and bake at 350° for about 25 minutes or until a cake tester inserted in center comes out clean. Makes 24 muffins.

Note — Muffins freeze beautifully.
  — Serve them warm with lots of sweet butter.
  — As a lovely extra, you may enjoy serving them with Almond Butter.

Almond Butter

1/2 cup butter (1 stick), unsalted and slightly softened (if butter is too soft, it will become oily)
1 cup sifted powdered sugar
1 teaspoon almond extract
1/4 cup finely chopped toasted almonds

Cream butter until it is light. Slowly beat in powdered sugar, almond extract and chopped almonds. Place butter in a crock and refrigerate before serving. Makes about 1 cup flavored butter.

Honey Apple Bran Muffins

2 cups raisin bran cereal
3/4 cup orange juice
1 egg, beaten
1/4 cup oil
2 tablespoons honey

1 apple, peeled, cored and grated

1 cup flour
2-1/2 teaspoons baking powder
1/2 teaspoon salt
2 teaspoons cinnamon
1/2 cup sugar
1 tablespoon grated orange peel

Stir together the raisin bran, orange juice, egg, oil and honey until the mixture is blended. Stir in the apple. Add the remaining ingredients all at once and stir until the mixture is moistened and even. Do not overmix.

Divide the batter between 12 paper-lined muffin cups and bake in a 400° oven for 25 minutes or until a cake tester inserted in center comes out clean. Makes 12 muffins.

Note — *These muffins freeze beautifully.*
   — *Serve them warm with sweet, creamy whipped butter.*

Almond Strawberry Butter

1/4 cup butter, softened
1/4 cup cream cheese, softened
1/4 cup toasted slivered almonds
1/2 cup strawberry preserves

Cream butter and cream cheese until light and fluffy. Add remaining ingredients and blend. Chill. Makes 1-1/4 cups.

Banana Orange Bran Muffins

1 cup Raisin Bran Flake Cereal
1/2 cup All Bran Cereal
3/4 cup orange juice
1 egg, beaten
1/4 cup oil

1 banana, mashed
1/2 orange, grated (remove any large pieces of membrane but use the peel, juice and pulp)

1 cup flour
2-1/2 teaspoons baking powder
1/2 teaspoon salt
2 teaspoons cinnamon
1/2 cup sugar

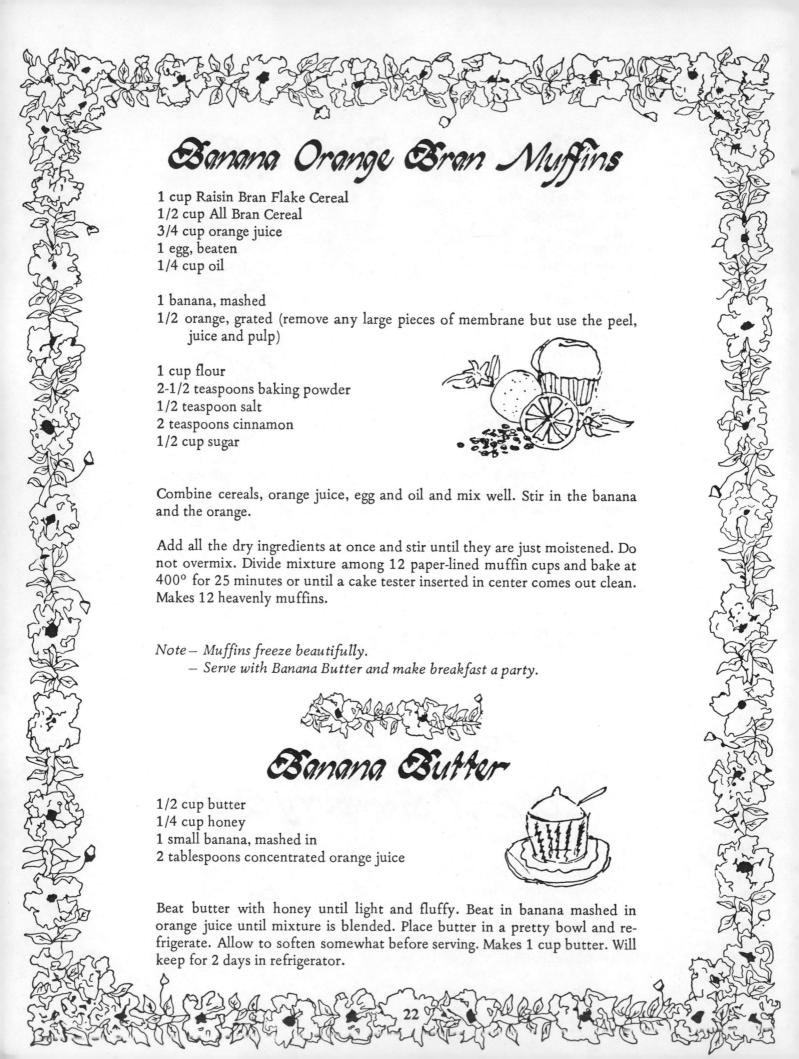

Combine cereals, orange juice, egg and oil and mix well. Stir in the banana and the orange.

Add all the dry ingredients at once and stir until they are just moistened. Do not overmix. Divide mixture among 12 paper-lined muffin cups and bake at 400° for 25 minutes or until a cake tester inserted in center comes out clean. Makes 12 heavenly muffins.

Note — Muffins freeze beautifully.
— Serve with Banana Butter and make breakfast a party.

Banana Butter

1/2 cup butter
1/4 cup honey
1 small banana, mashed in
2 tablespoons concentrated orange juice

Beat butter with honey until light and fluffy. Beat in banana mashed in orange juice until mixture is blended. Place butter in a pretty bowl and refrigerate. Allow to soften somewhat before serving. Makes 1 cup butter. Will keep for 2 days in refrigerator.

Hors D'Oeuvres & Small Entrees

I sometimes wonder what it is about dunking that is just fun, fun, fun. I cannot imagine people, not liking each other and dunking together. I cannot even picture a person sitting around a table, dunking and having a gloomy or grumpy look on his face. It seems almost impossible to dunk without chattering and laughing and feeling friendly. What fun, to sit around a table with family or friends, dunking into a heaven-sent Fondue Swiss, all the while bubbling with conversation and sparkling with laughter.

Yes, yes, yes. . . fondues are fun! Cheese fondues are notable for their utter simplicity and complete ease of preparation. Use a good quality Swiss or Gruyere cheese and grate it on the third largest size of the conventional four-side grater. Store the cheese in a plastic bag until ready to use. If you do not have a fondue maker, use an alcohol burner and a chafing dish and adjust the flame so that the cheese remains hot with a slow bubble.

Cheese fondues usually are made with white wine and Kirsch. The following recipe is my absolute favorite and is made with champagne. Use long forks or spears, piercing the soft part of the bread first and then the crust so that the bread is more secure. Dip the bread into the bubbly fondue and stir it around and around until it is completely coated. Give it a turn or two as you lift it out to avoid dripping. And then one bite . . . one bite is worth my thousand words.

Instant Fondue Swiss with Chives & Champagne

1 pound Swiss cheese, grated and tossed with 4 teaspoons flour

2 tablespoons butter
1 clove garlic, put through a press
1/4 cup finely chopped chives (or use 1 heaping tablespoon dried chives)

1-1/2 cups champagne
2 teaspoons Dijon-style mustard
pinch of salt and white pepper
pinch of nutmeg

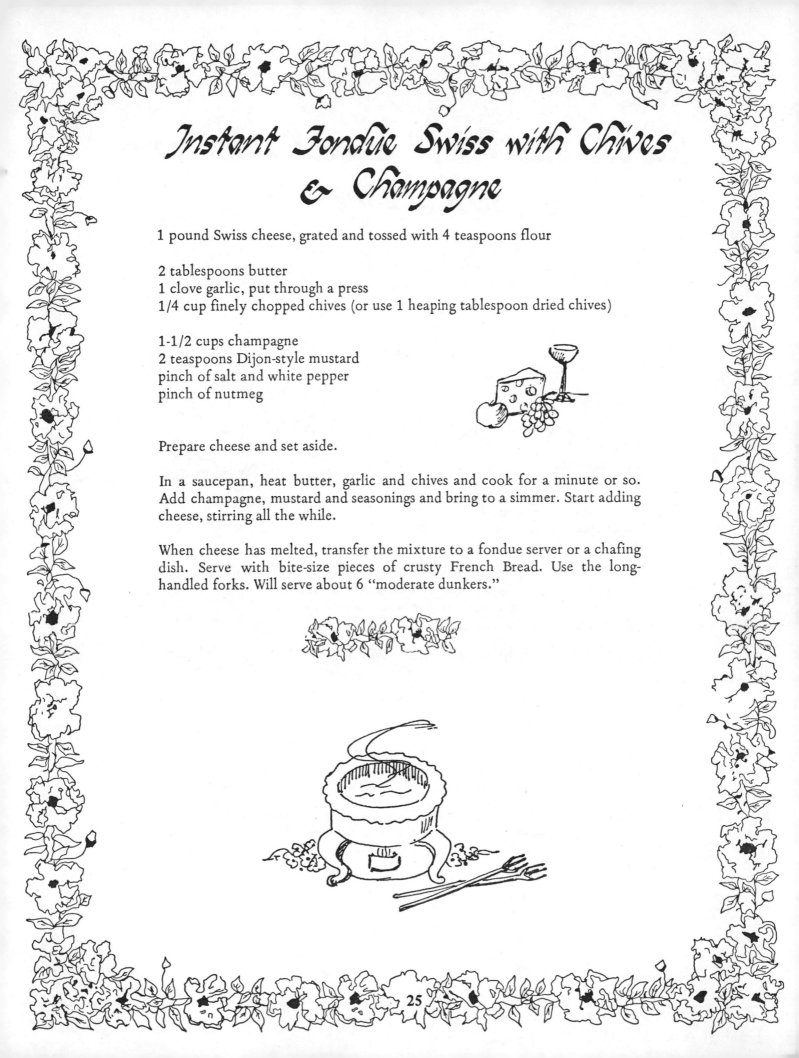

Prepare cheese and set aside.

In a saucepan, heat butter, garlic and chives and cook for a minute or so. Add champagne, mustard and seasonings and bring to a simmer. Start adding cheese, stirring all the while.

When cheese has melted, transfer the mixture to a fondue server or a chafing dish. Serve with bite-size pieces of crusty French Bread. Use the long-handled forks. Will serve about 6 "moderate dunkers."

Roulade Soufflé with Creamed Mushrooms & Herb Filling

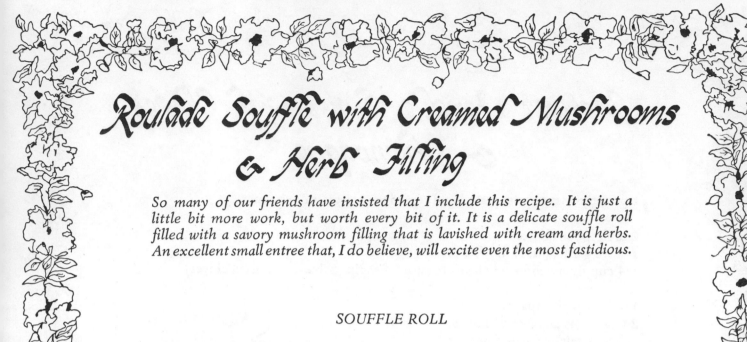

So many of our friends have insisted that I include this recipe. It is just a little bit more work, but worth every bit of it. It is a delicate souffle roll filled with a savory mushroom filling that is lavished with cream and herbs. An excellent small entree that, I do believe, will excite even the most fastidious.

SOUFFLE ROLL

4 tablespoons butter
1/2 cup flour
1-1/2 cups milk
1/2 cup cream
1 teaspoon sugar

4 egg yolks
4 egg whites, beaten stiff but not dry
1 tablespoon grated Parmesan cheese

In a saucepan, cook together the butter and flour for about 2 minutes, stirring all the while. Add the milk and cream and continue cooking for about 5 minutes, stirring constantly, until mixture is thick. Remove from heat and beat in the sugar and the egg yolks. (You can do this with a wire whip.)

Gently fold in the beaten egg whites. Butter a 10x15-inch jelly roll pan. Line it with wax paper extended 2 inches longer on each end. Butter the wax paper. Spread batter evenly in prepared pan and bake it in a 350° oven for 35 to 40 minutes or until top is golden and souffle is set. Sprinkle top of souffle roll with the grated Parmesan cheese.

Invert pan onto overlapping strips of wax paper that are about 18 inches long. Carefully remove the baking paper. Spread top with Creamed Mushroom Herb Filling and carefully roll it up, lifting the wax paper to help you.

Place filled souffle on a lovely porcelain server, seam side down, and heat in a 350° oven for 15 minutes or until heated through. Slice at the table and serve 10 as an hors d'oeuvre or 6 as a small entree.

Note – Get ready for a standing ovation.

Creamed Mushrooms & Herb Filling

6 tablespoons butter (3/4 stick)
1 onion, finely chopped
1 pound mushrooms, thinly sliced
1/2 teaspoon thyme
1/4 (scanty) teaspoon poultry seasoning
salt and pepper to taste

4 tablespoons flour
1 cup cream
1 cup sour cream

Saute onion in butter until onion is transparent. Add mushrooms and continue sauteing until mushrooms are tender. Add seasonings and flour and cook for 2 minutes, stirring all the while. Add cream and sour cream and continue cooking and stirring until mixture has thickened.

Note — Entire dish can be assembled 1 day earlier and refrigerated. Remove from the refrigerator about 30 minutes before reheating. Heat in a 350° oven for about 15 minutes or until heated through.

Curried Crab with Sour Cream & Chives

1 cup sour cream
1/4 pound cream cheese
2 tablespoons butter
1 tablespoon dried chopped chives
1 tablespoon chopped yellow raisins
1 clove garlic mashed
1 tablespoon lemon juice
1/2 teaspoon curry powder (or more to taste)

1/2 pound cooked crabmeat (picked over for bones)

Combine first eight ingredients in a pan and cook over low heat until the mixture is thoroughly blended. Stir in the crabmeat. Place mixture in a chafing dish and serve with thin slices of French bread or black bread. Can also be served as a small entree on a triangle of toasted bread. Garnish with thin slices of lemon and a sprinkling of chopped chives.

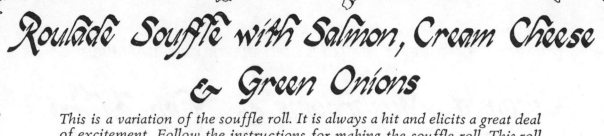

Roulade Soufflé with Salmon, Cream Cheese & Green Onions

This is a variation of the souffle roll. It is always a hit and elicits a great deal of excitement. Follow the instructions for making the souffle roll. This roll does not need to be heated for it is served chilled. Decorate it with cherry tomatoes and green onion frills.

1 10x15-inch Souffle Roll, inverted on overlapping strips of wax paper. Carefully remove the baking paper.

Salmon, Cream Cheese & Green Onion Filling

1/4 pound smoked salmon
1 package (8 ounces) cream cheese, room temperature
1/2 cup sour cream
2 tablespoons lemon juice (or more to taste)
4 tablespoons finely minced green onions (use only the tops)
1 tablespoon minced parsley

Beat together the salmon, cream cheese, sour cream and lemon juice until the mixture is light and fluffy. Beat in the green onions and parsley until blended. Place cooked souffle roll on overlapping strips of wax paper and remove baking paper.

Spread top with the prepared filling and carefully roll it up, lifting the wax paper to help you. Place filled souffle on a pretty oval platter, seam side down, and refrigerate until serving time. Decorate with lots of parsley, cherry tomatoes and green onion frills. Serves 12 as an appetizer.

Note— Green onion frills are made in the following manner: Cut 1-inch sections of green onions. With a sharp knife, cut the ends of each piece about 1/4-inch down being careful not to cut through the onion. Do this also with the green onion leaves and place all the pieces in a bowl of water and refrigerate overnight. All the cut sections will have curled and they make a very pretty garnish, indeed.

Giant Piroshkis with Chicken, Mushrooms & Sour Cream

This is a particularly delicious luncheon dish, unique in shape and texture. It's a grand way of serving leftover chicken or turkey. Don't reserve this dish for lunch alone. It's fun for dinner as well.

1 package frozen patty shells (6 shells), thawed
1 egg, beaten
6 teaspoons grated Parmesan cheese

Roll out each patty to measure about 6 inches. Place 1/6 of the Chicken Mushroom Sour Cream Filling in center of each patty shell. Moisten the edges and fold over. Trim the edges and press them down with the tines of a fork. Scallop them, if you have the time.

Brush tops with beaten egg and pierce tops with a fork. Sprinkle top with grated Parmesan cheese. Place piroshkis on a greased cookie sheet.

Bake in a 400° oven for 20 to 25 minutes or until pastry is puffed and top is a rich golden brown. Serve with fresh fruit or a buttered vegetable. Serves 6 for lunch.

Chicken, Mushrooms & Sour Cream Filling

1 onion, finely chopped
1/4 pound mushrooms, thinly sliced
2 tablespoons butter

2 tablespoons flour
1 cup sour cream
salt and pepper to taste

2 cups cooked chicken, cut into small dice

Saute onions and mushrooms in butter until onions are soft. Add flour and cook for a minute or two. Add the sour cream and cook until sauce thickens, about 2 minutes. Stir in the cooked chicken. Will fill 6 patty shells.

Teriyaki Chicken Wings
with Honey Glaze

Do not reserve this delectable dish solely for special occasions. Try it for dinner some evening soon and Voila! you're at a party.

3 pounds chicken wings, remove wing tips. Cut each wing in half by cutting through the joint. Place in one layer in a 9x13-inch pan and sprinkle with salt, pepper and garlic powder. Baste generously with Teriyaki Marinade or Soy Sauce.

Bake chicken wings in a 350° oven for about 20 minutes. Baste heavily with Honey Glaze 2 or 3 times during the remainder of the cooking time, about 40 minutes. Turn once during baking. Chicken will be a deep golden brown and glazed on all sides. Yields about 32 pieces.

Honey Glaze

1-1/2 cups honey
1/2 cup butter (1 stick)
1 cup chili sauce
6 tablespoons lemon juice
3 teaspoons Dijon-style mustard
3 tablespoons Teriyaki Marinade or Soy Sauce
salt to taste

Combine all the ingredients in a saucepan and simmer mixture for 10 minutes. Brush on chicken. Store remaining glaze in the refrigerator.

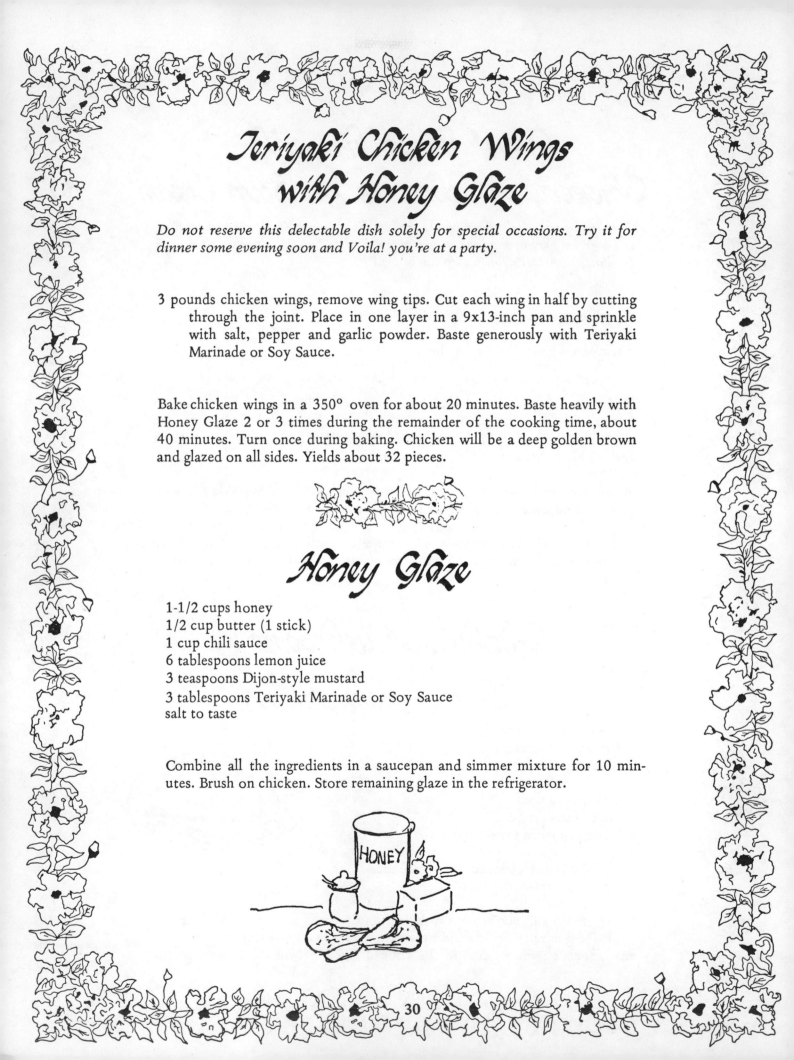

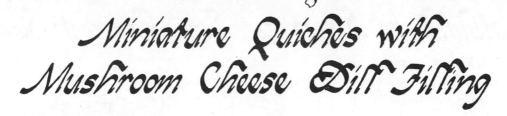

Miniature Quiches with Mushroom Cheese Dill Filling

THE PASTRY

1 cup butter (2 sticks)
1 package (8 ounces) cream cheese
2 cups flour
1/4 teaspoon salt

In your electric mixer, cream butter and cream cheese until blended. Add flour and salt and mix at low speed until the flour is incorporated and even. Do not overmix. Place dough on floured wax paper, shape it into an 8-inch circle, wrap it in the wax paper and refrigerate it overnight.

Divide dough into four parts. Working one part at a time, roll it out on a floured pastry cloth until the dough is about 1/8-inch thick. Cut into rounds with a 2-1/2-inch cookie cutter and accumulate scraps in the refrigerator to roll out at the end.

Place rounds in hors d'oeuvre-size muffin pans that have been lightly greased. (Teflon pans should be greased also.) Place a few sauteed mushrooms into each round. Pour egg mixture into each shell and bake in a 350° oven for about 20 or 25 minutes or until custard is set and pastry is lightly browned on the bottom. Makes 50 divine hors d'oeuvres. Heat quiches in a 350° oven before serving.

Mushroom Cheese Dill Filling

1/2 pound mushrooms, thinly sliced
1 clove garlic, mashed or put through a press
2 tablespoons butter

EGG MIXTURE

4 eggs, beaten
2 cups cream
3/4 cup grated Swiss cheese
1/2 cup grated Parmesan cheese
1/4 teaspoon dried dill weed
salt and pepper to taste

Saute mushrooms and garlic in butter until mushrooms are tender and liquid is evaporated. Set mixture aside. In a 1-quart measuring glass, beat together the eggs, cream, cheeses and seasonings until blended. (Using the 1-quart measuring glass will facilitate pouring.)

Meatballs in Sweet & Sour Currant Sauce

1-1/2 pounds ground beef
1 cup herb seasoned stuffing mix, soaked in 1/4 cup milk
1 small onion, grated
2 eggs
1/4 cup golden raisins
1/4 cup sunflower seeds, shelled
salt and pepper to taste

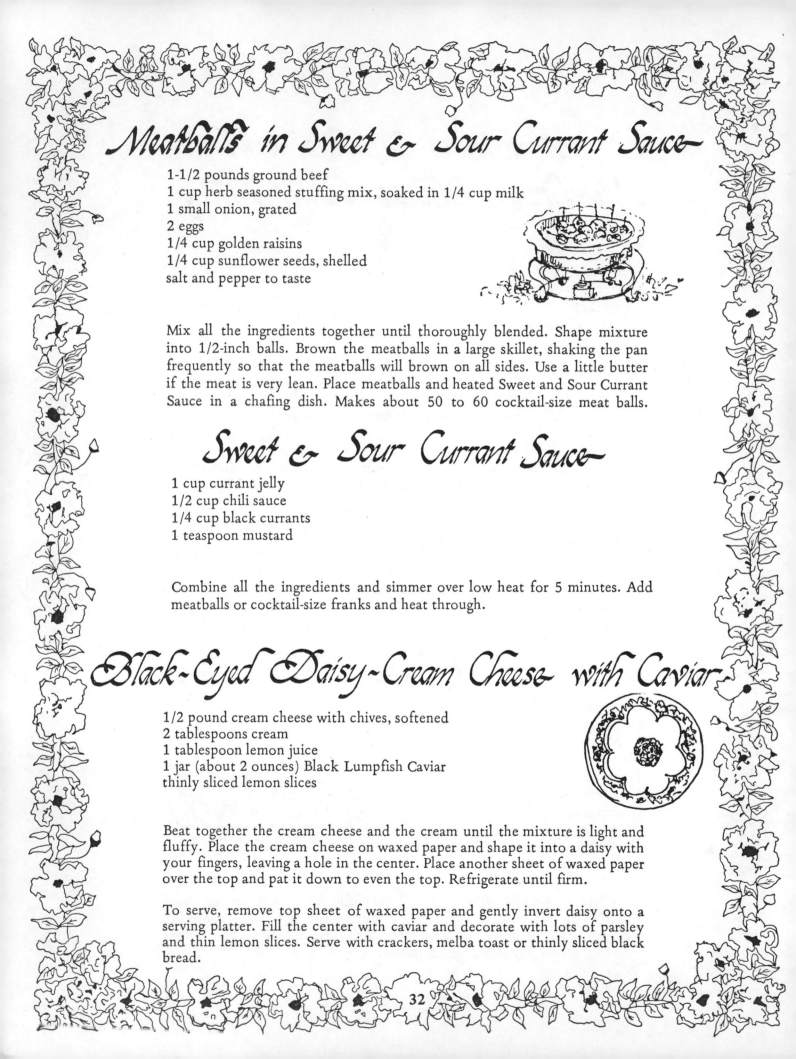

Mix all the ingredients together until thoroughly blended. Shape mixture into 1/2-inch balls. Brown the meatballs in a large skillet, shaking the pan frequently so that the meatballs will brown on all sides. Use a little butter if the meat is very lean. Place meatballs and heated Sweet and Sour Currant Sauce in a chafing dish. Makes about 50 to 60 cocktail-size meat balls.

Sweet & Sour Currant Sauce

1 cup currant jelly
1/2 cup chili sauce
1/4 cup black currants
1 teaspoon mustard

Combine all the ingredients and simmer over low heat for 5 minutes. Add meatballs or cocktail-size franks and heat through.

Black-Eyed Daisy-Cream Cheese with Caviar

1/2 pound cream cheese with chives, softened
2 tablespoons cream
1 tablespoon lemon juice
1 jar (about 2 ounces) Black Lumpfish Caviar
thinly sliced lemon slices

Beat together the cream cheese and the cream until the mixture is light and fluffy. Place the cream cheese on waxed paper and shape it into a daisy with your fingers, leaving a hole in the center. Place another sheet of waxed paper over the top and pat it down to even the top. Refrigerate until firm.

To serve, remove top sheet of waxed paper and gently invert daisy onto a serving platter. Fill the center with caviar and decorate with lots of parsley and thin lemon slices. Serve with crackers, melba toast or thinly sliced black bread.

Mushrooms Stuffed with Shrimp, Cheese & Chives

1 pound medium-sized mushrooms, remove stems and reserve them for another use. Clean the mushroom caps and then brush them with melted butter.

1/4 pound cooked tiny bay shrimp, coarsely chopped
3 packages (3 ounces each) cream cheese and chives, softened
1/2 cup garlic croutons, crushed into crumbs
1/2 cup grated Swiss cheese

Parmesan cheese, grated
paprika

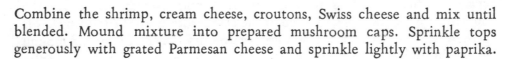

Combine the shrimp, cream cheese, croutons, Swiss cheese and mix until blended. Mound mixture into prepared mushroom caps. Sprinkle tops generously with grated Parmesan cheese and sprinkle lightly with paprika.

Bake in a 350° oven until piping hot. Broil for a few seconds. Serve immediately.

Clams with Cream Cheese, Green Onions & Dill

1 can (7 ounces) chopped clams, drained
4 tablespoons finely minced green onions (use only the tops)
2 tablespoons sour cream
2 tablespoons lemon juice
1/2 pound cream cheese, room temperature
1/8 teaspoon dill

Beat together all the ingredients until blended. Line a pretty mold with plastic wrap. Pour mixture into lined mold and pat down to even. Cover with the overlapping ends of plastic wrap and refrigerate overnight.

To unmold, remove plastic cover and invert on a lovely serving dish. Peel off the plastic wrap and decorate with lots of parsley and lemon slices. Serve with thin slices of black bread or a subtle soda cracker.

Mushrooms Stuffed with Clams & Herbs

1/2 pound mushrooms, clean and remove stems. Brush with some melted butter.

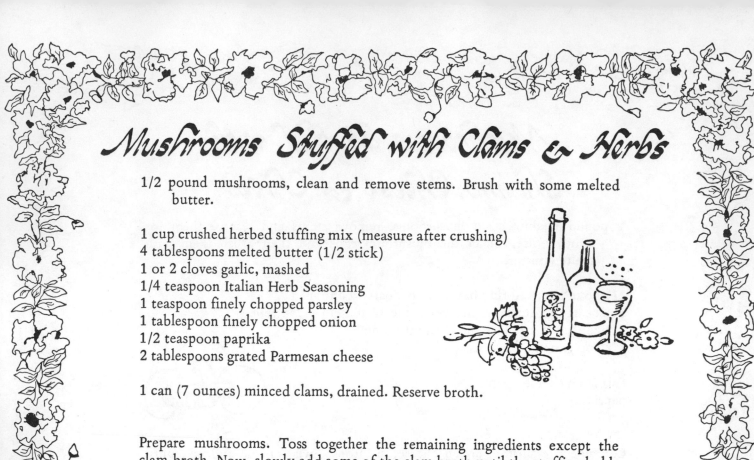

1 cup crushed herbed stuffing mix (measure after crushing)
4 tablespoons melted butter (1/2 stick)
1 or 2 cloves garlic, mashed
1/4 teaspoon Italian Herb Seasoning
1 teaspoon finely chopped parsley
1 tablespoon finely chopped onion
1/2 teaspoon paprika
2 tablespoons grated Parmesan cheese

1 can (7 ounces) minced clams, drained. Reserve broth.

Prepare mushrooms. Toss together the remaining ingredients except the clam broth. Now, slowly add some of the clam broth until the stuffing holds together. Stuffing should not be soggy or too dry. Divide filling and mound into mushroom caps, filling them loosely. Sprinkle tops with a little extra grated Parmesan and paprika. Place on cookie sheet and heat at 350° until piping hot. Broil for a few seconds to brown.

Mushrooms Stuffed with Feta, Green Onions & Garlic

1 pound medium mushrooms, clean and remove stems. Baste with melted butter.

8 ounces Feta cheese, mashed
1/2 cup cream cheese
1/2 cup grated Parmesan cheese
1/2 cup chopped green onions
1/4 cup finely chopped parsley
1 egg
1/2 cup garlic croutons, crushed into crumbs

Prepare mushrooms, Combine the remaining ingredients and stir until the mixture is well blended. Fill the mushrooms, mounding the mixture high into the caps. Bake in a 350° oven until piping hot. Broil for a few seconds to lightly brown. Serves 6 as an appetizer.

Shrimp Puffs with Water Chestnuts & Ginger

1/4 pound tiny bay shrimp, cooked
4 water chestnuts, finely chopped
1 green onion, finely chopped
2 egg whites, beaten
1/4 teaspoon ginger
salt and pepper to taste
4 tablespoons sour cream
1 tablespoon lemon juice

4 slices white bread, crusts removed and toasted crisp

In a bowl, combine all the ingredients except the bread and stir until the mixture is well mixed.

Spread the mixture on the prepared bread slices. Cut each slice into fourths, either into squares, triangles or long fingers. Place canapes on a cookie sheet and broil until they are puffy and golden. Watch carefully so that they do not burn. Makes 16 canapes.

Cocktail Franks in Sweet & Sour Cranberry Sauce

1 pound cocktail-size franks

1 cup whole cranberry sauce
1/2 cup barbecue sauce
2 to 3 tablespoons brown sugar
1 teaspoon grated orange peel

Heat together all the ingredients and simmer mixture for 5 minutes. Place it all in a chafing dish and serve with picks or spears.

Batter Fried Chicken with Hot Lemon Mandarin Sauce

4 whole chicken breasts. Ask the butcher to remove the bones and skin and to cut them in 3/4-inch squares. Sprinkle with salt, pepper and garlic powder. Dust lightly with flour.

Batter

1 cup flour
1/2 cup corn starch
1 teaspoon baking powder
1 egg
1-1/2 cups water (about)
1/8 teaspoon salt

Combine the batter ingredients and beat with a rotary beater until the batter is smooth and blended. Add only enough water to make batter the consistency of heavy cream.

Dip chicken pieces in batter and fry them in hot oil until golden brown on both sides. Remove from oil and drain. Serve with Hot Lemon Mandarin Sauce on the side for dipping. Serve with fancy picks. Be sure to spear the mandarin orange sections with the chicken.

Hot Lemon Mandarin Sauce

1 cup orange marmalade
6 tablespoons lemon juice
3 tablespoons brown sugar
3 tablespoons chili sauce
pinch of powdered ginger
1 can (8 ounces) mandarin orange sections, drained. Reserve juice.*

In a saucepan, combine all the ingredients and simmer the mixture for 5 minutes. Allow sauce to cool for a few minutes and serve warm. Makes about 1-1/2 cups sauce.

Note – Sauce can be made earlier in the week and reheated at time of serving.
   – Chicken can be cooked earlier in the day and refrigerated. Heat in a 350° oven until heated through.
   *– *Thin the sauce with a little of the juice, if necessary.*

Beef Won Tons
with Chinese Red Hot Sauce

1 package prepared won ton skins (about 45 to 50 in a package)

1 pound lean ground beef
1 teaspoon beef seasoned stock base
2 teaspoons dried onion flakes
1/4 pound finely chopped mushrooms
12 finely chopped water chestnuts
1/4 cup finely chopped green onions
1/8 teaspoon garlic powder
salt and pepper to taste

Combine all the ingredients except the won ton skins in a large skillet and stir fry them until the beef is thoroughly cooked.

Place 1 tablespoon (scanty) of filling in center of each skin. Moisten the edges with water and fold the won ton wrappers in half, either lengthwise or on the diagonal. Press your fingers around the edges to seal.

Fry filled won tons in hot oil until golden brown on both sides. Drain. Serve hot with Chinese Red Hot Sauce or Hot Plum Sauce for dipping.

Chinese Red Hot Sauce

1/2 cup ketchup
1/2 cup chili sauce
1 teaspoon soy sauce
1/2 teaspoon Colemans dry mustard (or to taste)

Combine all the ingredients and stir until blended. Makes about 1 cup sauce.

Hot Plum Sauce

1 cup plum preserves
2 tablespoons vinegar
1/4 cup chili sauce
2 tablespoons soy sauce
1 tablespoon brown sugar

Combine all the ingredients and simmer for a few minutes. Allow to cool a few minutes and serve warm. Yields about 1-1/2 cups.

Creamed Chicken & Mushrooms in Patty Shells

6 frozen patty shells, baked according to the directions on the package

1/4 pound mushrooms, thinly sliced
2 tablespoons butter
pinch of poultry seasoning
salt and pepper to taste

1 cup finely chopped cooked chicken
3 packages (3 ounces each) cream cheese with chives, softened
1 egg

Saute mushrooms in butter with the seasonings until the mushrooms are tender and liquid is evaporated. Stir in the cooked chicken.

Beat together the cream cheese and egg until the mixture is blended. Stir in the cooked chicken and mushrooms.

Just before serving, heat the patty shells in a 350° oven for 5 minutes. Heat chicken and mushroom mixture until hot, but do not let it boil. Spoon it into the warmed shells and serve it with spiced apricots or buttered broccoli. Serves 6 for lunch.

Note— Patty shells can be baked earlier in the day. Creamed chicken and mushroom filling can be assembled earlier in the day. Heat just before serving.

Scallop Shells filled with Shrimp & Mushrooms in a Sour Cream Wine Sauce

This is a beautiful first course. Served in attractive scallop shells, it will add a touch of excitement and festivity to your dinner.

1 onion, finely chopped
4 tablespoons butter
1/2 pound mushrooms, thinly sliced

4 tablespoons flour
1 cup cream
1 cup sour cream

salt and white pepper to taste
2 tablespoons sherry or sauterne
1/2 pound tiny bay shrimp

3 tablespoons Ritz cracker, crushed into fine crumbs
2 tablespoons grated Parmesan cheese

Saute onion in butter until onions are soft, but not brown. Add the mushrooms and continue sauteing until mushrooms are tender. Add the flour and cook, stirring, for 2 minutes. Add the cream and cook over low heat, stirring, until sauce thickens.

Add sour cream, seasonings, wine and shrimp and stir until blended. Divide mixture into 8 scallop shells. Combine cracker crumbs and cheese and sprinkle the mixture over the filled shells.

Heat in a 350° oven until heated through, about 20 minutes. Broil for a few seconds to lightly brown the crumb topping. Garnish with a little chopped parsley. Serves 8 with pride.

Note— Entire dish can be assembled earlier in the day and refrigerated. Reheat just before serving.

Salmon Mousse with Dilled Sauce Verte

A lovely pink mousse sparkled with a green dressing is an important looking hors d'oeuvre. Using the blender simplifies preparation time and makes results foolproof. If you own a 1-quart fish mold, it would be just lovely. A ring mold is fine also. Serve with simple soda crackers so that the flavor is not disturbed. Don't wait for a party, however. This is a delight for lunch.

1 envelope (1 tablespoon) unflavored gelatin
1/4 cup cold water

1/2 cup cream, heated to boiling point
1/4 teaspoon paprika
1/4 teaspoon dill

2 green onions (do not use the green tops)
1 can (1 pound) pink salmon, drained
3 tablespoons lemon juice
2/3 cup mayonnaise
salt and pepper to taste

Soften gelatin in cold water and liquefy it over hot water. Place in blender container. With blades running, add the remaining ingredients in order listed, until the mixture is well blended. (If your blender does not have enough room for the mayonnaise, stir it in by hand.) Pour the mixture into an oiled ring mold and refrigerate until set.

Unmold on a lovely platter and garnish with lemon slices. Fill the center with Dilled Sauce Verte. Serve with crackers.

Note – Make this mold 1 day earlier.

Dilled Sauce Verte

1 cup mayonnaise
1/2 cup sour cream
4 sprigs parsley, remove stems
2 green onions
1-1/2 tablespoons lemon juice
1/4 teaspoon dried dill weed

1/2 cup frozen chopped spinach, defrosted and drained

Blend first 6 ingredients until smooth. Add drained spinach and stir until well mixed. Refrigerate until serving time.

Molded Egg Salad with Lemon Mustard Mayonnaise

10 eggs, hard cooked and mashed
salt to taste
3/4 cup mayonnaise
2 tablespoons Dijon-style mustard
4 tablespoons lemon juice
2 teaspoons dried onion flakes
1 teaspoon dried chopped chives

1 envelope unflavored gelatin
1/4 cup cold water

Combine first 6 ingredients and mix until blended. Soften gelatin in 1/4 cup cold water. (Use a metal measuring cup, 8 ounce size.) Place measuring cup in a pan of boiling water and liquefy the gelatin.

Add the gelatin to the egg mixture and stir to thoroughly blend. Now, take a large piece of plastic wrap and place it over a pretty 1-quart heart-shaped mold. Place the egg-gelatin mixture into the plastic-lined heart mold. Refrigerate until firm.

To serve, invert mold onto a pretty serving platter, remove plastic wrap and decorate with lots of parsley and lemon slices. Serve with crackers or thinly sliced black bread.

Note — *You might like to add a border of sour cream and pink caviar on top of the mold, for an exciting touch.*
— *Using the plastic wrap is a little secret I will share with you that will facilitate removing even the most stubborn molds. You will be amazed at how easily this works and at how foolproof this method is.*

Liver Pate with Apples & Brandy

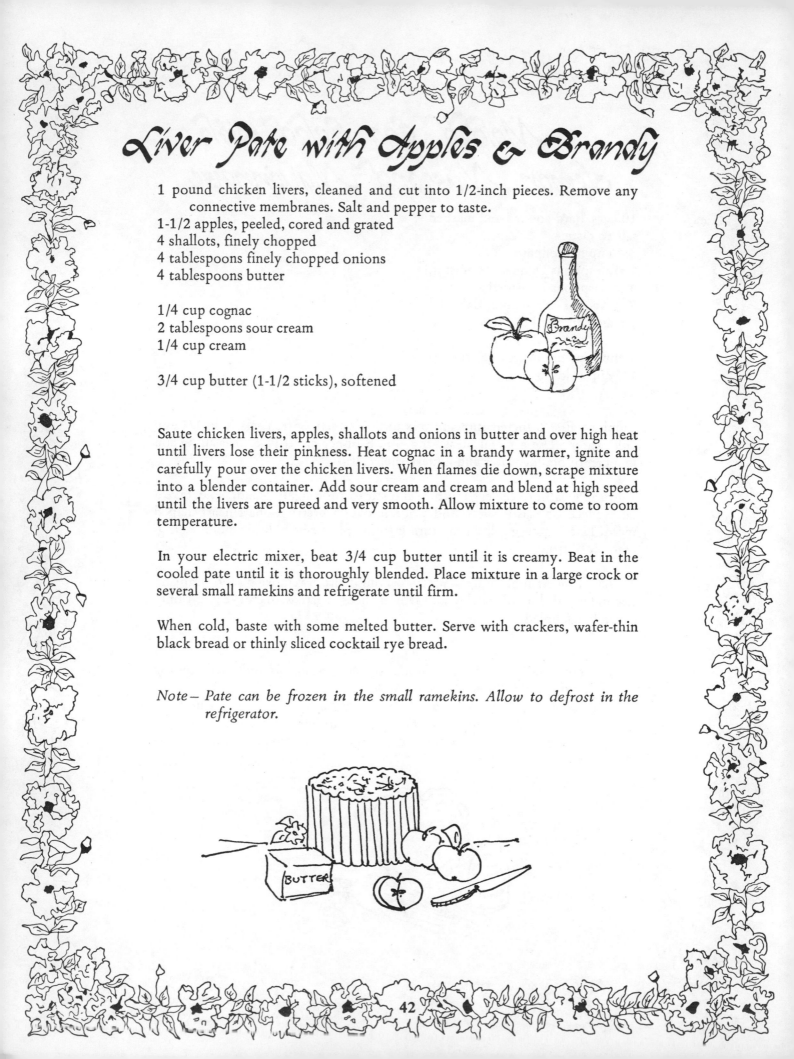

1 pound chicken livers, cleaned and cut into 1/2-inch pieces. Remove any connective membranes. Salt and pepper to taste.
1-1/2 apples, peeled, cored and grated
4 shallots, finely chopped
4 tablespoons finely chopped onions
4 tablespoons butter

1/4 cup cognac
2 tablespoons sour cream
1/4 cup cream

3/4 cup butter (1-1/2 sticks), softened

Saute chicken livers, apples, shallots and onions in butter and over high heat until livers lose their pinkness. Heat cognac in a brandy warmer, ignite and carefully pour over the chicken livers. When flames die down, scrape mixture into a blender container. Add sour cream and cream and blend at high speed until the livers are pureed and very smooth. Allow mixture to come to room temperature.

In your electric mixer, beat 3/4 cup butter until it is creamy. Beat in the cooled pate until it is thoroughly blended. Place mixture in a large crock or several small ramekins and refrigerate until firm.

When cold, baste with some melted butter. Serve with crackers, wafer-thin black bread or thinly sliced cocktail rye bread.

Note — Pate can be frozen in the small ramekins. Allow to defrost in the refrigerator.

Casseroles

Zucchini Onion Swiss Soufflé

Sauteed zucchini and onions topped with a very delicate cheese souffle. Excellent for brunch or lunch or for a light supper. You'll enjoy the fact that it can be assembled early in the day and refrigerated until 1 hour before serving.

4 medium zucchini, peeled and thinly sliced
1 cup chopped onions
1/4 cup butter (1/2 stick)

8 eggs
1 cup cream (can use half and half)
1 package (8 ounces) cream cheese, softened
2 cups grated Swiss cheese
1 cup grated Parmesan cheese
salt and pepper to taste (go easy on the salt as you are using a lot of
        Parmesan)

Saute zucchini and onion in butter until zucchini is tender and onions are soft. Place mixture in an 8x12-inch porcelain* casserole.

In the large bowl of your electric mixer, combine the remaining ingredients and beat 3 minutes. Pour egg mixture over the zucchini. Bake in a 350° oven for 30 to 40 minutes or until top is browned and eggs are set. Serve with a green salad or fresh fruit. Serves 6.

Note — Casserole can be assembled earlier in the day and refrigerated. Bake as directed above.
   *— *Use any 8x12-inch casserole. The advantage of using porcelain or a pretty baker is that you can serve from it directly.*
   — While the custard will settle a bit, leftovers are delicious. Warm slightly, before serving.

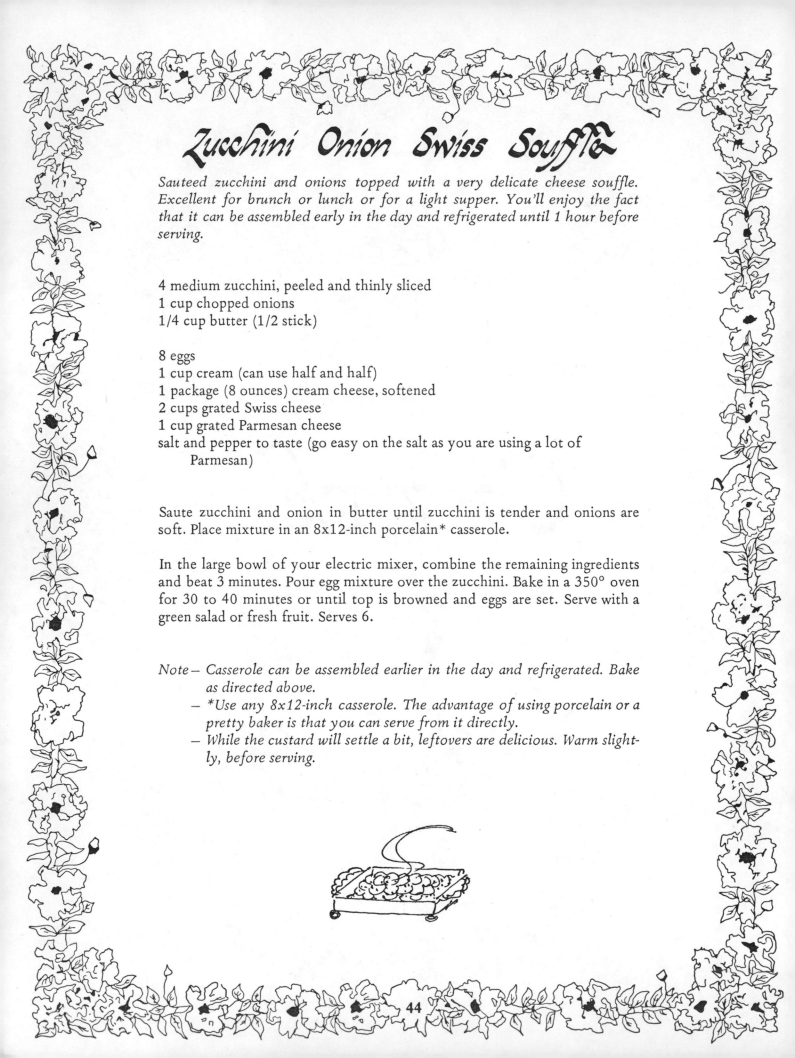

Banana Cream Cheese Casserole with Strawberries & Cream

1/2 cup butter (1 stick), melted
1/2 cup sugar
2 eggs
1 cup flour
1/2 cup milk
3 teaspoons baking powder, double acting
1 teaspoon vanilla
pinch of salt

1 tablespoon cinnamon sugar

In the small bowl of your electric mixer, beat all the above ingredients together, except the cinnamon sugar, until the mixture is well blended. Pour 1/2 the batter in a buttered 9x13-inch baking pan. Drop the Banana Cream Cheese Filling by teaspoonsful evenly over the batter. Top with the remaining batter. Sprinkle top with cinnamon sugar.

Bake casserole in a preheated 300° oven for about 45 minutes or until batter is cooked through and top is golden brown. Cut into squares and serve hot with a dollup of sour cream and a tablespoon of defrosted strawberries or raspberries in syrup. (Strawberry or raspberry jam is good too.) Serves 6 very lucky people. An outstanding dish for brunch or lunch.

Note — Entire casserole can be assembled a few hours before baking.
— Casserole can be baked earlier in the day and reheated before serving. Can be frozen after it is baked.

Banana Cream Cheese Filling

1 pound cream cheese (2 packages, 8 ounces each) at room temperature
1 pint (16 ounces) cottage cheese (small curd or whipped)
2 eggs
3/4 cup sugar
3 tablespoons lemon juice
2 bananas, sliced
1/2 teaspoon vanilla
pinch of salt

Beat cream cheese until light and fluffy. Add cottage cheese, eggs, and sugar and beat until blended. Toss banana slices in the lemon juice. Now add the bananas, vanilla and salt to the cheese mixture and stir the mixture until it is blended.

Mini~Lasagna with Meat Sauce & Mozzarella

3/4 pound noodles, cooked and drained (use the wide egg noodles or the
    extra-wide lasagna noodles)
1 cup grated Mozzarella cheese
1 pound Ricotta cheese
1/2 cup grated Parmesan cheese

1/2 cup additional Mozzarella cheese, grated

Mix together the noodles, Mozzarella, Ricotta and Parmesan cheese. In a
9x13-inch lasagna pan, lay alternate layers of Meat Sauce and noodle mixture, starting and ending with the meat sauce. Sprinkle top with additional
Mozzarella.

Bake casserole in a 350° oven for 30 minutes or until piping hot. Makes 6
servings.

Meat Sauce

1 onion, finely chopped
1 tablespoon butter
1 pound lean ground beef

1 can (1 pound 12 ounces) tomato puree
1 tablespoon sugar
1 teaspoon Italian Herb Seasoning
1 bay leaf
1 tablespoon chopped parsley
salt and pepper to taste

Saute onion in butter until onions are soft. Add ground beef and saute until
meat loses its pinkness. Add the remaining ingredients and simmer mixture
for 10 minutes. Remove bay leaf. Use on spaghetti and lasagna.

Cabbage Rolls German Style with Sauerkraut & Ginger Snap Sauce

1 large head cabbage
1 onion, chopped, sauteed in 1 tablespoon butter
1 pound lean ground beef
1/2 cup raw rice
1 egg
1/4 cup cold water
pinch of garlic powder
salt and pepper to taste

Wash cabbage and remove the core. Stand it up and cook it in boiling water for 10 to 12 minutes. Remove and refresh under cold water. Carefully remove the outer leaves. When the leaves get too small to roll, chop them finely and place them in a large Dutch-oven type casserole.

Combine the onion, beef, rice, egg, water, garlic powder and seasonings and mix them until they are well blended. Place about 2 tablespoons meat mixture on bottom of cabbage leaf. Tuck in the sides and roll it. Place rolls in Dutch oven. Pour Sauerkraut and Ginger Snap Sauce over the rolls and cook them, covered, for about 1-1/2 hours over low heat. Makes about 12 cabbage rolls.

Sauerkraut & Ginger Snap Sauce

1 cup sauerkraut
1/2 cup yellow raisins
3 tablespoons granulated sugar
2 tablespoons brown sugar
1 teaspoon Bovril (Beef Extract)
1 tablespoon lemon juice
1 can (10-1/2 ounces) beef broth

2 ginger snaps, crushed into crumbs

Combine all the ingredients except the ginger snaps and pour sauce over the cabbage rolls. When rolls are completely cooked, add the ginger snap crumbs to slightly thicken the sauce.

Curry Cheddar Cheese Soufflé
(Made in your blender)

5 eggs
1 slice white bread, remove crust

1/2 cup cream
1/2 pound cream cheese (8 ounces), cut into 4 pieces
6 ounces Cheddar cheese, cubed
1/4 cup Parmesan cheese, grated
1/2 teaspoon curry powder
1/4 teaspoon salt

In a blender container, blend eggs with bread. Continue blending the ingredients in order listed. Blend until mixture is smooth, about 15 seconds after the last addition.

Place mixture in a buttered 1-1/2-quart souffle dish and bake at 375° for about 50 minutes to 1 hour. Serves 4 or 5.

Note – Can be assembled several hours earlier and refrigerated. Bake as described above.

Florentine Casserole with Spinach & Cheese

2 packages (10 ounces, each) frozen chopped spinach, defrosted and drained
4 green onions, chopped
1 pound Ricotta cheese, room temperature
8 ounces cream cheese, room temperature
1/2 cup seasoned bread crumbs
1/2 cup Parmesan cheese, grated
1/4 teaspoon ground nutmeg
salt and pepper to taste
4 eggs

Combine all the ingredients in a large bowl of your electric mixer and beat mixture for 3 minutes at medium speed. Pour mixture into a buttered 9x13-inch pan and bake at 375° for about 40 minutes or until mixture is set and top is golden. Serves 8.

Rice Casserole with Eggplant, Tomatoes & Onions Sauce

1-1/2 cups long-grain rice
1 can (10-1/2 ounces) chicken broth
1-1/2 cups water
2 teaspoons chicken seasoned stock base
3 tablespoons butter
salt and pepper to taste

Combine all the ingredients in a saucepan and simmer until liquid is absorbed and rice is tender but firm. When rice is cooked toss with Eggplant, Tomato, Onion Sauce until well mixed. Place mixture in a buttered casserole and heat in a 350° oven until heated through. Serves 6.

Eggplant, Tomatoes & Onions Sauce

1 eggplant, medium-sized, peeled and cut into 1/4-inch slices
salt and pepper to taste
olive oil

1 cup chopped onions
2 cloves garlic
2 tablespoons butter
1 can (1 pound) stewed tomatoes, drained and chopped
pinch of thyme
salt and pepper to taste

1/2 cup grated Parmesan cheese

Place eggplant slices on a lightly greased cookie sheet, sprinkle with salt and pepper and brush lightly with oil. Cover pan tightly with foil and bake eggplant in a 400° oven for about 20 minutes or until eggplant is soft.

Meanwhile, saute onion and garlic in butter until onions are soft. Add tomatoes and seasonings and simmer mixture for 15 minutes. Add the cooked eggplant and stir to blend. Stir in the grated cheese. Delicious also when served as a side dish of vegetables.

*Note— Entire casserole can be assembled earlier in the day and refrigerated.
Reheat in a 350° oven for about 30 minutes or until piping hot.*

Eggplant with Lamb & Mushrooms in Tomato Sauce

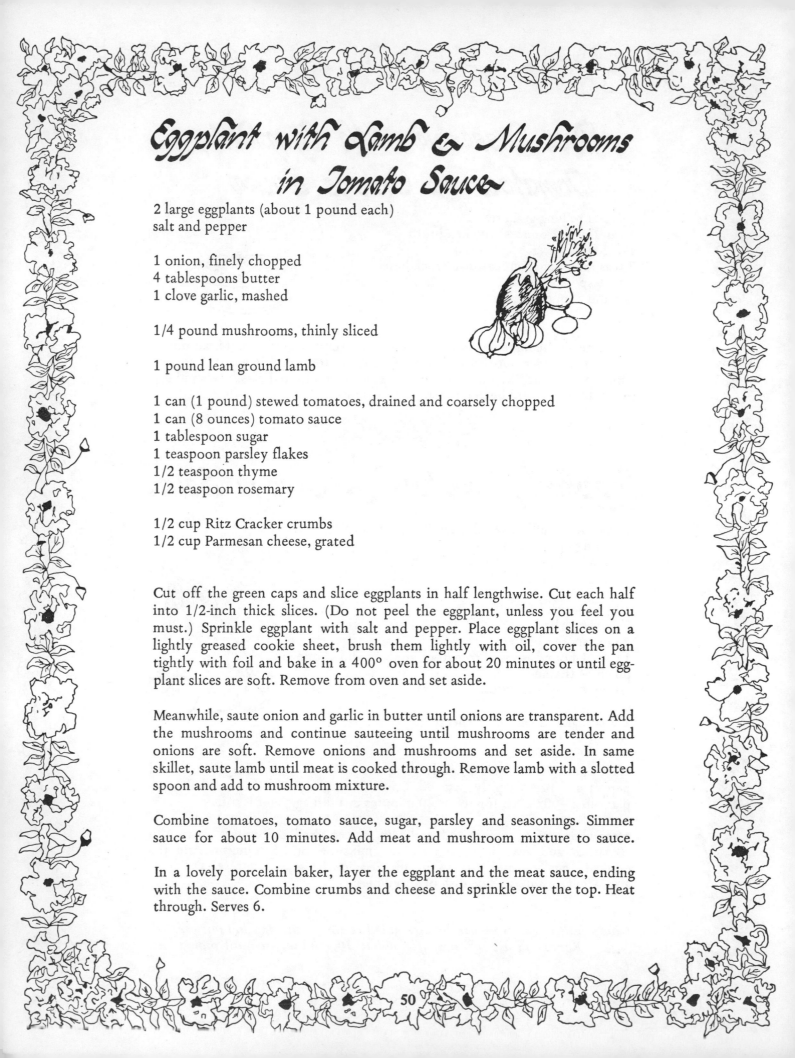

2 large eggplants (about 1 pound each)
salt and pepper

1 onion, finely chopped
4 tablespoons butter
1 clove garlic, mashed

1/4 pound mushrooms, thinly sliced

1 pound lean ground lamb

1 can (1 pound) stewed tomatoes, drained and coarsely chopped
1 can (8 ounces) tomato sauce
1 tablespoon sugar
1 teaspoon parsley flakes
1/2 teaspoon thyme
1/2 teaspoon rosemary

1/2 cup Ritz Cracker crumbs
1/2 cup Parmesan cheese, grated

Cut off the green caps and slice eggplants in half lengthwise. Cut each half into 1/2-inch thick slices. (Do not peel the eggplant, unless you feel you must.) Sprinkle eggplant with salt and pepper. Place eggplant slices on a lightly greased cookie sheet, brush them lightly with oil, cover the pan tightly with foil and bake in a 400° oven for about 20 minutes or until eggplant slices are soft. Remove from oven and set aside.

Meanwhile, saute onion and garlic in butter until onions are transparent. Add the mushrooms and continue sauteeing until mushrooms are tender and onions are soft. Remove onions and mushrooms and set aside. In same skillet, saute lamb until meat is cooked through. Remove lamb with a slotted spoon and add to mushroom mixture.

Combine tomatoes, tomato sauce, sugar, parsley and seasonings. Simmer sauce for about 10 minutes. Add meat and mushroom mixture to sauce.

In a lovely porcelain baker, layer the eggplant and the meat sauce, ending with the sauce. Combine crumbs and cheese and sprinkle over the top. Heat through. Serves 6.

Beef Burgundy with Mushrooms in Wine

2 pounds beef chuck, cut into 1-inch cubes and sprinkled with salt and
    pepper and dredged in flour
3 tablespoons butter
2 cloves garlic, mashed

1/2 pound mushrooms, thickly sliced
12 small white onions, remove the skins
1 can (10-1/2 ounces) beef broth
1/2 cup Burgundy wine
2 tablespoons brown sugar
2 tablespoons currant jelly, cut into smaller pieces
1 tablespoon chopped parsley
pinch of thyme

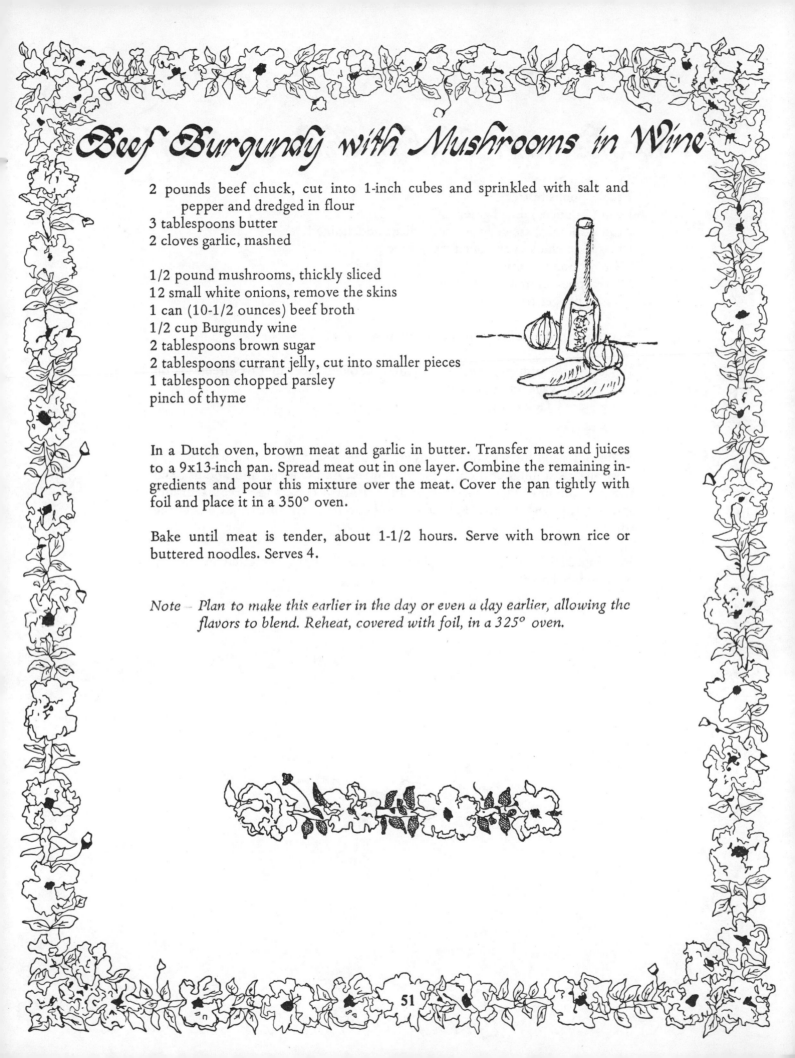

In a Dutch oven, brown meat and garlic in butter. Transfer meat and juices
to a 9x13-inch pan. Spread meat out in one layer. Combine the remaining ingredients and pour this mixture over the meat. Cover the pan tightly with
foil and place it in a 350° oven.

Bake until meat is tender, about 1-1/2 hours. Serve with brown rice or
buttered noodles. Serves 4.

*Note – Plan to make this earlier in the day or even a day earlier, allowing the
flavors to blend. Reheat, covered with foil, in a 325° oven.*

Noodles with Chicken, Chiles & Tomatoes

2 onions, chopped
2 tablespoons butter
1 can (4 ounces) diced green chiles
1 can (1 pound) stewed tomatoes, diced and drained, reserve juice
1 teaspoon chicken seasoned stock base
1/4 teaspoon tumeric
1/8 teaspoon cumin
salt and pepper to taste

3 cups cooked chicken, cut into large dice

1 package (8 ounces) medium noodles, cooked according to directions on
    the package and drained
1 cup grated Jack cheese

Saute onions in butter until onions are tender. Add chiles, tomatoes, chicken base and seasonings and cook for 5 minutes. Add chicken and noodles and toss to combine. Place mixture in an 8x12-inch cook and serve baker and sprinkle top with cheese. Pour about 1/4 cup reserved tomato juice over the top.

Heat in a 350° oven until piping hot and cheese topping is melted and lightly browned. Serves 6.

Spanish Chicken with Rice

2 onions, chopped
2 cloves garlic, mashed
3 tablespoons butter
1/2 pound sliced mushrooms
1 cup rice

2 tomatoes, coarsely chopped
1 can (10-1/2 ounces) chicken broth
1 jar (2 ounces) pimento strips
1/4 teaspoon turmeric
salt and pepper to taste

3 cups cooked chicken
1 package (10 ounces) frozen green peas

Saute onions and garlic in butter until onions are transparent. Add mushrooms and continue sauteeing until mushrooms are tender. (Add a little butter, if necessary.) Add rice and saute for 5 minutes, tossing and turning.

Now add the remaining ingredients and stir until blended. Cover and simmer mixture until rice is cooked and liquid is absorbed. Stir and serve hot. Serves 4.

Curried Chicken with Raisins & Rice

This is a very delicious and quick curry dish that can make leftover chicken or turkey grand enough for a dinner party and yet is easy enough to serve on an evening when you are running late.

2 onions, chopped
3 tablespoons oil
1-1/2 cups long-grain rice

1 apple, peeled, cored and grated
3/4 cup golden raisins
1 tablespoon brown sugar
2 teaspoons curry powder
2 cans (10-1/2 ounces each) chicken broth
1 tablespoon lemon juice
salt to taste
3 cups cooked chicken or turkey cut into large dice
1/2 cup toasted slivered almonds

In a Dutch oven, saute onion in oil until onions are soft. Add rice and saute it for 3 minutes, stirring and turning. Add the remaining ingredients, except the almonds, and stir until they are well blended.

Cover and simmer casserole until rice is tender and liquid is absorbed. Serve with chutney and several condiments, such as coconut flakes, grated cucumber or bacon bits. Serves 6.

Note — Casserole can be made earlier in the day and refrigerated. Reheat carefully over low heat to prevent rice from scorching.

Cracker Quiche with Bacon, Onions & Swiss Cheese

1-1/2 cups Ritz cracker crumbs (about 34 crackers)
1/4 cup butter (1/2 stick), melted

3 eggs, beaten
1/4 cup milk
1/2 cup sour cream
1 cup Swiss cheese, grated
6 strips bacon, cooked crisp and crumbled
2 teaspoons dried onion flakes
1 teaspoon chopped parsley
salt and pepper to taste

Combine cracker crumbs and melted butter and mix until blended. Pat mixture evenly on the bottom and sides of a 9-inch pie pan. Bake crust in a 350° oven for 8 minutes or until top is lightly browned. Set aside to cool.

Meanwhile, beat eggs with milk and sour cream until light. Stir in the remaining ingredients. Pour mixture into prepared crust and bake in a 350° oven about 40 minutes or until custard is set. Serves 4 for lunch.

Note — To make crumbs, place the crackers in a 1-gallon plastic bag and roll them into crumbs with a rolling pin.
— Quiche can be made earlier in the day and reheated at time of serving.

Clam Quiche with Bacon & Green Onions

2 9-inch frozen pie shells (purchase the shallow shells, about 1-inch deep)

4 eggs
1 package (8 ounces) cream cheese
1/2 cup cream
1/2 teaspoon dried dill weed
4 tablespoons grated Parmesan cheese

2 cans (7 ounces, each) minced clams, drained
1/2 cup finely chopped green onions
6 strips bacon, cooked crisp, drained and crumbled
salt and pepper to taste

Bake frozen pie shells in a 400° oven for about 10 minutes or until lightly golden.

Beat eggs with cream cheese, cream, dill and grated cheese. Add clams, onions, bacon and salt and pepper to taste. Divide mixture evenly between the 2 pie shells.

Bake quiches on a cookie sheet and bake in a 350° oven for 40 to 45 minutes or until quiche is set. Each pie serves 4.

Note — *As with all pie shells, if the edges are beginning to brown too quickly, place a strip of foil along the rim.*
— I do not recommend freezing this quiche.

Country French Eggplant Quiche with Tomatoes & Cheese

2 9-inch frozen pie shells (purchase the shallow shells, about 1 inch deep)
2 teaspoons Dijon-style mustard
1 eggplant, about 1-1/2 pounds
salt and pepper to taste

1 can (1 pound) stewed tomatoes, drained and cut up into small dice. Reserve juice for another use.
2 cups grated Swiss cheese
4 strips bacon, cooked crisp, drained and crumbled
4 eggs, well beaten
2 tablespoons parsley, finely chopped
2 tablespoons tomato paste
1/2 cup grated Parmesan cheese

Bake frozen pie shells in a 400° oven for about 10 minutes or until lightly browned. Brush bottom of shells with 1 teaspoon mustard, each.

Peel and slice eggplant into 1/4-inch slices. Sprinkle with salt and pepper. Place eggplant slices on a lightly greased cookie sheet, brush lightly with oil, cover pan with foil and bake in a 400° oven for about 30 minutes or until eggplant slices are soft.

In a large bowl, combine eggplant and remaining ingredients and stir until they are well mixed. Divide this mixture into the 2 prepared pie shells. Sprinkle top with additional grated Parmesan cheese.

Place quiches on a cookie sheet and bake in a 350° oven for 45 to 50 minutes or until quiche is set. Each pie serves 4.

Note – This is extremely delicious and a perfect blend of flavors. Serve with a Green Pea, Tomato and Onion salad for an interesting variation.
– Can be made earlier in the day but do not freeze.

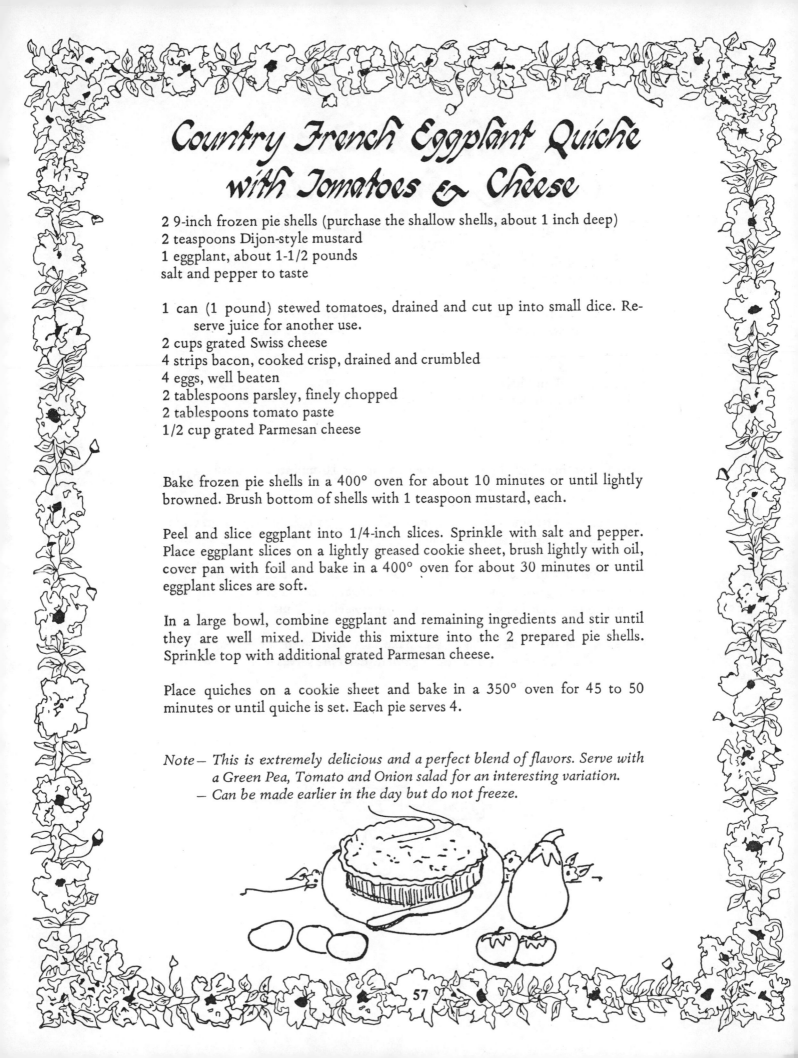

Quiche with Bacon, Onions & Swiss Cheese

2 9-inch frozen pie shells (purchase the shallow shells, about 1 inch deep)

1 large onion, finely chopped
2 tablespoons butter

1/4 pound bacon, cooked crisp, drained and crumbled
1 cup grated Swiss cheese

3 eggs
1-1/2 cups half and half
1/4 cup grated Parmesan cheese
salt and pepper to taste

Bake frozen pie shells in a 400° oven for about 10 minutes or until lightly golden.

Meanwhile, saute onion in butter until onions are soft. In another pan, cook the bacon until crisp. Then drain and crumble.

Divide onion and bacon between the two pie shells. Beat together the eggs and cream for 2 minutes at medium speed. Beat in the cheese and salt and pepper to taste. Divide egg mixture evenly between the 2 pie shells.

Place quiches on a cookie sheet and bake in a 350° oven for 40 to 45 minutes or until custard is set and top is golden. Each pie serves 4.

Crepes

&

Pancakes

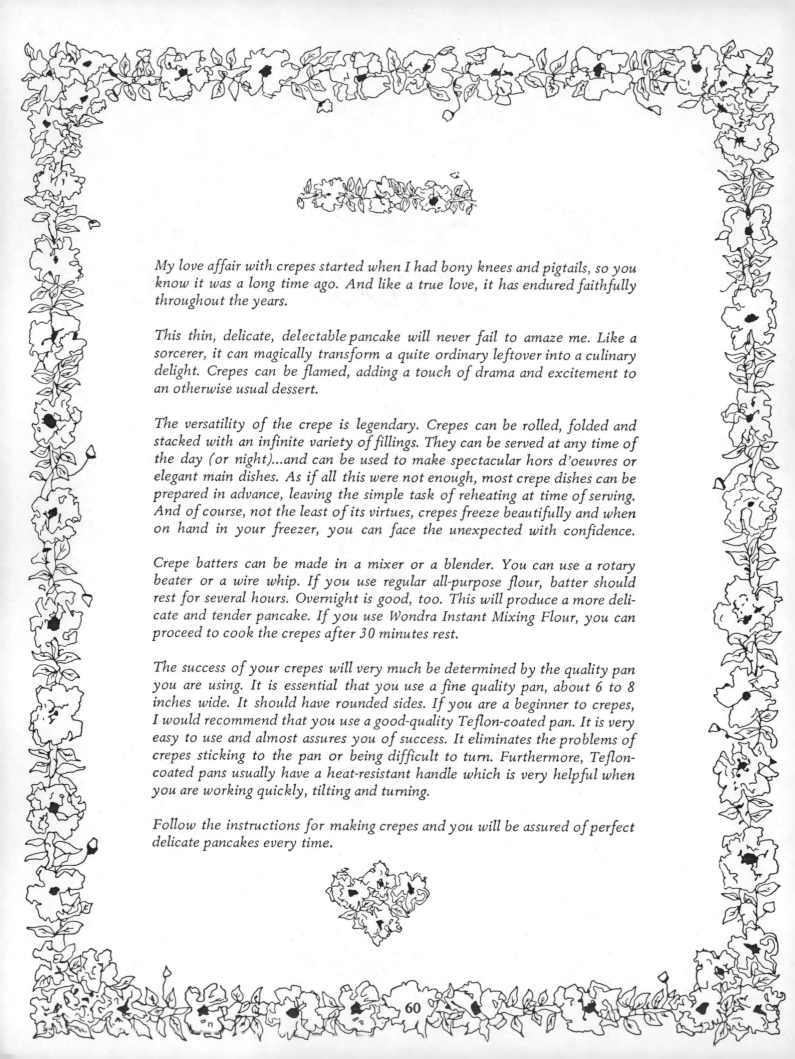

My love affair with crepes started when I had bony knees and pigtails, so you know it was a long time ago. And like a true love, it has endured faithfully throughout the years.

This thin, delicate, delectable pancake will never fail to amaze me. Like a sorcerer, it can magically transform a quite ordinary leftover into a culinary delight. Crepes can be flamed, adding a touch of drama and excitement to an otherwise usual dessert.

The versatility of the crepe is legendary. Crepes can be rolled, folded and stacked with an infinite variety of fillings. They can be served at any time of the day (or night)...and can be used to make spectacular hors d'oeuvres or elegant main dishes. As if all this were not enough, most crepe dishes can be prepared in advance, leaving the simple task of reheating at time of serving. And of course, not the least of its virtues, crepes freeze beautifully and when on hand in your freezer, you can face the unexpected with confidence.

Crepe batters can be made in a mixer or a blender. You can use a rotary beater or a wire whip. If you use regular all-purpose flour, batter should rest for several hours. Overnight is good, too. This will produce a more delicate and tender pancake. If you use Wondra Instant Mixing Flour, you can proceed to cook the crepes after 30 minutes rest.

The success of your crepes will very much be determined by the quality pan you are using. It is essential that you use a fine quality pan, about 6 to 8 inches wide. It should have rounded sides. If you are a beginner to crepes, I would recommend that you use a good-quality Teflon-coated pan. It is very easy to use and almost assures you of success. It eliminates the problems of crepes sticking to the pan or being difficult to turn. Furthermore, Teflon-coated pans usually have a heat-resistant handle which is very helpful when you are working quickly, tilting and turning.

Follow the instructions for making crepes and you will be assured of perfect delicate pancakes every time.

Crepes ~ Technique

1. With a rotary beater, beat ingredients until they are blended. Refrigerate batter for about 1 hour.

2. Remove batter from the refrigerator and stir it if it has separated. Add a little water if the batter has thickened.

3. Crepes are made over moderately high heat. Heat pan and butter it with a napkin or paper towel. Wipe off any excess butter. Pan should be very hot, but butter should not brown.

4. Lift pan off heat. With the other hand, pour about 1/8 cup of batter into the pan. Quickly tilt and turn the pan so that the bottom is completely covered with batter. Pour out any excess batter.

5. Place pan back on the heat and continue cooking the crepe for about 45 seconds or until top is dry. Turn and cook other side for about 15 seconds. Remove crepe onto a platter.

6. Heat and grease pan and start again from Step 3.

THE CRUCIAL POINT IS THAT THE PAN MUST BE HOT WHEN THE BATTER IS POURED. IT MUST THEN BE TILTED AND TURNED IMMEDIATELY TO COVER THE BOTTOM WITH A THIN LAYER OF BATTER.

Note— Unfilled crepes may be stored and frozen between layers of waxed paper.

Light, Light Crepes

3 eggs
1/2 cup flour
1/2 cup Wondra flour
1 cup Non-Fat milk (or Lo-Fat milk)
pinch of salt

In a mixing bowl, combine ingredients and proceed as above.

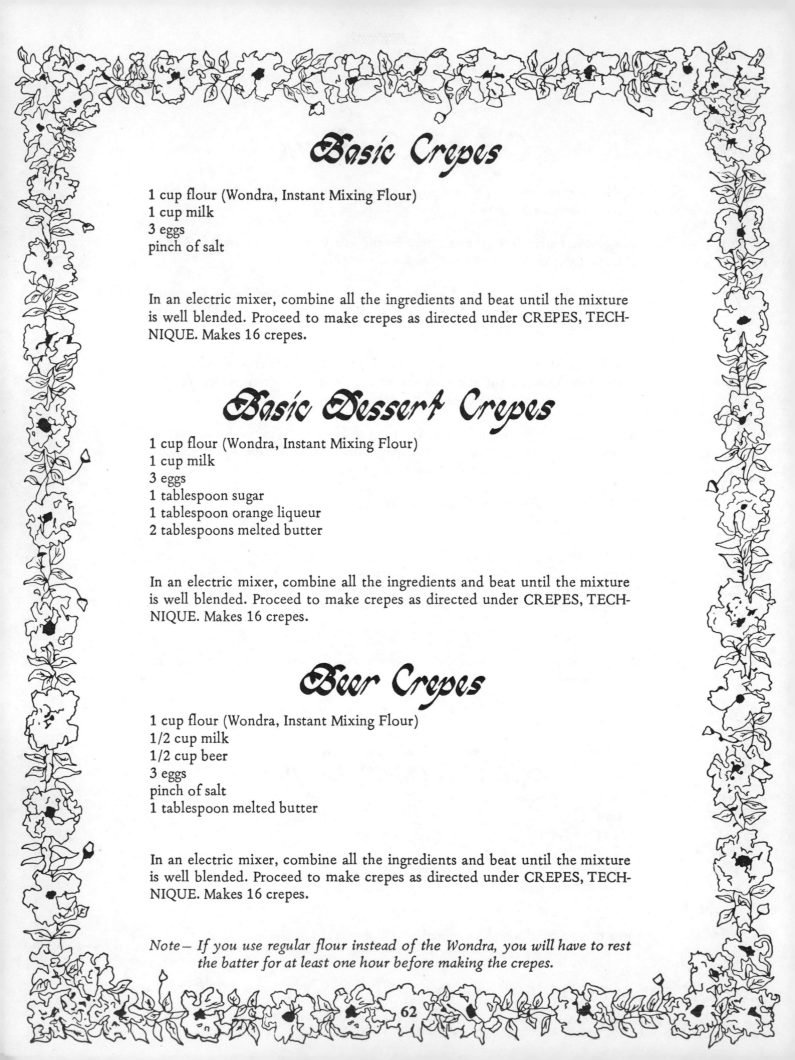

Basic Crepes

1 cup flour (Wondra, Instant Mixing Flour)
1 cup milk
3 eggs
pinch of salt

In an electric mixer, combine all the ingredients and beat until the mixture is well blended. Proceed to make crepes as directed under CREPES, TECHNIQUE. Makes 16 crepes.

Basic Dessert Crepes

1 cup flour (Wondra, Instant Mixing Flour)
1 cup milk
3 eggs
1 tablespoon sugar
1 tablespoon orange liqueur
2 tablespoons melted butter

In an electric mixer, combine all the ingredients and beat until the mixture is well blended. Proceed to make crepes as directed under CREPES, TECHNIQUE. Makes 16 crepes.

Beer Crepes

1 cup flour (Wondra, Instant Mixing Flour)
1/2 cup milk
1/2 cup beer
3 eggs
pinch of salt
1 tablespoon melted butter

In an electric mixer, combine all the ingredients and beat until the mixture is well blended. Proceed to make crepes as directed under CREPES, TECHNIQUE. Makes 16 crepes.

Note— If you use regular flour instead of the Wondra, you will have to rest the batter for at least one hour before making the crepes.

Green Crepes with Herbs

1 cup flour (Wondra, Instant Mixing Flour)
1 cup milk
3 eggs
1 tablespoon dried chopped chives
1/4 cup frozen chopped spinach, squeezed dry
1 tablespoon melted butter

Place all the ingredients in a blender container and blend for 30 seconds or until spinach is completely incorporated in the batter. Proceed to make crepes as directed under CREPES, TECHNIQUE. Makes 16 crepes.

Crepes with Herbs

1 cup flour (Wondra, Instant Mixing Flour)
3/4 cup milk
1/4 cup sour cream
3 eggs
1 teaspoon dried chives
1 teaspoon parsley flakes
1 tablespoon oil

Beat together all the ingredients until the mixture is well blended. Proceed to make crepes as directed under CREPES, TECHNIQUE. Makes 16 crepes.

Crepes with Cheese

1 cup flour (Wondra, Instant Mixing flour)
1 cup milk
1/4 cup water
3 eggs
1/4 cup grated Parmesan cheese
1 tablespoon oil

Beat all the ingredients together in your electric mixer until the mixture is well blended. Proceed to make crepes as directed under CREPES, TECHNIQUE. Makes 16 crepes.

Note— If you use regular flour instead of the Wondra, then you will have to rest the batter for at least one hour before making the crepes.

Crepes Italienne with Cheese in a Light Tomato Sauce

16 7-inch Crepes with Herbs

FILLING

1 pint Ricotta cheese
2 eggs
1/2 cup grated Mozzarella cheese
1/2 cup Saltine cracker crumbs
1/2 cup grated Parmesan cheese
1 tablespoon minced fresh parsley
1 tablespoon dried chives

Combine all the filling ingredients and stir until well blended. Place 2 table-spoons filling on end of each crepe. Roll them up and place them, seam side down on a buttered porcelain baker. Spoon Light Tomato Sauce over the top and sprinkle with additional Parmesan cheese.

Heat in a 350° oven for about 20 minutes or until piping hot. Serves 8 for lunch.

Light Tomato Sauce

1 can (1 pound) stewed tomatoes, finely chopped
1 can (8 ounces) tomato sauce
1-1/2 teaspoons Italian Herb Seasoning
1 teaspoon parsley flakes
1/8 teaspoon garlic powder
1 tablespoon olive oil

Combine all the ingredients and simmer for 20 minutes, uncovered.

Note— Crepes can be made and filled a day before serving. Remove from the refrigerator and spoon sauce over the crepes just before placing in the oven to heat.
— Sauce can be made a day earlier and refrigerated.

Crepes Royal
with Chicken, Raisins & Almonds

12 7-inch Light, Light Crepes

3 cups diced cooked chicken
1/2 cup chopped golden raisins
1/2 cup toasted slivered almonds
1 cup sour cream
salt to taste

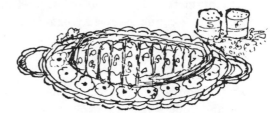

Combine the chicken with the rest of the ingredients and stir to mix well. Divide the filling between the crepes. Place about 2 tablespoons filling on each crepe, roll it up jelly roll fashion and place each crepe, seam side down, in a single layer in a buttered porcelain baker. Spread Sour Cream Mushroom Sauce over the top and heat in a 350° oven until heated through. Serves 4 for dinner or 6 for lunch.

Sour Cream Mushroom Sauce

1/4 pound mushrooms, thinly sliced
1/4 cup finely minced onion
2 tablespoons butter

1 tablespoon flour
1/2 cup half and half
1/2 cup sour cream
1 tablespoon dry white wine
salt and white pepper to taste

In a saucepan, saute mushrooms and onion in butter until the onions are soft. Add flour and cook for a minute or two, stirring now and again. Add cream and cook over low heat, stirring, until sauce thickens. Add the remaining ingredients and heat through. Do not allow to boil.

Note— Entire dish can be assembled earlier in the day and refrigerated. Allow to come to room temperature before reheating.

Crepes with Chicken, Tomatoes & Chiles

12 7-inch Basic Crepes

3 cups diced cooked chicken
2 medium tomatoes, peeled, seeded and finely chopped. (You may substitute 2 canned stewed tomatoes.)
1 can (4 ounces) diced chiles
1 cup grated Swiss cheese
1 cup sour cream
3 tablespoons finely minced chives
salt and pepper to taste

Combine the chicken with the rest of the ingredients and stir to mix well. Divide the filling between the crepes, roll, and place each crepe, seam side down, in a single layer in a lovely porcelain baker. Spread Instant Cheese Sauce over the top and heat in a 350° oven until piping hot and cheese is melted. Serves 4 (for dinner) or 6 (for lunch).

Instant Cheese Sauce

1-1/2 cups sour cream
1 cup grated Swiss cheese
2 tablespoons grated Parmesan cheese
2 tablespoons finely minced chives
salt and pepper to taste

Mix all the ingredients together until they are well blended.

Note — *Entire casserole can be assembled earlier in the day and even a day before you are planning to serve it. Remove casserole from the refrigerator about 1 hour before you are planning to reheat it. Then heat it at 350° for about 30 minutes.*
— This is a lovely luncheon or party dish. If you have any leftover chicken, it will be an extraordinarily simple dish.
— Serve with canned pears sprinkled with brown sugar and pecans and broiled until sugar is melted.

Crepes Filled with Spinach & Mushrooms with Instant Swiss Parmesan Sauce

12 7-inch Basic Crepes

1/4 pound mushrooms, thinly sliced
1 onion, finely chopped
3 tablespoons butter

2 tablespoons Cognac
2 tablespoons flour

1/4 cup cream
1 package (3 ounces) cream cheese, at room temperature
salt and pepper to taste
pinch of nutmeg
1 package (10 ounces) frozen chopped spinach, drained very dry

Saute mushrooms and onion in butter until onions are soft. Heat 2 tablespoons Cognac in a brandy warmer or very small saucepan. Ignite Cognac with a match and very carefully pour flaming Cognac over the mushrooms.

When the flames die down, add flour and cook for 2 minutes, tossing and turning. Add the cream, cream cheese, seasonings and continue cooking and stirring until mixture is blended. Stir in the prepared spinach until thoroughly combined.

Divide filling between the 12 crepes. Roll up the crepes and place them, seam side down, in one layer in a buttered casserole. Spread Instant Parmesan Swiss Sauce over the top and heat casserole in a 350° oven until heated through and cheese sauce is melted. Brown for a few seconds under the broiler. Serves 6 for lunch or 4 for dinner.

Instant Swiss Parmesan Sauce

1 cup sour cream
1 cup grated Swiss cheese
1/2 cup grated Parmesan cheese

Combine all the ingredients and stir to blend.

Note— Entire casserole can be prepared earlier in the day and refrigerated. Remove from the refrigerator and allow to come to room temperature before reheating.

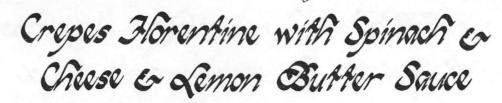

Crepes Florentine with Spinach & Cheese & Lemon Butter Sauce

12 7-inch Crepes with Cheese

1 package (10 ounces) frozen chopped spinach, defrosted in a strainer and
    pressed dry
6 strips bacon, cooked crisp and crumbled
2 green onions, finely chopped
1/2 cup Ricotta cheese
1 cup grated Mozzarella cheese
1/2 cup grated Parmesan cheese
salt and freshly ground pepper to taste
pinch of nutmeg

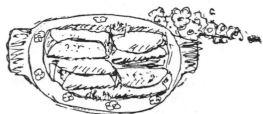

Combine the spinach with the remaining ingredients and stir to blend well.
Divide filling onto the crepes. Roll up each crepe and place in a buttered
porcelain baker, seam side down.

Baste crepes with Lemon Butter Sauce and sprinkle with extra grated Parmesan cheese to taste. Heat in a 350° oven until heated through, about 20 minutes. Serves 4 for dinner or 6 for lunch.

Lemon Butter Sauce

1/2 cup butter (1 stick)
2 tablespoons lemon juice
1/4 cup grated Parmesan cheese

Combine the ingredients and stir until blended.

Note — Entire casserole can be assembled earlier in the day and refrigerated.
      Baste with Lemon Butter Sauce before heating, not earlier.
  — Do not freeze.

Cannelóni with Meat in Mushroom Tomato Sauce

12 7-inch Green Herb Crepes

FILLING

1 pound ground beef
1 egg
2 tablespoons dehydrated onion soup
1/4 cup crushed garlic croutons soaked in 1/4 cup water
1 tablespoon parsley flakes
1/8 teaspoon garlic powder
salt and pepper to taste

In a skillet, cook the ground beef, turning and stirring, until the meat loses its pinkness. Do not overcook the meat. Add the remaining ingredients and stir until well blended.

Place 2 tablespoons meat mixture on end of each crepe. Roll them up and place them, seam side down, on a buttered porcelain baker. Spoon Mushroom Tomato Sauce over the top and sprinkle with grated Parmesan cheese.

Heat in a 350° oven for about 20 minutes or until piping hot. Serves 4.

Mushroom Tomato Sauce

1/2 pound mushrooms, cleaned and thinly sliced
2 tablespoons oil
1 onion, finely chopped
1 clove garlic, mashed
1 can (1 pound) stewed tomatoes, finely chopped
1 can (6 ounces) tomato paste
1 tablespoon minced parsley (fresh) or 1 teaspoon dried
1 teaspoon Italian Herb Seasoning
1 bay leaf
1 tablespoon sugar
salt and pepper to taste

Saute mushrooms, onion and garlic in oil until onions are transparent. Add the remaining ingredients and simmer sauce for 15 minutes.

Dessert Crepes with Cream Cheese & Apricot Raisin Jam

12 7-inch Basic Crepes

FILLING

2 packages (8 ounces, each) cream cheese, softened
1/2 cup sugar
3 tablespoons lemon juice
1 tablespoon grated lemon peel

3 tablespoons melted butter

Beat together the cream cheese, sugar, lemon juice and lemon peel until the mixture is blended.

Place 2 tablespoons of filling on each crepe. Roll them up and place them, seam side down, on a buttered casserole in one layer. Brush them with the melted butter.

Heat in a 350° oven until heated through. Serve them with a dollup of sour cream and a teaspoon of Apricot Raisin Jam. Serves 6.

Apricot Raisin Jam

1 cup apricot jam, cut up any large pieces of fruit
1 teaspoon grated lemon peel
1/4 cup yellow raisins
1/2 cup coarsely chopped walnuts
12 maraschino cherries, sliced
2 tablespoons lemon juice

Place all the ingredients in a pint jar with a lid. Stir mixture until blended. Refrigerate until ready to use. Delicious on muffins and toast. Yields 2 cups.

Dessert Crepes with Apricots & Walnuts

12 7-inch Basic Dessert Crepes

FILLING

1 cup finely chopped toasted walnuts
1 cup apricot jam, puree or chop any large pieces of fruit
1 tablespoon orange liqueur

Combine the filling ingredients and stir to mix well. Spread 2 tablespoons filling over each crepe and roll them up jelly-roll fashion. Refrigerate until ready to serve. Before serving, heat in a 350° oven for about 10 minutes.

At serving time, spoon a teaspoon (or two) of Instant Hot Fudge Sauce over each crepe. Sprinkle with additional finely chopped toasted walnuts. Serves 6.

Instant Hot Fudge Sauce

1 package (6 ounces) semi-sweet chocolate chips
1 tablespoon orange liqueur

1 cup whipping cream
1 teaspoon vanilla

Place chocolate chips and orange liqueur in blender container. Heat cream just to boiling point and pour into blender. Blend for a few seconds until chocolate is melted. Add vanilla and blend for another few seconds. Serve immediately. Makes 1-1/2 cups sauce.

Note — You can make Hot Fudge Sauce in advance and reheat it in a double boiler over hot, not boiling water.
— If you would like to add a dramatic touch, flame the crepes before serving. To Flame: Heat 2 tablespoons brandy in an 8-ounce copper or metal saucepan. Ignite the brandy with a match and pour carefully over the crepes. When flames die down, serve as described above.
— Entire dish can be assembled earlier in the day. Spoon the chocolate sauce just before serving.

Cottage Cheese Pancakes with Orange Butter Honey

1 cup cottage cheese
3 eggs
1/3 cup flour
pinch of salt
2 tablespoons sugar
2 tablespoons melted butter
1 teaspoon baking powder
1/2 teaspoon vanilla

Place all the ingredients in a mixing bowl and beat with a fork until they are combined. Do not overmix.

Pour batter on a lightly greased, preheated Teflon griddle. When bottom of pancake is golden brown and top is bubbly, turn and brown other side.

Serve warm with a dollup of sour cream and defrosted strawberries in syrup. It is also very good with applesauce sprinkled with cinnamon. If you like syrup with your pancakes, you will enjoy the unusual Orange Butter Honey. Makes 12 pancakes.

Orange Butter Honey

1/2 cup butter (1 stick)
1/2 cup honey
1 tablespoon undiluted orange juice (frozen concentrate)
1 tablespoon lemon juice
1/8 teaspoon cinnamon

Combine all the ingredients in a saucepan and simmer mixture for 2 minutes. Yields about 1 cup.

Note— If you have a fussy, picky eater, you might want to try these protein pancakes. They are light and fluffy, and I do believe, the kind of pancakes that kids remember with nostalgia when they are fully grown.

Apple Pancakes with Honey Almond Cream Syrup

3 eggs, beaten
1 cup flour
3 teaspoons baking powder
1/4 teaspoon salt
1 tablespoon brown sugar
2 tablespoons melted butter
3/4 cup milk

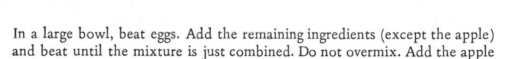

1 small apple, peeled, cored and grated

In a large bowl, beat eggs. Add the remaining ingredients (except the apple) and beat until the mixture is just combined. Do not overmix. Add the apple and stir to mix.

Pour about 1/8 cup batter on a lightly greased, preheated griddle. (Use more or less batter, depending on the size pancake you wish to make.) When bottom of the pancake is golden brown and top is bubbly, turn and brown the other side. Serve warm with Honey Almond Cream Syrup. Makes about 12 pancakes.

Honey Almond Cream Syrup

1/2 cup butter
1/2 cup honey
1/2 cup cream
4 tablespoons finely chopped toasted almonds
2 tablespoons brown sugar
1 teaspoon vanilla

In a saucepan, simmer together all the ingredients (except the vanilla) for 5 minutes, or until syrup thickens. Stir in the vanilla. Serve warm. Makes about 1-1/2 cups.

Note — If you enjoy a stronger almond flavor, add 1/2 teaspoon almond extract with the vanilla.

Banana Orange Pancakes

1 cup flour
2 teaspoons baking powder
pinch of salt
2 tablespoons melted butter
2 tablespoons sugar
2 eggs
1 teaspoon vanilla
3/4 cup milk

1 medium banana, mashed
1 tablespoon grated orange peel

Orange Honey

Mix together the first eight ingredients until blended. Do not overmix. Fold in the banana and orange peel.

Pour about 1/8 cup batter on a lightly greased, preheated griddle. (Use more or less batter, depending on the size pancake you wish to make.) When bottom of the pancake is golden brown and top is bubbly, turn and brown the other side. Serve warm with Orange Honey. Makes about 12 pancakes and serves 4.

Orange Honey

1/2 cup honey
1/2 cup orange marmalade

Mix together the honey and marmalade until mixture is blended. Store in a covered jar in the refrigerator. Remove from the refrigerator about 20 minutes before serving and allow to come to room temperature.

Soups

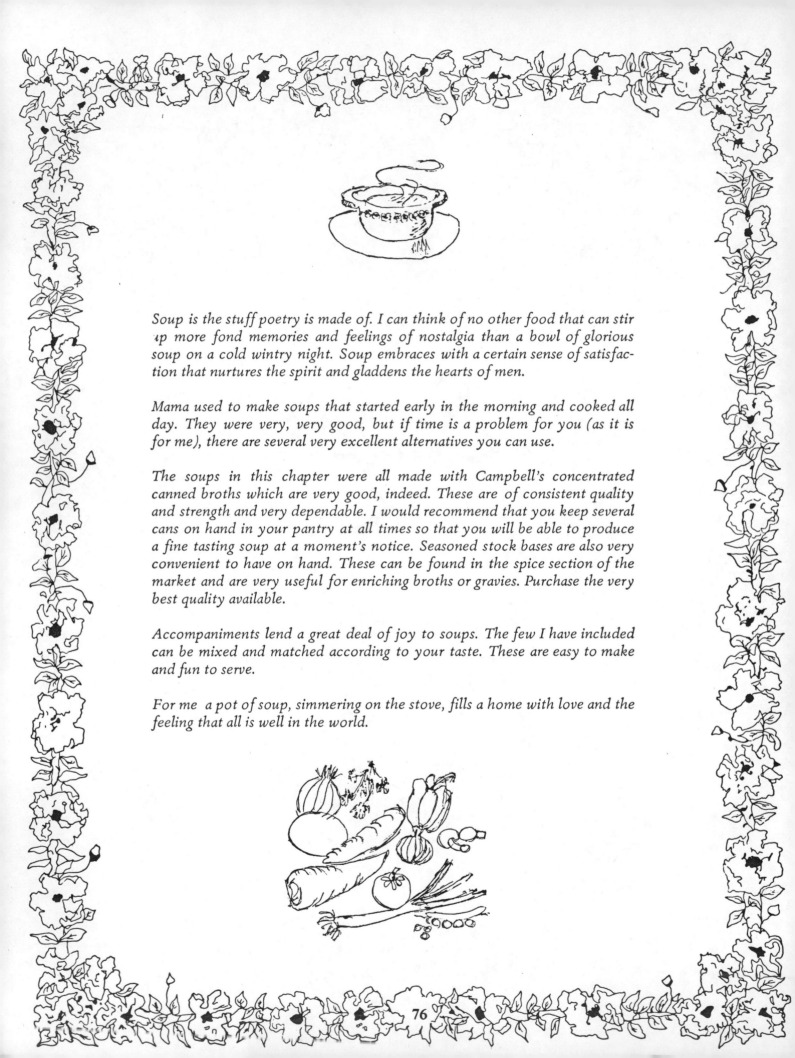

Soup is the stuff poetry is made of. I can think of no other food that can stir up more fond memories and feelings of nostalgia than a bowl of glorious soup on a cold wintry night. Soup embraces with a certain sense of satisfaction that nurtures the spirit and gladdens the hearts of men.

Mama used to make soups that started early in the morning and cooked all day. They were very, very good, but if time is a problem for you (as it is for me), there are several very excellent alternatives you can use.

The soups in this chapter were all made with Campbell's concentrated canned broths which are very good, indeed. These are of consistent quality and strength and very dependable. I would recommend that you keep several cans on hand in your pantry at all times so that you will be able to produce a fine tasting soup at a moment's notice. Seasoned stock bases are also very convenient to have on hand. These can be found in the spice section of the market and are very useful for enriching broths or gravies. Purchase the very best quality available.

Accompaniments lend a great deal of joy to soups. The few I have included can be mixed and matched according to your taste. These are easy to make and fun to serve.

For me a pot of soup, simmering on the stove, fills a home with love and the feeling that all is well in the world.

Mama's Hearty Barley Beef Soup with Onion Roulades

2 pounds flanken ribs, meaty and lean (sometimes called short ribs)
2 medium onions, chopped
3 medium carrots, thinly sliced
1 can beef broth (10-1/2 ounces)
1 can chicken broth (10-1/2 ounces)
1 cup water
salt and pepper to taste
1 clove garlic put through a press
1 cup cooked barley*

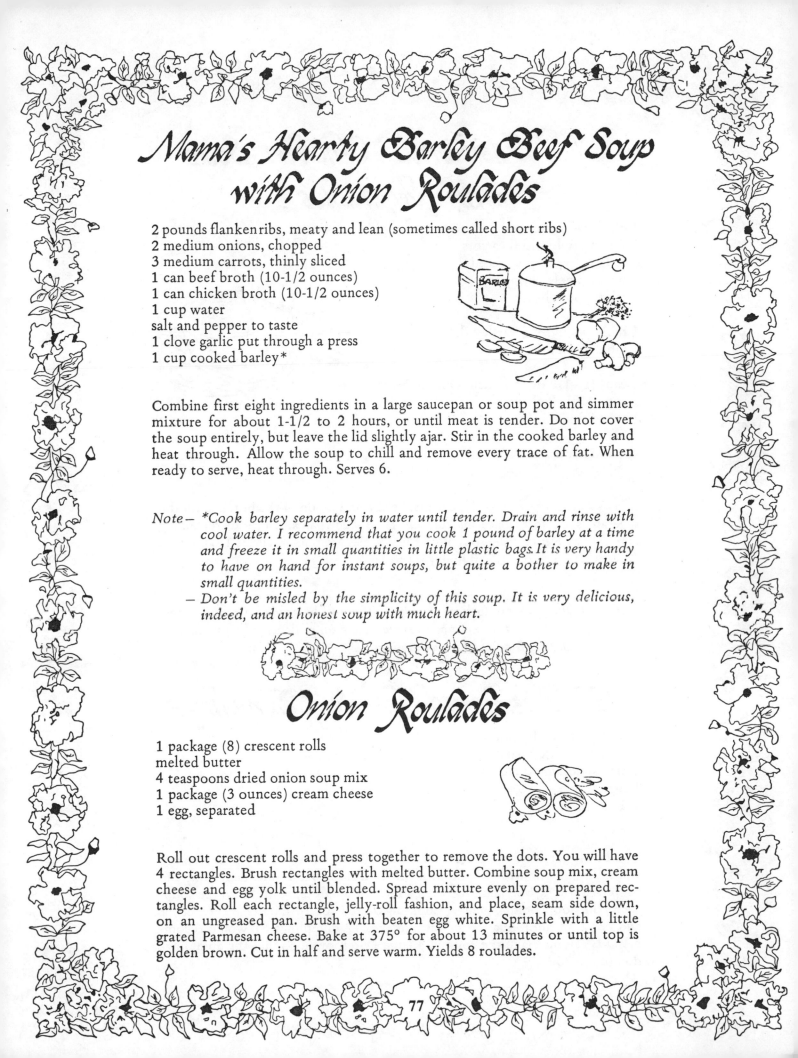

Combine first eight ingredients in a large saucepan or soup pot and simmer mixture for about 1-1/2 to 2 hours, or until meat is tender. Do not cover the soup entirely, but leave the lid slightly ajar. Stir in the cooked barley and heat through. Allow the soup to chill and remove every trace of fat. When ready to serve, heat through. Serves 6.

Note— *Cook barley separately in water until tender. Drain and rinse with cool water. I recommend that you cook 1 pound of barley at a time and freeze it in small quantities in little plastic bags. It is very handy to have on hand for instant soups, but quite a bother to make in small quantities.
— Don't be misled by the simplicity of this soup. It is very delicious, indeed, and an honest soup with much heart.

Onion Roulades

1 package (8) crescent rolls
melted butter
4 teaspoons dried onion soup mix
1 package (3 ounces) cream cheese
1 egg, separated

Roll out crescent rolls and press together to remove the dots. You will have 4 rectangles. Brush rectangles with melted butter. Combine soup mix, cream cheese and egg yolk until blended. Spread mixture evenly on prepared rectangles. Roll each rectangle, jelly-roll fashion, and place, seam side down, on an ungreased pan. Brush with beaten egg white. Sprinkle with a little grated Parmesan cheese. Bake at 375° for about 13 minutes or until top is golden brown. Cut in half and serve warm. Yields 8 roulades.

Old Fashioned Chicken Soup with Vegetables

1 clove garlic, mashed
1/2 cup thinly sliced carrots
1 stalk celery, thinly sliced
1 onion, finely chopped
3 tablespoons butter

1 tablespoon dried parsley flakes
1 tablespoon dried chives

3 cans (10-1/2 ounces each) chicken broth
1 cup diced chicken
1/2 cup fine noodles

salt and pepper to taste

In a skillet, saute the garlic, carrots, celery and onion in the butter until the vegetables are soft. Place mixture in a large sauce pan and add the remaining ingredients. Simmer the soup until the noodles are tender, about 15 minutes. Serve with hot biscuits and honey. Serves 6.

Note — If you happen to have the time, it would be so nice to make some old fashioned dumplings to serve in the soup. Especially good would be Old Fashioned Chive Dumplings.

Old Fashioned Chive Dumplings

2 cups prepared biscuit mix
2 teaspoons dried parsley
1 tablespoon dried chives
1 egg, beaten
1/2 cup milk

In a bowl, combine the biscuit mix, parsley and chives. Add the beaten egg and milk and stir with a fork until the mixture is barely blended. Bring the soup to a rolling boil and drop the batter by the tablespoonful into the soup. Keep the soup boiling gently. Cook uncovered for 10 minutes. Then cover and cook an additional 10 minutes. Makes 12 dumplings. (I would recommend that you make the soup in a large Dutch oven, so that the dumplings do not crowd.)

Country French Vegetable Soup

3 carrots, thinly sliced
3 potatoes, cubed
3 cans (10-1/2 ounces, each) chicken broth
1 cup water
salt and pepper to taste
1 can (8 ounces) tomato sauce
1/4 cup chopped parsley leaves

1/4 cup butter
3 shallots, finely chopped
3 onions, finely chopped
2 cloves garlic, put through a press
1 package (10 ounces) frozen peas

In a large saucepan or soup pot, cook together the first seven ingredients and simmer mixture for 45 minutes or until vegetables are tender. Do not cover the soup pot entirely, but leave the lid slightly ajar.

Meanwhile, saute together the remaining ingredients until the onions are tender. Add this mixture to the soup pot and continue simmering for 15 minutes. Divide mixture between 6 or 8 oven-proof soup bowls. Float a slice of French Bread with Garlic Swiss on top and broil for a few seconds until top is lightly browned. Serves 6 to 8.

French Bread with Garlic Swiss Cheese

1 egg white
1 clove garlic, put through a press
1 cup grated Swiss cheese

6 slices French bread, lightly toasted

Combine egg white, garlic and cheese and stir until blended. Spread mixture on toasted French bread.

Broccoli Mushroom Cream Soup

1/4 pound mushrooms, cleaned and sliced
2 tablespoons butter
2 packages (10 ounces each) frozen chopped broccoli
2 onions, sliced
2 shallots, minced
4 tablespoons butter

2 cans (10-1/2 ounces each) Campbell's Chicken Broth, undiluted
1-1/2 cups half and half
salt and pepper to taste
pinch of garlic powder
pinch of dried dill weed

Saute mushrooms in 2 tablespoons butter until mushrooms are tender. Remove mushrooms with a slotted spoon and set aside. Saute broccoli, onions and shallots in same skillet with the 4 tablespoons butter, until the vegetables are tender.

Blend the vegetables with some of the chicken broth until they are pureed and smooth. Blend a few at a time. Don't attempt them all at once.

Pour the pureed vegetables into a saucepan. Add the sauteed mushrooms and the remaining ingredients. Simmer the soup for 10 minutes. Serve with Toasted Buttered Dill Rounds. Serves 6.

Toasted Buttered Dill Rounds

6 slices white bread
6 teaspoons butter
dill weed
grated Parmesan cheese

With a 2-inch biscuit cutter cut rounds out of each slice of bread. Reserve the trimmed crusts for making crumbs at another time. Toast the rounds in a 200° oven until they are fairly dry. Spread each round with about 1 teaspoon butter, sprinkle with dill weed and grated Parmesan cheese. Broil for a few seconds and serve warm.

Note — Soup can be made earlier in the day and reheated at time of serving. Reheat over low heat.

— Toasted rounds can be made earlier and broiled at time of serving.

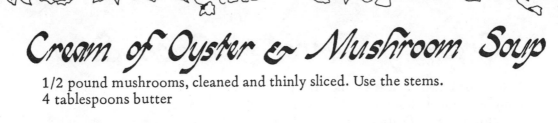

Cream of Oyster & Mushroom Soup

1/2 pound mushrooms, cleaned and thinly sliced. Use the stems.
4 tablespoons butter

2 tablespoons flour

1 can (8 ounces) oysters, coarsely chopped
2 cans (10-1/2 ounces each) chicken broth
1 tablespoon lemon juice
1 tablespoon dried parsley flakes

1/2 cup vermicelli, crushed
salt and pepper to taste
1-1/2 cups half and half

Saute mushrooms in butter until they are tender. Add the flour and cook for two minutes, stirring now and again. Do not let flour brown.

Add the oysters, chicken broth, lemon juice and parsley and heat through. Add the vermicelli and salt and pepper and cook for 10 or 12 minutes until noodles are tender. Add the cream and heat through. Serve with Herbed Muffins with Cheese. Serves 6.

Herbed Muffins with Cheese

2 eggs, beaten
1 cup small curd cottage cheese
2 tablespoons sour cream
1 tablespoon oil
1 teaspoon sugar
1/2 cup grated Parmesan cheese
1 teaspoon dried parsley flakes
1 teaspoon dried chives
1/2 cup Bisquick, prepared biscuit mix

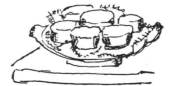

Combine all the ingredients in the large bowl of your electric mixer and beat until the mixture is well blended. Butter 24 teflon-coated hors d'oeuvre-size muffin tins and fill 1/2 full with batter.

Bake in 350° oven for 25 minutes or until puffed and golden brown. Yields 24 muffins.

Cream of Carrot & Onion Soup

1/2 pound carrots, cleaned and grated
2 onions, finely chopped
1/4 cup butter (1/2 stick)
1 apple, peeled, cored and grated
1/4 cup minced parsley (or 1 tablespoon dried parsley flakes)

2 cans (10-1/2 ounces) chicken broth

1 teaspoon sugar
salt and pepper to taste

1 cup cream
1 cup sour cream

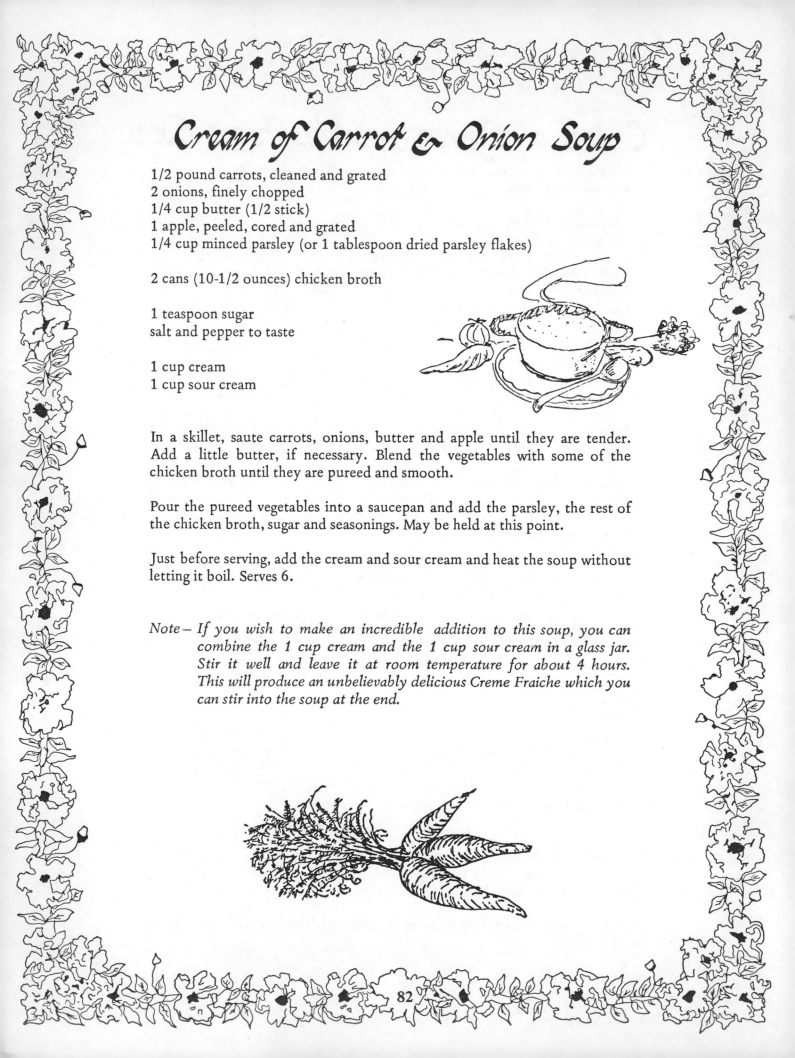

In a skillet, saute carrots, onions, butter and apple until they are tender. Add a little butter, if necessary. Blend the vegetables with some of the chicken broth until they are pureed and smooth.

Pour the pureed vegetables into a saucepan and add the parsley, the rest of the chicken broth, sugar and seasonings. May be held at this point.

Just before serving, add the cream and sour cream and heat the soup without letting it boil. Serves 6.

Note – *If you wish to make an incredible addition to this soup, you can combine the 1 cup cream and the 1 cup sour cream in a glass jar. Stir it well and leave it at room temperature for about 4 hours. This will produce an unbelievably delicious Creme Fraiche which you can stir into the soup at the end.*

Quick Mushroom Soup with Cheese Chewies

1 pound mushrooms, cleaned and sliced. Use the stems.
1/4 cup butter (1/2 stick)

2 tablespoons flour
1 tablespoon lemon juice
2 cans (10-1/2 ounces, each) beef broth

1 cup half and half
1/2 cup sour cream
1/4 teaspoon dried thyme
salt and pepper to taste
1 tablespoon dried parsley flakes

Saute the mushrooms in the butter until the mushrooms are tender. Add the flour and cook and stir for 2 minutes. Add the lemon juice and broth and continue cooking and stirring until the mixture is thoroughly blended.

Beat together the cream and sour cream until the mixture is blended. Stir the cream into the soup along with the seasonings and the parsley. Bring the soup to a simmer and simmer for 5 minutes. Do not boil. Serves 6. Serve with warm Cheese Chewies and sweet butter.

Cheese Chewies

4 tablespoons butter, at room temperature
2 tablespoons sugar
1 egg
3/4 cup milk
1 cup grated Swiss cheese
1/2 cup grated Parmesan cheese

1-1/2 cups flour
2 teaspoons baking powder
1/4 teaspoon salt

Beat together the butter, sugar, egg and milk until the mixture is blended. Stir in the Swiss and Parmesan cheeses. Stir in the remaining ingredients and stir until the dry ingredients are just moistened.

Divide the mixture between 12 paper-lined muffin cups and sprinkle top generously with additional grated Parmesan cheese. Bake in a 400° oven for about 25 minutes or until a cake tester, inserted in center, comes out clean. Serve warm with sweet whipped butter. Yields 12 muffins.

Sweet Pea Potato Soup

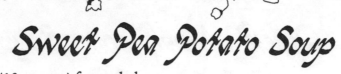

1 package (10 ounces) frozen baby peas
3 tablespoons butter
1 clove garlic, mashed

2 potatoes, peeled, boiled and very finely chopped
6 strips bacon, cooked crisp and crumbled, drained
2 cans (10-1/2 ounces each) chicken broth, undiluted
1 cup half and half
1 cup sour cream
Salt to taste

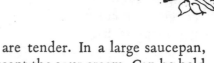

Saute peas and garlic in butter until peas are tender. In a large saucepan, place peas and the remaining ingredients, except the sour cream. Can be held at this point.

Just before serving, stir in the sour cream and heat the soup through. Do not let it boil. Serve with Toast Points with Butter and Garlic. Serves 6.

Toast Points with Butter & Garlic

6 slices very thinly sliced Westphalian Pumpernickel (From the refrigerated
    section in your market)
6 teaspoons butter
garlic powder
grated Parmesan cheese
paprika

Butter each slice of bread and sprinkle with garlic powder, grated Parmesan cheese and paprika. Cut each slice into four triangles. Just before serving, place under the broiler for a few seconds until butter melts and cheese is bubbly. Bread is very thin and will become crisp.

Note— *Soup can be made earlier and refrigerated. Add the sour cream just*
    before heating.
    — Bread can be prepared earlier and wrapped carefully in plastic wrap.
    Remove wrap before broiling.

Country Style Pumpkin Soup with Honey

1 onion, minced
2 tablespoons butter

2 cups canned pumpkin puree
2 cans (10-1/2 ounces each) chicken broth
3 tablespoons honey
1/2 teaspoon pumpkin pie spice
salt and pepper to taste

1/2 cup orange juice
1 pint half and half

Saute the onion in the butter until the onions are soft. Puree the onions in the blender. (Use a little chicken broth, if your blender needs it to whip smoothly.)

Pour the pureed onions into a Dutch oven. Add the pumpkin, chicken broth, honey and spices. Add the orange juice and stir until well blended. Heat carefully and when hot, slowly add the cream. Bring to a simmer and cook for 10 minutes. Simmer gently, but do not boil.

Serve with a dollup of sour cream. Serve hot or cold. Serves 6.

Note— Soup can be made up to 2 days earlier and kept refrigerated. Take care in reheating. Allow soup to come to room temperature and then heat carefully.
— If you are planning to serve the soup cold, sweeten it with an additional tablespoon or two of honey or with a little brown sugar.

Curried Chicken Soup with Apples & Coconut

1 apple, peeled, cored and grated
2 tablespoons butter
2 tablespoons flour
1 tablespoon curry powder

1 can (10-1/2 ounces) chicken broth
3/4 cup apple juice
salt to taste

1-1/2 cups half and half
1 cup cooked chicken, cut into julienned strips

1/2 cup cream, whipped
1/2 cup sweetened coconut flakes, toasted

Saute apple in butter until apple is soft. Add flour and curry powder and cook for 1 minute, stirring now and again. Stir in chicken broth and apple juice and continue cooking and stirring until mixture is heated through. Add the salt, half and half and chicken and simmer for 5 minutes. Serve with a dollup of whipped cream and a sprinkling of toasted coconut flakes. Serve with Pita Bread with Butter, Sesame Seeds and Honey. Serves 4.

Pita Bread with Butter Sesame Seeds & Honey

With a scissors trim about 1/8-inch off the edge of the pita bread. You will have two flat circles of bread. Cut each half in quarters, spread with sweet butter and honey. Sprinkle with a few sesame seeds. Broil for a few seconds only. Bread should not brown, but will be very crisp. Make at least 2 pitas for 4 people.

Hardy Tomato Soup with Croustades of Tomato & Cheese

4 slices bacon, cut into 1-inch pieces
2 onions, chopped
2 carrots, thinly sliced
1 clove garlic, put through a press
salt and pepper to taste
1/4 teaspoon thyme

2 cans stewed tomatoes (1 pound, each) finely chopped
2 cans chicken broth (10-1/2 ounces, each)

Saute together the first six ingredients until the onions are transparent. In a large saucepan or soup pot, place onion mixture, stewed tomatoes (reserve 2 tomatoes for croustades) and broth and simmer mixture for about 40 minutes or until vegetables are tender. Do not cover the soup entirely, but leave the lid slightly ajar while cooking.

Blend the soup in small quantities in your blender and place in individual oven-proof soup bowls. Place a Croustade of Tomato and Cheese on the top and heat in a 350° oven until piping hot and cheese is melted. Broil for a second or two under the broiler. Serves 6, very fortunate individuals.

Croustades of Tomato & Cheese

2 tomatoes (reserved from above), finely chopped
1 clove garlic, put through a press
2 tablespoons chopped chives
1 tablespoon butter
salt and pepper to taste

3/4 cup grated Jack cheese
6 slices French bread

Cook together the first 5 ingredients for 5 minutes, stirring now and again. Allow to cool. Stir in the grated cheese. Spread mixture on sliced French bread.

Tomato & Dill Soup

2 cans stewed tomatoes (16 ounces each)

1 onion, chopped
1 carrot, chopped
1 clove garlic, mashed
2 green onions, chopped
4 tablespoons butter

2 cans (10-1/2 ounces, each) chicken broth
2 tablespoons tomato paste
1/2 teaspoon dried thyme
1/4 teaspoon dried basil
1/2 teaspoon dried dill weed
1/2 teaspoon sugar (or a little more if the tomatoes are too acid)
salt and pepper to taste.

1 cup sour cream

Puree the stewed tomatoes in your blender and pour it in a large saucepan. In a skillet, saute the onion, carrot, garlic and green onions in the butter, until the vegetables are soft.

Puree the vegetables in the blender using some of the chicken broth to aid the blades in turning. Pour the mixture into the saucepan with the tomatoes.

Now add the remaining ingredients and simmer the soup for 15 minutes over low heat, stirring now and again, making certain that the soup does not scorch.

Serve with a dollup of sour cream and a sprinkling of dill. Serves 6.

Note— Soup can be made several days earlier and refrigerated. Allow to come to room temperature before reheating. Reheat over low heat, stirring, to prevent scorching.

Salads

&

Dressings

Chicken Salad Italienne

3 cups cooked chicken, diced
1 jar (2 ounces) sliced pimentos (drained)
1/4 cup pine nuts

In a large bowl, place the chicken, pimentos and pine nuts. Pour Olive Lemon Dressing and toss to combine. Refrigerate overnight to allow flavors to blend. Serves 6.

Olive Lemon Dressing

1/4 cup olive oil
1/4 cup salad oil
2 tablespoons wine vinegar
2 tablespoons lemon juice
1 clove garlic, put through a garlic press
1 tablespoon capers, rinsed and drained
salt and pepper to taste

Combine all the ingredients in a glass jar with a tight lid and shake contents until dressing is well blended.

Curried Chicken Salad with Pineapple & Almonds

1/2 cup mayonnaise
1/4 cup sour cream
2 tablespoons lemon juice
1/2 teaspoon curry powder

2 cups cooked chicken, diced
1/2 cup crushed pineapple, drained
1/2 cup toasted slivered almonds
1/2 cup yellow raisins

Combine mayonnaise, sour cream, lemon juice and curry powder until mixture is blended. Toss together the chicken, pineapple, toasted almonds and raisins. Add mayonnaise mixture and stir until blended. Serve in individual lettuce cups. As a festive touch, you can serve the salad in halved cantaloupes or papayas. Serves 4.

Mushroom Salad Parisienne

1 pound mushrooms, cleaned and thinly sliced

1/4 cup red wine vinegar
1/4 cup Dijon-style mustard
1/4 teaspoon oregano
1/4 teaspoon tarragon
1 tablespoon chopped chives (or 1 teaspoon dried chives)
1 tablespoon chopped parsley (or 1 teaspoon dried parsley)
salt and pepper to taste

3/4 cup oil

Place vinegar, mustard, oregano, tarragon, chives, parsley and salt and pepper into your blender container. Blend for 2 seconds. Slowly drizzle in the oil, while the blender continues running. Refrigerate dressing in a glass jar.

Just before serving, toss dressing with the sliced mushrooms and serve. Serves 6.

Shrimp Salad with Lemon Mustard Mayonnaise

1 pound tiny bay shrimp, cooked. You can use 1 pound of mixed shellfish, crab, lobster and shrimp.

Lemon Mustard Mayonnaise

Combine shellfish and Lemon Mustard Mayonnaise to taste. Serve on lettuce greens or stuff into scooped-out tomatoes or cucumbers. Serves 4.

Lemon Mustard Mayonnaise

1 cup mayonnaise
1-1/2 tablespoons Dijon-style mustard
2 tablespoons lemon juice
1 tablespoon dried green onion flakes
1 teaspoon parsley flakes

Stir together all the ingredients until the mixture is thoroughly blended. Store unused dressing in the refrigerator. Makes about 1-1/4 cups dressing.

French Green Bean & Tomato Salad with Lemon Parmesan Dressing

1 can (1 pound) French-style green beans, drained. Discard the liquid.
2 green onions, finely chopped
2 tomatoes, coarsely chopped
1 teaspoon dried parsley flakes (or 1 tablespoon fresh)

Place all the ingredients in a bowl. Pour Lemon Parmesan Dressing over the vegetables. Stir to coat them thoroughly.

Cover bowl and refrigerate it for at least 4 hours (overnight is also good) to allow flavors to blend. Serves 4.

Lemon Parmesan Dressing

6 tablespoons oil
3 tablespoons lemon juice
1 tablespoon wine vinegar
1 clove garlic, put through a press
1/4 cup grated Parmesan cheese
salt and freshly ground pepper to taste

Combine all the ingredients in a jar and shake to blend. Yields about 3/4 cup sauce.

Spinach Salad with Creamy Dreamy Dressing

8 cups fresh chopped spinach, carefully washed free of every trace of sand

2 tomatoes, chopped
4 green onions, finely chopped
8 slices bacon, cooked crisp, drained and crumbled
4 hard cooked eggs coarsely chopped
8 large mushrooms, cleaned and thinly sliced

In a large salad bowl, place all the ingredients and refrigerate until ready to serve. Pour Creamy Dreamy Dressing over the salad and toss to evenly coat the leaves. Serve with Onion Cheese Croissants and sweet butter. Serves 4.

Creamy Dreamy Dressing

1/2 cup mayonnaise
1/2 cup sour cream
1 teaspoon sugar
2 green onions, including the green tops
1 teaspoon Dijon-style mustard
1 clove garlic
1 tablespoon dried parsley flakes
3 tablespoons lemon juice
salt and pepper to taste

Place all the ingredients in a blender container and blend until the mixture is smooth. Store dressing in a covered jar in the refrigerator until ready to serve. Makes 1-1/2 cups dressing.

Note — Salad can be assembled earlier in the day and refrigerated.
— Dressing can be made 2 or 3 days earlier and refrigerated.

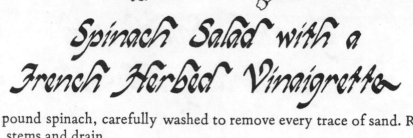

Spinach Salad with a French Herbed Vinaigrette

1/2 pound spinach, carefully washed to remove every trace of sand. Remove stems and drain.

8 slices bacon, crisped and crumbled
4 hard cooked eggs, finely chopped

Set spinach on 4 salad plates. Sprinkle each plate with 1/4 of the bacon and 1/4 of the chopped eggs. Sprinkle with salt and drizzle with French Herbed Vinaigrette. Serves 4.

French Herbed Vinaigrette

1 egg
1 tablespoon dried parsley
2 green onions
6 tablespoons white vinegar
2 tablespoons mayonnaise
1 teaspoon Dijon-style mustard
1/8 teaspoon garlic powder
2 teaspoons sugar
1 cup oil

Place first eight ingredients in a blender container and blend for 10 seconds. Now add oil in a steady trickle until oil is incorporated. Store in a covered jar in the refrigerator.

Heavenly Potato Salad

8 medium-sized potatoes, rubbed, tubbed and scrubbed. Do not peel.

1 medium onion, grated
2 tablespoons sugar
3 tablespoons lemon juice
1 tablespoon vinegar
1 teaspoon Dijon-style mustard
salt and pepper to taste

1/4 cup chopped parsley
2 hard-cooked eggs, chopped
3/4 cup mayonnaise
1/2 cup sour cream

Cook the unpeeled potatotes in boiling water until they are tender, but still firm. Do not overcook or they will fall apart when you slice them. Immediately immerse them in cold water and let them cool. Peel the potatoes and slice them thinly. Place them in a large bowl.

Toss potatoes with onion, sugar, lemon juice, vinegar, mustard and seasonings and let mixture rest for 10 minutes, stirring now and again. Now add the remaining ingredients and toss to combine. Refrigerate overnight to allow flavors to blend. Serves 8.

Lemon Dressing with Garlic & Dill

1 cup sour cream
1 cup cream
3 small green onions, remove only the whiskers
1/8 teaspoon garlic powder
1/4 teaspoon salt
1 teaspoon sugar
1/4 teaspoon dill weed (or more to taste)
3 tablespoons lemon juice

Place the ingredients in the blender container and blend at high speed until mixture is blended. Remove dressing to a jar with a tight lid and refrigerate. Keeps for 1 week in the refrigerator.

Note— Serve with salad greens, zucchini, cucumbers, tomatoes or any combination.

3 ~ Bean Salad in a Mild Vinaigrette Dressing

1 can (1 lb) cut green beans, drained
1 can (15 ounces) red kidney beans, drained
1 can (1 lb) cici peas (garbanzos), drained
4 green onions, finely chopped
salt and pepper to taste

Combine all the ingredients in a large bowl. Toss with 1 cup Mild Vinaigrette Dressing and refrigerate for at least 1 day. (Salad will keep for 1 week.) Good for serving to a large group. Will serve 12.

Mild Vinaigrette Dressing

1/3 cup olive oil
1/3 cup salad oil
1/3 cup red wine vinegar
1 clove garlic, put through a press
1 tablespoon chopped parsley
1 tablespoon chopped onion
1 teaspoon Dijon-style mustard
salt and pepper to taste

Place all the ingredients in a glass jar with a tight fitting lid and shake until it is blended. Store any unused dressing in the refrigerator. Yields about 1 cup.

Cucumber & Tomato Salad with Lemon Garlic Dressing

2 cucumbers, peeled and sliced
2 tomatoes, chopped coarsely
2 green onions, finely chopped

Combine all the ingredients in a salad bowl. Toss with Lemon Garlic Dressing and serve at once. Serves 4.

Lemon Garlic Dressing

1/3 cup salad oil
1/3 cup olive oil
1/3 cup lemon juice
1 clove garlic, put through a press
1/4 teaspoon dill weed
1 tablespoon chopped parsley
salt and pepper to taste

Combine all the ingredients in a glass jar and shake to combine. Makes 1 cup dressing. Store unused dressing in the refrigerator.

Cold Vegetable Platter with Guacamole

Arrange a large platter of sliced zucchini, mushrooms, carrots, celery, cucumbers, cherry tomatoes, jicama, in any combination you desire. Slice the vegetables into pretty shapes, on the diagonal, into sticks, curls, circles, etc. Arrange them on a bed of lettuce. (Dip the ends of the lettuce leaves in paprika for an exciting effect.) Place the guacamole in the center and toss some lemon peel curls over all. It will look very dramatic and exciting and the dip is just delicious too.

Guacamole with Tomatoes & Chiles

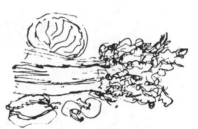

4 avocados, mashed
1/4 cup finely chopped onions
1 can (4 ounces) chopped green chiles (or diced)
1 teaspoon salt
1/4 cup lemon juice
1 medium tomato, finely chopped

Combine all the ingredients and stir until blended. Place mixture in a lovely serving dish and refrigerate until serving time.

The Best Guacamole Salad Dressing

1 cup mayonnaise
1/4 cup cream
2 tablespoons lemon juice
1/2 teaspoon garlic powder
6 sprigs parsley (remove the stems and use the leaves)
2 or 3 green onions (remove the whiskers and use the bulb and green leaves)
1/8 teaspoon MSG (optional)
salt and pepper to taste

2 ripe avocados, mashed

Place first eight ingredients in a blender container and blend at high speed until mixture is smooth, about 1 minute. Stir in the mashed avocados. Store dressing in a covered glass jar in the refrigerator. Makes about 2 cups dressing. Serve over a lettuce or mixed green salad or a tomato and onion salad.

Fish

&

Shellfish

The Best Bouillabaisse Americaine

More than a soup and less than a stew, bouillabaisse is a hearty fish chowder. Traditionally made with many varieties of fish and shellfish, it is also amazingly delicious with only 1 kind of fish. Fish should be filleted and cut into slices about 1 to 2 inches. Vary the size of the slices. The chowder has a rich aroma and is very rich in taste.

1/4 cup oil
1 cup chopped onions
3 cloves garlic, mashed
1 can (1 pound) stewed tomatoes, chopped
1 can (7 ounces) minced clams
2 cups tomato juice
3 cups clam juice
1 tablespoon dried parsley flakes
1/4 teaspoon basil
1 teaspoon thyme flakes
2 teaspoons sugar
pinch of saffron
pinch of tumeric
salt and pepper to taste

1 pound each of perch, flounder and halibut fillets (or 3 pounds of assorted fish or shellfish, including cod, snapper, haddock, sole, scallops, clams, crab or lobster)

Combine all the ingredients, except the fish, in a Dutch oven and simmer the mixture, uncovered, for 20 minutes. Bring soup to a rolling boil and add the fish. Boil for about 5 minutes or until the fish becomes opaque. Serve in deep soup bowls with some crusty French bread. Serves 6.

Note — Soup base can be made earlier in the day and refrigerated. Bring to a boil and then add the fish just before serving.
  — You might like to add 2 or 3 cooked and thinly sliced potatoes (medium sized).

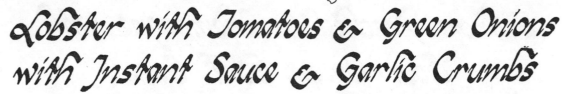

Lobster with Tomatoes & Green Onions with Instant Sauce & Garlic Crumbs

Please don't be misled by the long title. This is an extremely simple dish. The Cheese sauce assembles in minutes and if you buy the lobster already cooked, then just heat and serve. You can substitute shrimp with equally good results.

1-1/2 pound cooked lobster meat
2 or 3 finely chopped green onions
2 medium tomatoes, chopped
1/2 cup sour cream
salt and pepper to taste
2 tablespoons lemon juice

In a bowl, combine all the ingredients and mix them until they are blended. Place mixture in a shallow baking dish and top with Instant Cheese Sauce and sprinkle with Garlic Cheese Crumbs. Heat in a 350° oven for about 15 minutes or until heated through. Serve on toasted triangles with spiced peaches or apricots. Serves 4 or 5.

Instant Cheese Sauce

1 cup sour cream
1 cup grated Jack cheese
2 tablespoons lemon juice

In a bowl, stir all the ingredients together.

Garlic Cheese Crumbs

1/3 cup Waverly cracker crumbs
1/3 cup gated Parmesan cheese
4 tablespoons melted butter
1 clove garlic, mashed

In a bowl, combine all the ingredients and stir them until they are blended.

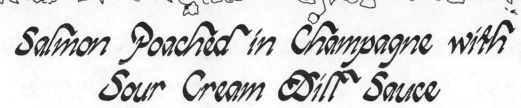

Salmon Poached in Champagne with Sour Cream Dill Sauce

6 slices salmon, about 1 inch thick

6 tablespoons butter
3 tablespoons lemon juice
1/2 cup champagne
2 tablespoons chopped chives

In pan you will cook salmon, melt the butter. Add the lemon juice, champagne and chives.

Place salmon in butter mixture and baste. Cover and cook over low heat about 30 minutes. Place salmon on a lovely platter and serve with Sour Cream Dill Sauce on the top.

Note — You may substitute dry white wine for the champagne.

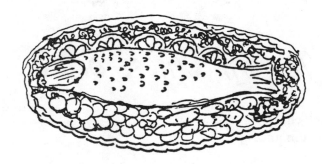

Sour Cream Dill Sauce

1/2 cup sour cream
1 tablespoon Dijon-style mustard
2 tablespoons lemon juice
1 tablespoon chopped chives
2 tablespoons sugar
1 teaspoon dried dill weed

Combine all the ingredients in a glass jar and stir until they are blended. Refrigerate sauce until serving time. Makes about 1 cup sauce.

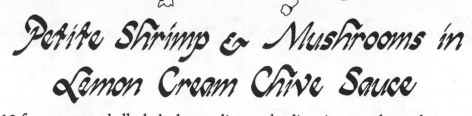

Petite Shrimp & Mushrooms in Lemon Cream Chive Sauce

12 frozen patty shells, baked according to the directions on the package

3 tablespoons butter
1/2 pound mushrooms, cleaned and sliced

2 eggs
6 ounces cream cheese and chives
3 tablespoons lemon juice

1/2 pound tiny bay shrimp, cooked
salt and pepper to taste
1/4 teaspoon dried thyme

Saute mushrooms in butter until mushrooms are golden. Beat together the eggs, cream cheese and lemon juice until the mixture is blended.

Combine the mushrooms, cream cheese mixture, shrimp, salt, pepper and thyme and stir until the mixture is thoroughly blended. Divide the mixture between the 12 cooked patty shells and sprinkle with some parsley flakes. Heat in a 350° oven until filling is hot, about 15 to 20 minutes. Serves 6.

Note   Entire dish can be assembled earlier in the day and refrigerated. Remove from the refrigerator about 30 minutes before reheating.
  — Serve with spiced apricots and buttered broccoli.

Shrimp Curry with Apples & Raisins

1 stick butter
2 onions, finely chopped
2 cloves garlic, put through a press

1/4 cup flour
1 tablespoon curry powder (or to taste)
salt to taste

2 large apples, peeled, cored and grated
2 tablespoons brown sugar
1 cup yellow raisins, plumped overnight in orange juice and drained
2 cups chicken broth
1 pint sour cream

2 pounds cooked shrimp

Saute onion and garlic in butter until onions are transparent. Add flour and curry powder and cook for a minute or so, stirring.

Add apples, brown sugar, raisins and chicken broth. Cook over low heat, stirring, until sauce thickens. (If the sauce is too thick, add a little more broth.) Stir in sour cream and heat through. Add shrimp and heat through. Do not allow to boil. Serves 6.

Note— Dish can be prepared ahead up to the point of adding the sour cream and shrimp, which should be done soon before serving.

Fillets of Sole with Sour Cream, Butter, Garlic Sauce

2 pounds fillets of sole, sprinkle with salt and white pepper

1/2 cup butter, softened
1/2 cup sour cream
1/4 cup chopped green onions
2 teaspoons dried parsley
1 clove garlic, mashed
3 tablespoons lemon juice

1 cup Waverly crackers, rolled into crumbs

In a 12x16-inch pan, arrange the fillets in one layer. Combine the next 6 ingredients and mix until blended. Spread this mixture over the fillets. Sprinkle the top evenly with the cracker crumbs.

Bake in a 350° oven for about 12 mintues or until the fish flakes easily with a fork. Do not overcook. Broil crumbs for a few seconds to brown lightly. Serves 6.

Fillets of Sole with Lemon Swiss Cheese Sauce

2 pounds fillets of sole, sprinkle with salt, white pepper and paprika

1/2 cup butter (1 stick) melted
2 cloves garlic, mashed
3 tablespoons lemon juice

1/2 cup sour cream
1/2 cup grated Swiss cheese

Arrange the fillets in one layer in a 12x16-inch pan. Combine the melted butter, garlic and lemon juice. Drizzle over the fillets. Combine the sour cream and the Swiss cheese and spread the mixture over the fillets. Bake in a 350° oven for about 12 minutes or until the fish flakes easily with a fork. Broil for a few seconds to brown lightly. Serves 6.

Note — Both recipes can be assembled earlier in the day and refrigerated.

Shrimp & Mushrooms in Garlic Sauce

Try this delightful dish on a night when you have little time for preparation. Serve it with some crusty French bread to mop up the sauce.

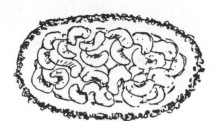

1/4 cup butter
1/4 cup olive oil
4 cloves garlic, mashed
1/2 pound mushrooms, cleaned and sliced
1 pound raw shrimp, peeled and deveined

2 tablespoons lemon juice
1 tablespoon finely minced parsley (or 1 teaspoon dried parsley flakes)
1 teaspoon dried snipped chives
salt and pepper to taste

In a 10-inch skillet, heat the butter with the olive oil. Add the garlic and the mushrooms and saute the mixture until the mushrooms are tender. Remove the mushrooms with a slotted spoon. Add the shrimp to the skillet (add a little butter, if necessary) and quickly saute the shrimp until they turn pink. *Do not overcook the shrimp.* They are tender and succulent when cooked just to the point when they turn pink.

Now, add the mushrooms and the remaining ingredients and heat through. Serve with herbed rice and a crisp salad. Serves 4.

Shrimp in Lemon Mustard Dressing

1 pound tiny bay shrimp, cooked

1/4 cup lemon juice
1/4 cup Dijon-style mustard
1/4 teaspoon thyme flakes (dried)
1 tablespoon chopped parsley (or 1 teaspoon dried parsley)
1 tablespoon chopped chives (or 1 teaspoon dried chives)
salt and pepper to taste
3/4 cup oil

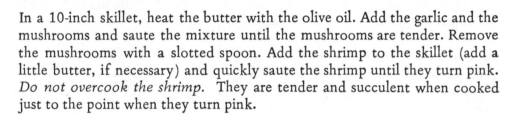

Place lemon, mustard, thyme, parsley, chives, salt and pepper into blender container. Blend for 2 seconds. Slowly drizzle in the oil, while the blender continues running.

Place shrimp in a large bowl and toss with the dressing. Refrigerate overnight. Toss and turn before serving. Serve on a bed of lettuce. Serves 6.

Fillets of Sole with Lemon Dill Sauce

2 pounds fillets of sole
6 tablespoons melted butter
4 tablespoons dry white wine
salt and pepper to taste

Place fillets in one layer in a 12x16-inch roasting pan. Drizzle them with melted butter and sprinkle with white wine. Salt and pepper them to taste.

Bake fillets in a 350° oven for about 15 minutes or until fish flakes easily with a fork. Do not overbake. Serve with *LEMON DILL SAUCE* on the side.

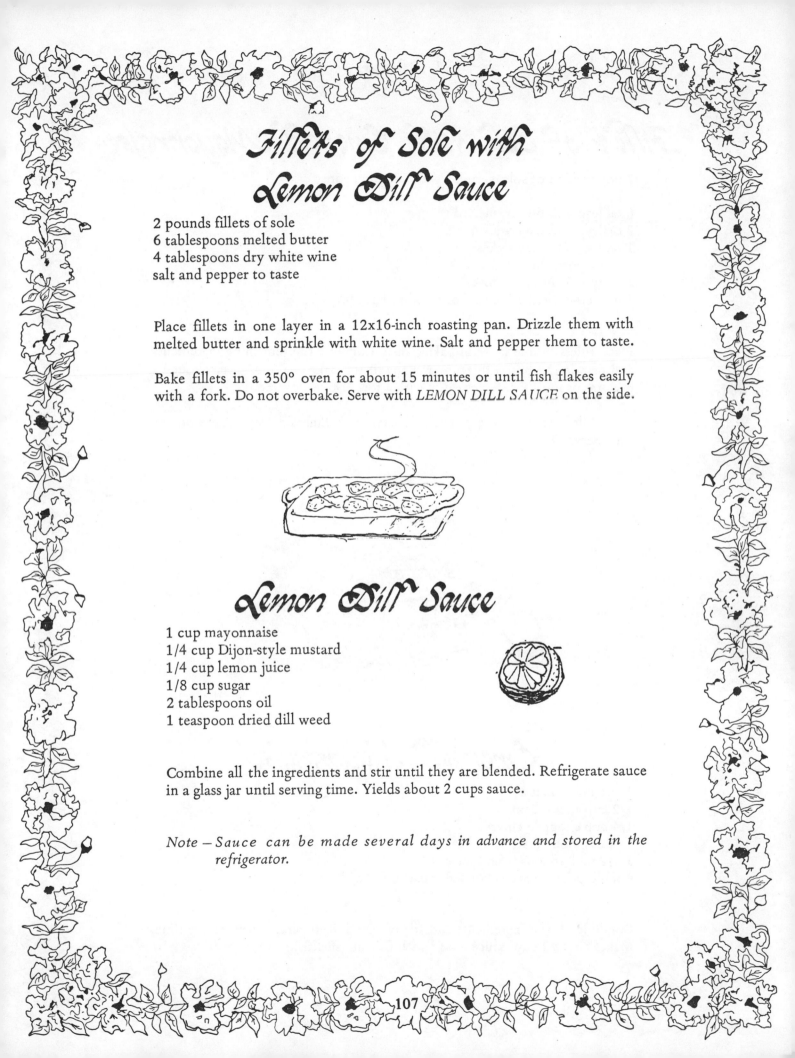

Lemon Dill Sauce

1 cup mayonnaise
1/4 cup Dijon-style mustard
1/4 cup lemon juice
1/8 cup sugar
2 tablespoons oil
1 teaspoon dried dill weed

Combine all the ingredients and stir until they are blended. Refrigerate sauce in a glass jar until serving time. Yields about 2 cups sauce.

Note – Sauce can be made several days in advance and stored in the refrigerator.

Fillet of Sole with Emerald Mayonnaise

1 pound fillet of sole, sprinkle with salt and pepper

6 tablespoons butter, melted
2 tablespoons lemon juice
1 teaspoon parsley flakes
1/2 teaspoon dill weed
1 teaspoon chopped chives
1 or 2 cloves garlic, minced or put through a press

Place fillets in one layer in baking dish. Combine the remaining ingredients and drizzle the butter mixture over the fillets. Bake in a 350° oven about 15 minutes or until fish flakes easily with a fork. Do not overcook.

Place fillets on a serving platter and serve with Emerald Mayonnaise on the side. Serves 4.

Emerald Mayonnaise

1 cup mayonnaise
1/2 cup sour cream
1/4 cup chopped chives
1 tablespoon parsley
1-1/2 tablespoons lemon juice
4 tablespoons frozen chopped spinach, drained dry

Combine all the ingredients and stir to blend. Refrigerate until serving time. Makes about 2 cups sauce Good with fish and shellfish.

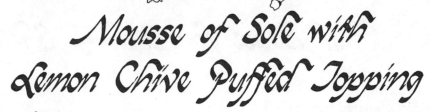

Mousse of Sole with Lemon Chive Puffed Topping

3 egg whites
1 pound fillets of sole, cut into small pieces
1 cup cream
2 tablespoons dry white wine
1 clove garlic
1/2 teaspoon dill weed
1 teaspoon parsley flakes
2 tablespoons lemon juice
salt and pepper to taste

Place egg whites in blender container and whip for a few seconds. Start adding the fish and the cream and continue blending until the fish is finely chopped. You might have to turn off the blender and stir the mixture several times. Mixture will be heavy. Blend in the remaining ingredients.

Place mixture into 6 buttered ramekins. Place ramekins on a cookie sheet and place in a 350° oven for about 40 minutes or until mousse is set.

Divide the Lemon Chive Topping over the top of the mousses and broil them until the top is puffed and golden. Serve at once. Serves 6 for lunch.

Lemon Chive Puffed Topping

3/4 cup mayonnaise
2 tablespoons lemon juice
1 tablespoon dried chives
1 egg white, beaten stiff

Stir together the mayonnaise, lemon juice and chopped chives. Fold in the stiffly beaten egg white. Use as a topping for fish and shellfish. Yields about 1 cup.

Note— If you own a food processor, proceed in the same fashion. However, be careful not to overblend. Mixture should be fairly smooth, but not pureed.

Red Cocktail Sauce for Fish & Shellfish

1/2 cup chili sauce
1/2 cup ketchup
1 teaspoon prepared horseradish
1 tablespoon lemon juice
1/4 cup sweet relish

In a glass jar, place all the ingredients and stir them until they are blended. Cover and refrigerate until serving time. Yields 1 cup of sauce.

Note — Sauce can be made several days earlier.

Herbed Mayonnaise for Fish & Shellfish

1 cup mayonnaise
1/4 cup sour cream
2 tablespoons chopped chives
4 tablespoons chopped parsley
1 hard-cooked egg, finely chopped
2 teaspoons Dijon-style mustard
2 tablespoons lemon juice

In a glass jar, place all the ingredients and stir them until they are blended. Cover and refrigerate until serving time. Yields 1-1/2 cups sauce.

Note — Sauce can be made several days earlier.

Meats

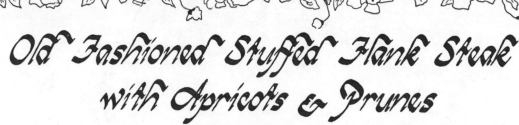

Old Fashioned Stuffed Flank Steak with Apricots & Prunes

1 flank steak, about 2 to 2-1/2 pounds. Ask your butcher to butterfly the
steak (split it on three sides so that it can be opened like a book.)
Sprinkle it with salt, pepper and garlic powder.

1 package (6 ounces) Stove Top Cornbread Stuffing Mix
1-1/2 cups apple juice
4 tablespoons butter (1/2 stick)
1/2 cup applesauce

Heat together the seasoning packet in the stuffing mix with the apple juice
and butter. Bring to a boil and add the bread cubes. Stir until the mixture is
well mixed. Stir in the applesauce.

Lay out the prepared flank steak, cut side up. Lay the stuffing mixture on
the long side (with the grain of the meat) and roll it up. Skewer it or tie it
securely with string, making certain to skewer the ends.

Place roast in a 9x13-inch pan, along with the Apricot and Prune Sauce ingredients. Cover the pan tightly with foil and bake in a 350° oven for 1-1/2
to 2 hours or until the meat is tender. Remove the skewers or string.

Slice and serve with the apricots and prunes on the side. Gravy is rich and delicious and can be served without any addition. Serves 4 or 5.

Apricots & Prune Sauce

1/4 cup apricot jam
3 tablespoons chili sauce
3/4 cup dry white wine
1/2 package dehydrated onion soup
12 dried apricots
12 pitted prunes

Combine all the ingredients and stir until they are mixed. Pour mixture
over the flank steak.

Note — If you like more meat, divide stuffing between 2 flank steaks.

112

Roulades of Beef with Herbed Stuffing & Mushroom Saute

12 thin spencer steaks, cut into 1/4-inch slices. Ask your butcher to cut the thin steaks from the small end. Sprinkle the steaks with salt, pepper and paprika.

HERBED STUFFING

4 cups fresh white bread cubes (about 12 slices). Remove crusts.
1/2 teaspoon poultry seasoning
1/2 teaspoon paprika
2 teaspoons beef seasoned stock base stirred into 1/2 cup water
3 tablespoons finely chopped onions
6 tablespoons melted butter
salt and white pepper to taste

Mash together all the ingredients until they are thoroughly blended. Add a little more water if needed to hold stuffing together.

Divide stuffing into 12 parts. Place 1 part stuffing in center of each steak. Roll steak and secure with toothpicks. Roll stuffed steak in Seasoned Flour and saute them in butter for about 5 minutes or until the meat loses its pinkness. Do not overcook. Meat is very tender.

Place beef rolls in a metal skillet. Heat 2 tablespoons cognac in a small pan, ignite and carefully pour over the roulades. When flames subside, heat steaks in a 350° oven until heated through. Serve with Mushroom Saute on the side. Serves 6.

SEASONED FLOUR

1/2 cup flour
1/2 cup grated Parmesan cheese
1/2 teaspoon paprika
1/8 teaspoon garlic powder
salt and pepper

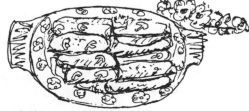

Mix together all the ingredients until blended.

MUSHROOM SAUTE

Saute 1 pound thinly sliced mushrooms in 1/2 cup butter until mushrooms are tender. Do this over high heat and make certain the liquid is evaporated. Salt and pepper to taste.

Country Kitchen Pot Roast with Peaches

4 pounds brisket of beef, lean and trimmed of fat. Sprinkle with salt, pepper and garlic powder.

1 package (6 ounces) dried peaches

1 envelope onion soup mix (about 1-1/2 ounces)
1/2 cup currant jelly
2 tablespoons brown sugar
1/4 cup ketchup
1 cup Burgundy or Rose wine

In a Dutch oven or 9x13-inch roasting pan, place meat. Snip the peaches and place them over the meat. Combine the remaining ingredients and pour the mixture over the brisket. Cover and bake in a 350° oven until meat is fork tender, about 2 hours. Remove from the oven and allow to cool.

Slice meat and return it to the pan with the gravy, from which all the fat has been removed. When ready to serve, heat in a 350° oven, covered, for another 30 minutes. Serves 6.

Note — Gravy is delicious and does not need to be thickened.
    — Entire dish can be prepared the day before with excellent results. Reheat at time of serving.
    —Serve with Glazed Buttered Carrots and Potato and Chive Casserole.

Imperial Prime Rib Roast with Horseradish Cream Sauce

1 standing prime rib roast. Ask your butcher to remove the chine bone, loosen the ribs and tie them back in place. Use a 6 or 7-pound roast (3 ribs) for 6 servings.

BASTING MIXTURE

1/2 cup butter
1 tablespoon paprika
4 cloves garlic, put through a press
1/2 teaspoon salt
1/8 teaspoon freshly ground pepper

Heat together all the ingredients and stir to blend. Simmer for 1 minute. Brush roast on all sides with basting mixture. Place roast, bone-side down, in a roasting pan and roast in a 300° oven until meat thermometer registers desired doneness.* Baste two or three times during the roasting period.

Remove roast from the oven. Remove the strings and place on a serving platter. Slice at the table and serve with majesty and pride. Serve with Horseradish Cream Sauce.

Note — *Meat thermometer should be inserted into the thickest part of the roast. Make certain that it does not touch the bone. Meat thermometer should register for:*

Very rare	-	*130°*
Rare	-	*140°*
Medium rare	-	*150°*
Medium	-	*160°*
Well done	-	*170°*

Horseradish Cream Sauce

1 cup sour cream
1 tablespoon prepared white horseradish or to taste

Combine sour cream and horseradish and stir until blended. Refrigerate. Remove from the refrigerator about 20 minutes before serving.

Meatballs in Thick Mushroom Tomato Sauce

1 cup herb seasoned stuffing mix
1/2 cup milk

2 pounds lean ground beef
1 small onion, grated
2 teaspoons beef seasoned stock base
1 clove garlic, put through a press
2 eggs
1 teaspoon dried parsley flakes
1/2 teaspoon Italian Herb Seasoning
salt and pepper to taste

Soak stuffing mix in milk until the bread is soft. In a large bowl, combine all the ingredients and mix until blended Shape mixture into 3/4-inch balls and saute them in a skillet until the meatballs are cooked through.

Place meatballs into a serving dish with Thick Mushroom Tomato Sauce. Makes about 50 to 60 meatballs.

Thick Mushroom Tomato Sauce

2 tablespoons olive oil
2 cloves garlic, mashed
2 cups chopped onions

1 can (1 pound 12 ounces) Italian tomatoes, finely chopped
1 can (6 ounces) tomato paste
2 tablespoons sugar
1 teaspoon Italian Herb Seasoning
2 bay leaves
salt and freshly ground pepper to taste

In a large saucepan, heat olive oil and saute the onions and garlic until the onions are soft. Add the remaining ingredients and simmer the sauce, uncovered, stirring now and again, for about 20 to 30 minutes. Now add:

1/2 pound mushrooms, sliced and sauteed in butter

Heat the sauce and serve.

Mama's
Beef & Spinach Dumplings

1 package (10 ounces) frozen chopped spinach, defrosted and drained
1 pound lean ground beef
2 large eggs
1/2 medium onion, grated (Must be grated, not chopped.)
1/2 cup cracker crumbs
2 teaspoons beef seasoned stock base
pinch of nutmeg
salt and pepper to taste

Combine all the ingredients in a large bowl and mix until thoroughly blended. Shape mixture into 2-inch balls. Roll them in flour and flatten them gently to about 3/4-inch thickness.

Place about 1/2 inch oil in a skillet and heat it until it is sizzling hot. Place a few dumplings in the skillet and saute them until they are browned. Turn and brown other side. Remove dumplings to a paper towel and drain.

Serve warm with a spoonful of sauteed mushrooms on top. Yields about 14 dumplings and serves 4 or 5.

Mushroom Saute

1/4 cup butter (1/2 stick)
1/2 pound mushrooms, thinly sliced
salt to taste

Over high heat, saute mushrooms in butter until they are tender.

Curried Beef with Apples, Raisins & Coconut

2 pounds sirloin steak, cut into 1/4-inch thick slices. Cut each slice into 1-inch pieces. (Slices should measure approximately 1 x 1 x 1/4-inches. Most butchers will do this for you.)

2 tablespoons flour
1/4 cup butter (1/2 stick)

2 cups chopped onions
1 clove garlic, pressed or mashed
1 apple, peeled, cored and grated
1 tablespoon brown sugar
1/2 cup golden raisins
1/4 cup flaked coconut
1 teaspoon lemon juice
2 teaspoons curry powder or to taste
salt and pepper to taste

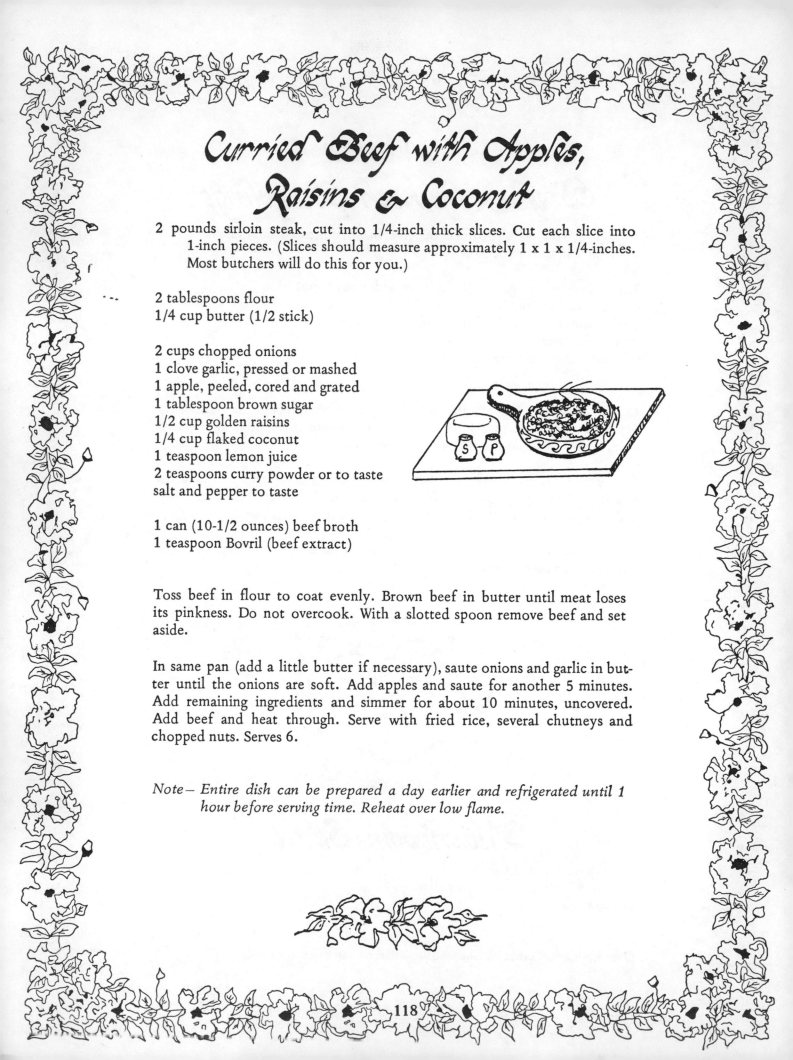

1 can (10-1/2 ounces) beef broth
1 teaspoon Bovril (beef extract)

Toss beef in flour to coat evenly. Brown beef in butter until meat loses its pinkness. Do not overcook. With a slotted spoon remove beef and set aside.

In same pan (add a little butter if necessary), saute onions and garlic in butter until the onions are soft. Add apples and saute for another 5 minutes. Add remaining ingredients and simmer for about 10 minutes, uncovered. Add beef and heat through. Serve with fried rice, several chutneys and chopped nuts. Serves 6.

Note— Entire dish can be prepared a day earlier and refrigerated until 1 hour before serving time. Reheat over low flame.

Lamb Curry Indian

3 pounds lamb (use a leg of lamb), have butcher cut the meat into 1/2-inch cubes. Sprinkle with salt to taste.

2 cups onions, finely chopped
1/2 cup butter (1 stick)
6 cloves garlic, mashed

1 can (1 pound 12 ounces) tomatoes, drained. Reserve juice for another use. Chop coarsely.

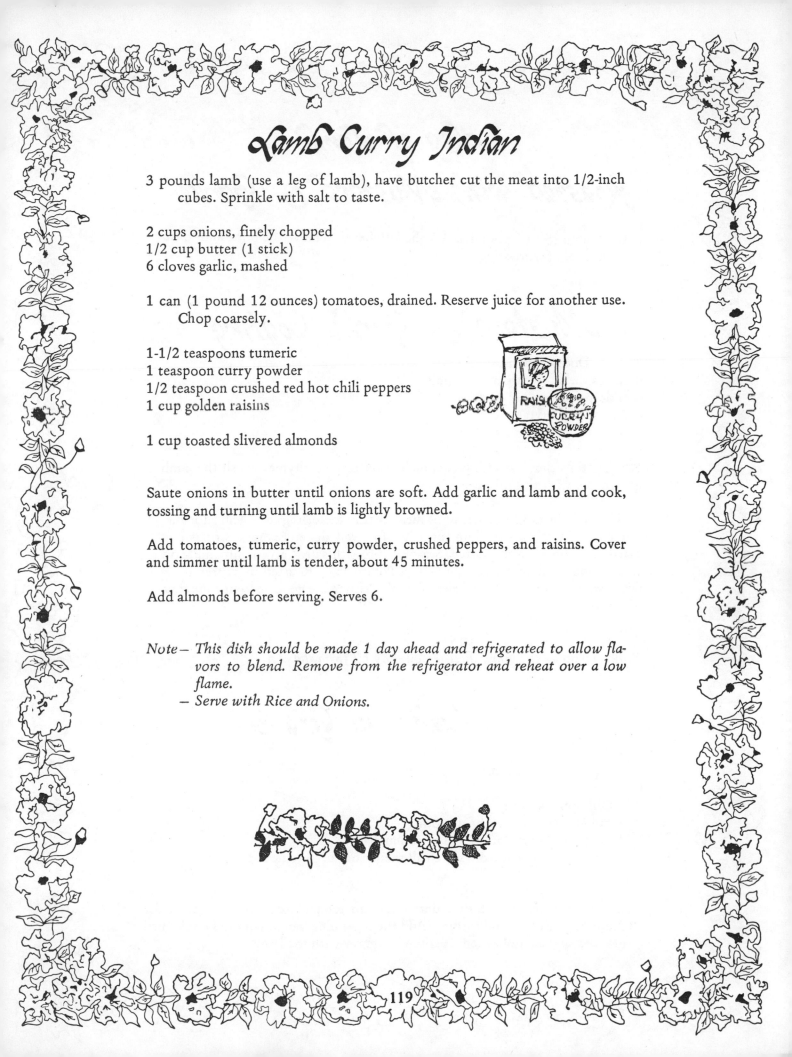

1-1/2 teaspoons tumeric
1 teaspoon curry powder
1/2 teaspoon crushed red hot chili peppers
1 cup golden raisins

1 cup toasted slivered almonds

Saute onions in butter until onions are soft. Add garlic and lamb and cook, tossing and turning until lamb is lightly browned.

Add tomatoes, tumeric, curry powder, crushed peppers, and raisins. Cover and simmer until lamb is tender, about 45 minutes.

Add almonds before serving. Serves 6.

Note— *This dish should be made 1 day ahead and refrigerated to allow flavors to blend. Remove from the refrigerator and reheat over a low flame.*
— Serve with Rice and Onions.

Leg of Lamb
Roasted with Mustard & Garlic

1 leg of lamb (5 to 6 pounds). Ask the butcher to remove the bone and to tie the lamb for roasting.

Mustard & Garlic Coating

1/2 cup Dijon-style mustard
4 cloves garlic, put through a press
4 tablespoons melted butter
1/2 teaspoon thyme

Stir together the mustard, garlic, melted butter and thyme. Brush the lamb generously with this mixture.

Roast lamb in a 350° oven until meat thermometer registers 150° for medium rare, 160° for medium or 170° for well done. Remove strings and place lamb on a warm platter. Season lamb with salt. Carve lamb and serve with a spoonful of Mushroom Gravy. Potato Fans Roasted in Butter along with Broiled Tomatoes with Herb Crumb Coating are good accompaniments. Serves 6.

Note—To make the gravy, first remove any fat from the pan.

Mushroom Gravy

1/4 cup butter
1/4 pound mushrooms

2 tablespoons flour
1 can (10-1/2 ounces) beef broth
1 teaspoon Bovril (broth and seasoning base)
1/2 cup lamb juices from which all the fat has been removed

Saute mushrooms in butter until they are tender. Add flour and cook for 2 minutes, stirring and turning. Add the remaining ingredients and cook until gravy is slightly thickened. Pass the hot gravy with the lamb.

Rack of Lamb with Garlic & Herbs

1 rack of lamb, about 2 pounds. Ask the butcher to crack the bone and to french the ribs about 1-1/2-inches down. Cover the end of each rib bone with aluminum foil. Sprinkle lamb with salt. Rub with 1 clove garlic put through a press and brush lamb with 1 tablespoon Dijon-style mustard.

1/3 cup bread crumbs
2 cloves garlic, put through a press
1 teaspoon chopped parsley
1/4 teaspoon dried thyme flakes
salt and pepper to taste

2 tablespoons butter, melted

Insert meat thermometer in thickest part of the meat, being careful not to touch the bone. Place lamb, fat side up (bones make a natural rack for lamb), in a shallow roasting pan. Roast lamb in a 375° oven for 30 minutes.

Meanwhile, combine crumbs, garlic, parsley, thyme, salt and pepper and mix until blended. Remove lamb from oven and allow it to rest for about 15 minutes.* Drizzle lamb with butter and sprinkle crumb mixture on top of lamb. Return lamb to oven and continue roasting until thermometer registers 175° for medium lamb or 180° for well-done lamb. (Time is approximately 1 hour 15 minutes to 1 hour 30 minutes.) Serves 2 or 3.

Note— *If you are extremely careful not to burn your fingers, you do not have to let the meat chill for 15 minutes. You may drizzle it with butter and sprinkle the crumb mixture and return to the oven with no interruption.

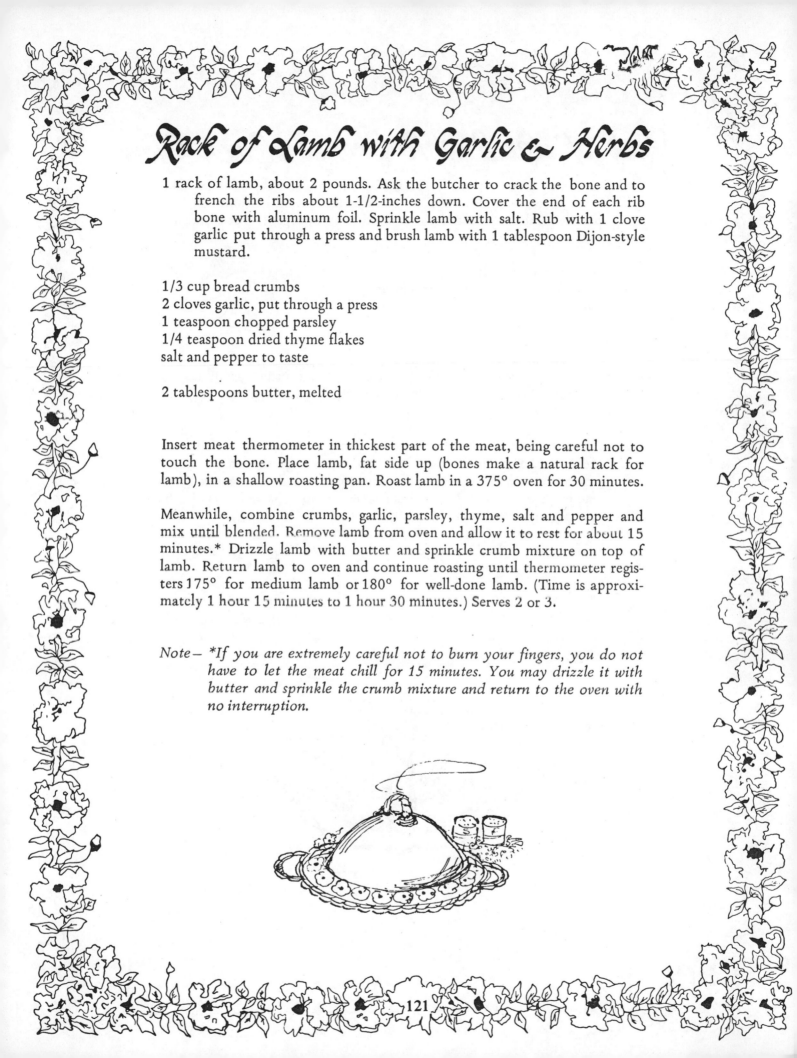

Rack of Lamb with Orange Lemon Glaze

1 rack of lamb, about 2 pounds. Ask the butcher to crack the bone to make for easier carving. Cover the end of each rib bone with aluminum foil. Sprinkle lamb with salt. Rub lamb with 1 clove garlic put through a press.

1/4 cup orange marmalade
2 ounces (1/3 can) orange juice concentrate
2 tablespoons lemon juice
4 tablespoons (1/2 stick) butter

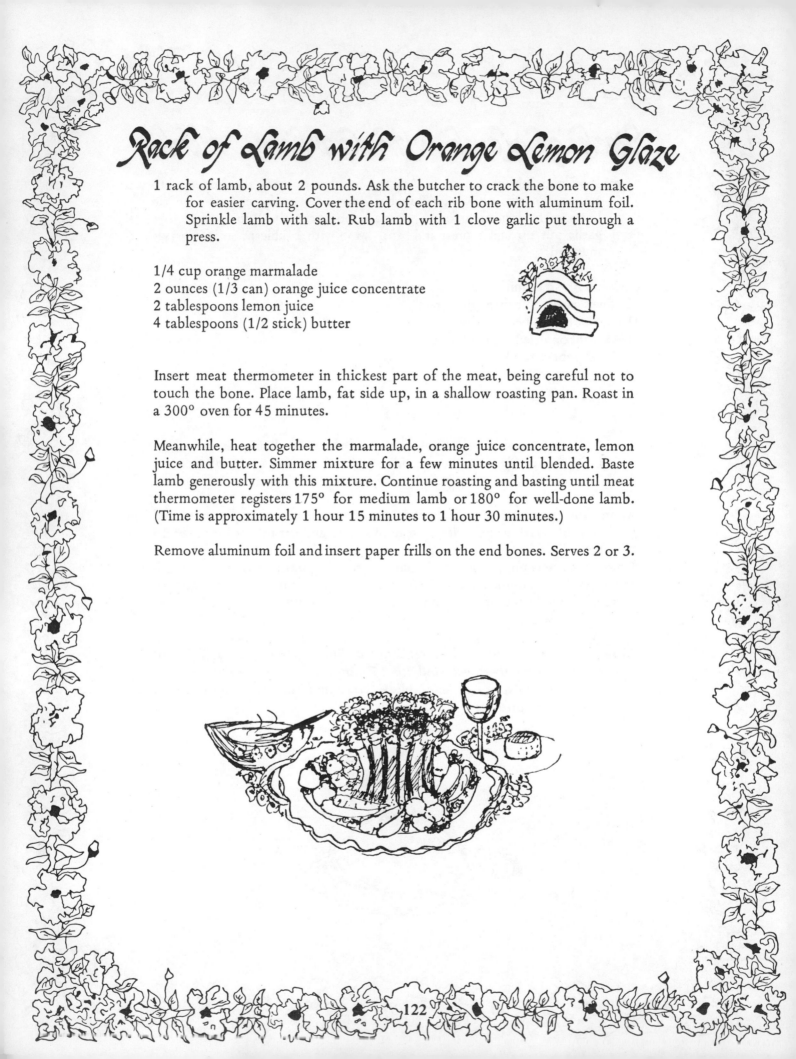

Insert meat thermometer in thickest part of the meat, being careful not to touch the bone. Place lamb, fat side up, in a shallow roasting pan. Roast in a 300° oven for 45 minutes.

Meanwhile, heat together the marmalade, orange juice concentrate, lemon juice and butter. Simmer mixture for a few minutes until blended. Baste lamb generously with this mixture. Continue roasting and basting until meat thermometer registers 175° for medium lamb or 180° for well-done lamb. (Time is approximately 1 hour 15 minutes to 1 hour 30 minutes.)

Remove aluminum foil and insert paper frills on the end bones. Serves 2 or 3.

Honey Glazed Ham with Brandy Orange Raisin Sauce

1 canned ham (about 5 pounds)

1/4 cup honey
1/4 cup brown sugar
1/4 cup barbecue sauce

Score ham on fatty side, about 1/2-inch deep. Combine honey, barbecue sauce and brown sugar and spread mixture on the top of the ham. Bake ham according to the instructions on can.

About 30 minutes before ham is finished, spread about 1 cup Brandy Orange Raisin Sauce on the top and continue baking for the 30 minutes.

Slice ham and serve with Brandy Orange Raisin Sauce on the side. Serves 8.

Note — Ham can be made earlier in the day and refrigerated. Reheat at 300° and tent loosely with foil.

Brandy Orange Raisin Sauce

1 cup raisins
1 cup orange marmalade
1 cup orange juice
1/4 cup brown sugar
1 tablespoon cognac or brandy
pinch of salt

Combine all the ingredients in a saucepan and simmer gently for 10 minutes. Yields about 3 cups sauce.

Baked Ham with Stewed Apples & Raisins

1 canned ham (about 5 pounds). Score top of ham in a diamond pattern with the tip of a knife. Do not cut deep into the meat. Place 1 clove in each diamond.

1 cup brown sugar
1/4 cup apple cider
1 teaspoon Dijon-style mustard
1 teaspoon vinegar

Bake ham according to the directions on the can. About 30 minutes before ham is finished cooking, combine sugar, cider, mustard and vinegar and spread this mixture on ham.

Return ham to a 350° oven and continue baking until ham is cooked. (Meat thermometer should register about 160°.) Allow ham to rest for about 10 minutes to facilitate carving. Pass Stewed Apples and Raisins on the side. Serves 8.

Stewed Apples & Raisins

1/2 cup apple cider
1/2 cup orange juice
3/4 cup sugar
2 tablespoons butter
6 medium apples, peeled, cored and sliced into quarters
1 cup golden raisins
1 tablespoon grated orange peel
2 slices lemon

1/2 teaspoon vanilla

In a saucepan, simmer together the first eight ingredients until apples are soft, about 20 minutes. Stir in the vanilla. This is a lovely accompaniment to pork or lamb. Serves 8.

Note — Fruit can be made earlier in the day and refrigerated. However, serve it warm or hot.

Country Style Spareribs with Honey Barbecue Sauce

3 pounds spareribs, cut into serving pieces. Sprinkle with salt, pepper and garlic powder.

Place ribs in a single layer in a shallow roasting pan. Roast in a 350° oven for 30 minutes. Brush ribs generously with Honey Barbecue Sauce and continue baking and basting until ribs are tender and beautifully glazed, about 1 hour more. Serve with a fried rice with green onions. Serves 4.

Honey Barbecue Sauce

3/4 cup honey
1/2 cup ketchup
1/4 cup butter (1/2 stick)
1 tablespoon vinegar
2 teaspoons Dijon-style mustard
2 tablespoons brown sugar
1 tablespoon soy sauce
1 clove garlic, put through a press

Combine all the ingredients in a sauce pan and simmer the mixture for 5 minutes. Makes about 1-1/2 cups sauce. Leftover sauce can be stored in the refrigerator for later use.

Tenderloin of Pork with Fruits & Currant Cinnamon Glaze

1 tenderloin of pork (about 1-1/2 pounds), sprinkle with salt, pepper, garlic powder and lemon juice

8 prunes
8 apricots
1/2 cup raisins
1 apple, peeled, cored and grated

3/4 cup sherry or sauterne
1/2 cup brown sugar

Place the tenderloin of pork in a shallow 6x12-inch roasting pan. (Pan should not be too large, but should fit roast with just a little room to spare.) Place fruit around the roast. Combine sherry or sauterne with the brown sugar and pour this mixture over the fruit.

Roast pork in a 350° oven for about 30 minutes. Tent it loosely with foil. Now baste pork with Currant and Cinnamon Glaze every 15 minutes until meat thermometer registers 180°, about another 30 minutes.

Place on a platter and surround with the cooked fruits. Serve with Cinnamon Rice as a delicious accompaniment. Serves 4.

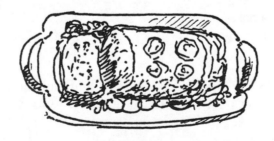

Currant Cinnamon Glaze

1/2 cup currant jelly
1/8 teaspoon cinnamon

Heat together the currant jelly and cinnamon until jelly is melted. Use to baste pork.

Veal Roast Tarragon
with Bearnaise Sauce

1 leg of veal, about 3-1/2 pounds. Ask your butcher to bone it and tie it.

1/2 cup olive oil
1/4 cup white wine vinegar
1 onion, minced
2 cloves garlic, put through a press
1 tablespoon parsley
1/4 teaspoon tarragon
salt and pepper to taste

In a large, deep bowl, stir together all the ingredients until they are well mixed. Place the veal in the marinade and turn it until it is completely coated. Leave the veal in the marinade for at least 4 hours in the refrigerator, (overnight is good, too), turning the veal in the marinade 2 or 3 times.

Remove veal from marinade and pat dry. Brush with some melted butter and roast in a 350° oven for about 2 hours or until veal is tender.

Slice the veal and spoon Bearnaise Sauce over the top. Serve additional Bearnaise Sauce at the table. Serves 6.

Bearnaise Sauce

3 egg yolks
1-1/2 tablespoons lemon juice
pinch of salt and white pepper
1 tablespoon tarragon vinegar
1 teaspoon dried parsley flakes
1 tablespoon dried shredded green onions
1/4 teaspoon dried tarragon or to taste

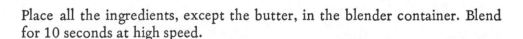

3/4 cup butter

Place all the ingredients, except the butter, in the blender container. Blend for 10 seconds at high speed.

Heat butter until it is sizzling hot and bubbly, but be careful not to brown it. Add the hot, sizzling butter, very slowly, in a steady stream, while the blender continues running at high speed. When the butter is completely incorporated, sauce will be thick and ready to serve. Makes about 1 cup.

Leg of Veal with Bacon Mushroom Herb Sauce

1 leg of veal, about 3 to 4 pounds. Ask the butcher to bone and tie it.

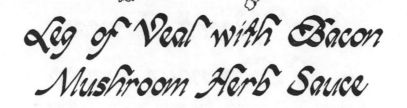

MARINADE

1/3 cup melted butter
1 teaspoon paprika
2 cloves garlic, mashed
1/4 teaspoon salt
1/8 teaspoon white pepper
2 tablespoons dry white wine

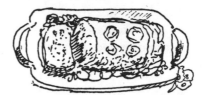

In a large bowl, place all the marinade ingredients. Roll the roast in the marinade and let stand at room temperature for 1 hour. Baste roast with marinade now and again.

Place roast and marinade in a roasting pan and roast in a 300° oven until meat thermometer registers 160°, about 2 hours.

Place roast on a serving platter and remove the strings. Reserve the pan juices for the sauce. Carve the roast and serve with Bacon Mushroom Herb Sauce on the side. Serves 6.

Bacon Mushroom Herb Sauce

4 tablespoons butter
1/2 pound mushrooms
1 onion, finely chopped

6 strips bacon, cooked crisp, drained and crumbled
1/2 cup pan juices
1 cup cream
1 tablespoon parsley flakes
1 tablespoon chopped chives

Saute mushrooms and onion in butter until onions are tender. Add remaining ingredients and cook until sauce thickens.

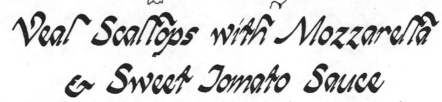

Veal Scallops with Mozzarella & Sweet Tomato Sauce

16 veal scallops, 1/4-inch thick. Sprinkle with salt, pepper and garlic powder. Dust lightly with flour.

2 eggs
2 tablespoons water

1 cup bread crumbs
1 cup grated Parmesan cheese
1/4 teaspoon garlic powder
2 tablespoons paprika

Sweet Tomato Sauce
1/2 cup grated Parmesan cheese
1/2 pound (8 ounces) Mozzarella cheese, grated

Beat together the eggs and water and set aside. Combine the bread crumbs, cheese, garlic powder and paprika. In a large skillet, heat about 1/4-inch of oil. Dip veal scallops into egg mixture and then into crumb mixture. Fry scallops until golden brown on both sides. Place scallops in a 9x13-inch pan, in one layer.

Spoon Sweet Tomato Sauce over the veal and sprinkle with the grated Parmesan cheese. Sprinkle top with the grated Mozzarella cheese. Bake veal in a 350° oven for 30 minutes or until it is heated through and cheese is melted and lightly browned. Serves 8.

Sweet Tomato Sauce

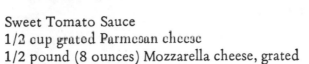

2 tablespoons oil
2 cans (8 ounces, each) tomato sauce
1 can (6 ounces) tomato paste
1 tablespoon dried onion flakes
2 tablespoons sugar
1/2 teaspoon Italian Herb Seasoning
1/2 cup chopped golden raisins
salt to taste
1/8 teaspoon garlic powder

Combine all the ingredients in a saucepan and simmer the sauce for 15 minutes over low heat and uncovered.

Stuffed Breast of Veal with Peach & Raisin Sauce

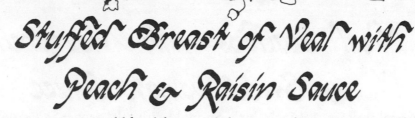

An inexpensive, yet incredibly delicious dish. Using the prepared stuffing mix saves a great deal of time and effort. A wonderful family dinner . . . and friends will love it too.

1 breast of veal, about 2-1/2 pounds. Ask your butcher to bone it. Sprinkle it with salt and pepper and lots of garlic powder.

1 package (6 ounces) Stove Top Chicken Flavored Stuffing Mix
1 can (10-1/2 ounces) chicken broth
1/4 cup water
1/2 cup raisins
1/4 cup butter (1/2 stick)

Heat together the seasoning packet in the stuffing mix with the broth, water, raisins and butter. Bring to a boil and add the bread cubes. Stir until the mixture is thoroughly blended.

Lay out the prepared breast of veal, cut side up. Place the stuffing mixture on the long side of the breast and roll it up. Skewer it or tie it securely with a string, making certain to skewer the ends.

Place roast in a 9x13-inch pan. Pour Peach and Raisin Sauce ingredients over the top. Cover the pan tightly with foil and bake in a 350° oven for 1-1/2 to 2 hours or until the meat is tender. Remove skewers or string.

Slice and serve with the peaches and raisins on the side. Gravy is rich and flavorful and can be served without any change. Serves 4.

Peach & Raisin Sauce

12 dried peaches, cut in half
1/2 cup golden raisins
3/4 cup dry white wine
1/2 package dry onion soup
3 tablespoons ketchup
1/4 cup peach jam

Combine all the ingredients and stir until they are mixed. Pour mixture over veal roast.

Poultry & Dressings

Chicken Paprikash Hungarian Style

1 broiler-fryer chicken (about 2-1/2 pounds, cut up) sprinkle with salt and
    pepper
2 tablespoons Dijon-style mustard

2 onions, finely chopped
2 tablespoons butter (1/2 stick)

2 tablespoons brown sugar
1/4 cup ketchup
1 teaspoon chicken seasoned stock base
1/2 cup white wine
1/2 cup tomato sauce
2 tablespoons paprika
salt and pepper to taste

1 cup sour cream

Toss chicken with mustard to coat evenly. Place in a roasting pan and cook
in a 350° oven for 1 hour.

Meanwhile, saute onions in butter until onions are soft. Add brown sugar
and saute until sugar is melted. Add ketchup, stock base, wine, tomato sauce,
paprika and seasonings and cook for about five minutes.

Add chicken to the sauce and simmer for 15 minutes. Taste for salt and pepper. Just before serving stir in the sour cream and heat through. Serve with
buttered noodles and honey glazed carrots. Serves 4.

*Note— Entire dish can be prepared the day before with the exception of the
sour cream which should be added just before serving.*

Chicken Burgundy in a Rich Wine Sauce

2 frying chickens, cut up, about 2-1/2 pounds, each. Sprinkle with salt, pepper and paprika.

1/4 cup butter
1 onion, finely chopped
2 carrots, finely chopped
2 cloves garlic, mashed

1 can (10-1/2 ounces) chicken broth
1/2 cup Burgundy wine
2 teaspoons Bovril, meat extract base
1 tablespoon tomato paste
1/4 teaspoon poultry seasoning
pinch of thyme
1 bay leaf

Place chicken pieces in one layer in a 12x16-inch roasting pan.

Saute the onion, carrots and garlic in the butter until the onions are transparent. Spoon this mixture over the chicken.

Combine the remaining ingredients and stir until blended. Pour this mixture over the chicken.

Roast chicken in a 325° oven for 1 hour 15 minutes, basting often with the sauce. Serve with Brown Rice with Mushrooms and pass the sauce on the side. Serves 6.

Note — Chicken can be made a day earlier and refrigerated. Reheat in a 325° oven until heated through.
— Sauce is rich and flavorful and does not need to be thickened. Serve it "natural" with some crusty French bread.

Chicken in Cream Sauce with Mushrooms & Swiss Cheese

4 whole chicken breasts, halved and sprinkled with salt, white pepper, garlic
    powder and paprika. Flatten a little to form a cutlet. Dust lightly with
    flour.
4 tablespoons butter
1/2 pound mushrooms, sliced thinly
1 tablespoon minced shallots
2 tablespoons butter

1 cup cream
1 cup extra rich chicken broth
salt and white pepper to taste

1-1/2 cups grated Swiss Cheese

In pan you will bake breasts, melt 4 tablespoons butter. Roll breasts in butter and bake in a 325° oven for about 1 hour. Keep warm.

Saute mushrooms and shallots in 2 tablespoons butter until mushrooms are
tender. Add cream and chicken broth and simmer over low heat until liquid
is reduced by 1/2 cup.

Add Swiss cheese and mix well. Continue cooking over low heat until cheese
is melted, about a minute or two.

Place chicken breasts on a lovely platter and spoon hot sauce over them.
Sprinkle with parsley and serve 8 with pride.

Note – You can make this dish earlier in the day with the following consid-
      erations. Chicken can be made earlier and heated before serving.
      Sauce can be made earlier except for the addition of the Swiss
      cheese. Heat the sauce before serving and at the last minute add the
      cheese and continue as above.
   – If you don't have extra rich broth on hand, you can use undiluted
      canned chicken broth.

Chicken with Apples & Honey Glaze

2 fryer chickens (2-1/2 to 3 pounds) cut up. Sprinkle with salt, pepper and garlic powder.

6 tablespoons butter (3/4 stick) melted

6 apples, cored, peeled and cut in quarters

1/2 cup honey
1/2 cup apple juice
2 tablespoons brown sugar

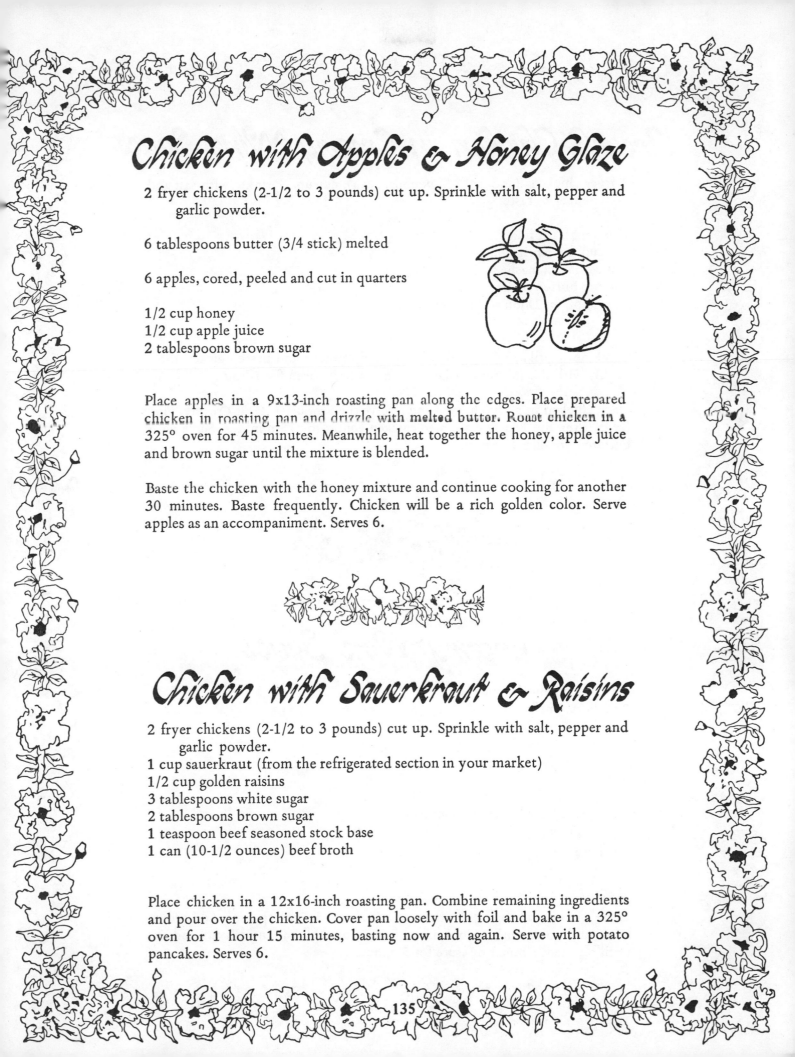

Place apples in a 9x13-inch roasting pan along the edges. Place prepared chicken in roasting pan and drizzle with melted butter. Roast chicken in a 325° oven for 45 minutes. Meanwhile, heat together the honey, apple juice and brown sugar until the mixture is blended.

Baste the chicken with the honey mixture and continue cooking for another 30 minutes. Baste frequently. Chicken will be a rich golden color. Serve apples as an accompaniment. Serves 6.

Chicken with Sauerkraut & Raisins

2 fryer chickens (2-1/2 to 3 pounds) cut up. Sprinkle with salt, pepper and garlic powder.
1 cup sauerkraut (from the refrigerated section in your market)
1/2 cup golden raisins
3 tablespoons white sugar
2 tablespoons brown sugar
1 teaspoon beef seasoned stock base
1 can (10-1/2 ounces) beef broth

Place chicken in a 12x16-inch roasting pan. Combine remaining ingredients and pour over the chicken. Cover pan loosely with foil and bake in a 325° oven for 1 hour 15 minutes, basting now and again. Serve with potato pancakes. Serves 6.

French Chicken in Creamy Wine Sauce

2 fryer chickens (about 2-1/2 pounds, each), cut up. Sprinkle with salt and
    pepper to taste.

1 teaspoon paprika
1/4 cup dry white wine
1 clove garlic, mashed
1/4 cup butter, melted
2 tablespoons Dijon-style mustard

Combine paprika, wine, garlic, butter and mustard and baste chicken thoroughly with this mixture. Bake chicken in a 350° oven for 1 hour.

Place chicken in a Dutch oven and reserve the pan juices. Pour Creamy Wine
Sauce over the top and simmer chicken gently for 15 minutes. Serve with
buttered noodles. Serves 6.

Creamy Wine Sauce

2 onions, finely chopped
2 shallots, finely chopped
2 tablespoons butter

2 tablespoons brown sugar

1/2 cup dry white wine
1 teaspoon Bovril, meat extract base
1 tablespoon paprika
1 cup cream
1/2 cup reserved pan juices

Saute onions and shallots in butter until onions are transparent. Add brown
sugar and cook until onions are soft. Combine all the ingredients and stir
until blended. Simmer mixture for 5 minutes.

Honey Glazed Chicken with Apricots & Raisins

2 fryer chickens, cut into pieces, sprinkle with salt, pepper and garlic powder
    and dust lightly with flour
1/4 cup butter
1/4 cup oil

In pan you will bake chicken, melt butter and mix in oil. Roll chicken pieces in butter, oil mixture and coat them evenly. Bake chicken in a 325° oven for 45 minutes. Now baste chicken with Honey Apricot Glaze and place apricots and raisins around chicken pieces. Continue basting every 10 minutes until chicken is tender, about 30 minutes more. Serves 6.

Honey Apricot Glaze

1/2 cup honey
1/2 cup reserved apricot syrup
2 tablespoons lemon juice
1/2 cup orange marmalade
1 tablespoon grated orange peel

In a pan, combine all the ingredients and heat through until the mixture is blended.

FRUIT MIXTURE

1 can (1 pound) apricots. Remove seeds and slice into fourths. Drain the fruit and reserve 1/2 cup of the syrup for the glaze.
1/2 cup golden raisins

Note— Entire dish can be cooked earlier in the day and refrigerated.

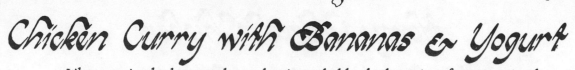

Chicken Curry with Bananas & Yogurt

When you've had a very busy day is probably the best time for using simple techniques that require very little extra time but add enchantment and excitement to everyday meals. Using curries is perhaps one of the very simplest; yet it can transform a quite ordinary dish into a culinary delight. Curries are the essence of simplicity, but by no means plain.

3 cups cooked chicken, diced

2 onions, finely chopped
1 clove garlic, mashed
4 tablespoons butter

2 tablespoons flour
1 teaspoon curry powder (or more to taste)
1 teaspoon tumeric
1 tablespoon brown sugar
1 cup chicken broth

1 cup yogurt
3 sliced bananas, tossed in lemon juice (about 1 or 2 teaspoons lemon juice)
salt to taste

Saute onion and garlic in butter until onion is soft but do not brown. Add flour, curry powder, tumeric and brown sugar and cook and stir for a minute or two. Add chicken broth and cook and stir until sauce thickens. If the sauce is too thick, add a little more broth.

Add yogurt and bananas and stir and heat through. Now add the cooked chicken and heat through. Serve with rice. Serves 5 or 6.

Note — Entire dish can be assembled and made a day earlier up to the point of adding the bananas and yogurt which I would add when reheating before serving.

Chicken with Orange Honey Glaze

2 fryer chickens, cut into pieces. Sprinkle with salt, pepper, garlic powder and ginger. Dust lightly with flour.
4 tablespoons butter, melted (1/2 stick)

Orange Honey Glaze

1/2 cup orange marmalade
1/2 cup honey
1 tablespoon lemon juice
1 tablespoon orange liqueur

Place prepared chicken in a 12x16-inch roasting pan and drizzle with the melted butter. Roast chicken in a 325° oven for 45 minutes.

Meanwhile, heat together the marmalade, honey, lemon juice and liqueur until the mixture is blended. Baste the chicken with Orange Honey Glaze and continue baking and basting for another 30 minutes. Chicken will have a deep golden color. Serves 6.

Chicken Teriyaki with Orange Plum Sauce

2 fryer chickens, cut into pieces. Sprinkle with salt, pepper, garlic powder and ginger. Baste generously with Lawry's Teriyaki Marinade.

Bake chicken in a 325° oven for about 45 minutes. Baste the chicken with the Orange Plum Sauce and continue baking and basting another 30 minutes, or until chicken is tender and a deep golden color. Serves 6.

Orange Plum Sauce

1 can (1 pound) purple plums, remove seeds and drain
1 can (6 ounces) frozen orange juice, undiluted
1 tablespoon vinegar
3 tablespoons brown sugar
2 tablespoons chili sauce
pinch of ginger

Blend all the ingredients until the plums are pureed.

Chicken with Maple Glaze & Pecans

2 frying chickens, cut into pieces, sprinkle with salt, garlic powder and
  paprika

1/4 cup butter, melted
2 tablespoons oil

1/2 cup maple syrup
1/2 cup coarsely chopped pecans

Mix butter and oil together and place in pan you will bake chicken. Roll
chicken pieces in butter, oil mixture and coat evenly. Bake chicken in a 325°
oven for 45 minutes. Baste chicken with maple syrup and bake another 20
minutes, basting frequently. Sprinkle with pecans and bake another 10
minutes until chicken is glazed a lovely caramel color. Serves 6.

Chicken with Garlic Crumbs

2 frying chickens, cut into pieces, sprinkle with salt, pepper, paprika

1/4 cup melted butter
1/4 cup Dijon-style mustard

1 cup bread crumbs
2 tablespoons dried parsley
4 cloves garlic, put through a press
1/4 cup butter, melted

Combine melted butter and mustard and coat chicken pieces with this mixture. Mix together the bread crumbs, parsley and garlic. Sprinkle crumb mixture over the chicken and bake in a 325° oven for 1 hour and 15 minutes,
basting from time to time with some of the extra butter. Serves 6.

Batter Fried Chicken with Hot Plum Sauce

8 whole chicken breasts. Ask your butcher to remove the bones and skin and
to cut them in half. Sprinkle with salt, pepper and garlic powder. Dust
lightly with flour.

1 cup flour
1/2 cup corn starch
1 teaspoon baking powder
1 egg
1-1/2 cups water
1/4 teaspoon salt

With a rotary beater, beat together all the ingredients, until the batter is
smooth. Batter should be the consistency of heavy cream.

Dip chicken in batter and fry the breasts in hot oil until they are golden
brown on both sides. Remove from the oil and drain. Place chicken in a
350° oven and bake for about 20 minutes or until chicken is cooked through.
Serve with Hot Plum Sauce on the side for dipping. Serves 8.

Hot Plum Sauce

1 cup plum preserves
6 tablespoons lemon juice
2 tablespoons grated lemon peel
6 tablespoons brown sugar
3 tablespoons chili sauce
pinch of ginger

In a saucepan, combine all the ingredients and simmer the mixture for 5 minutes. Allow sauce to cool for a few minutes and serve warm. Makes about
1-1/2 cups sauce.

Chicken in Sour Cream Mushroom Sauce

2 fryer chickens, cut into pieces, sprinkled with salt and garlic powder and
dusted lightly with flour

1/4 cup butter (1/2 stick)
1/4 cup oil

In pan you will bake chicken, melt butter and mix in oil. Roll chicken pieces
in butter, oil mixture and coat evenly. Bake chicken in a 325° oven for
about 1 hour and 15 minutes, basting 3 or 4 times. Pour Sour Cream Mushroom Sauce over the chicken and continue baking until heated through.
Serves 6.

Sour Cream Mushroom Sauce

1/4 pound fresh mushrooms, sliced
1/4 cup finely minced onion
2 tablespoons butter
2 tablespoons flour
1/2 cup extra rich chicken broth
1/2 cup sour cream
salt and white pepper to taste
2 tablespoons champagne

Saute mushrooms and onion in butter until onions are soft. Add flour and
cook for a minute or two. Add broth, sour cream, salt, pepper and champagne and heat through. Do not boil.

*Note — Entire dish can be made earlier in the day with the following consid-
erations: Cook chicken and refrigerate. Make sauce and refrigerate.
Reheat chicken and sauce separately, taking special care not to boil
the sauce. Heat the sauce over low heat just until heated through.
Serve over the hot chicken as above.*

Crusty Chicken in an Herbed Tomato Wine Sauce

2 chickens, 2-1/2 pounds each, fryers or broilers, cut up, sprinkle with
  salt and pepper

2 egg whites, slightly beaten
2 tablespoons Dijon-style mustard

1 cup bread crumbs
1 cup Parmesan cheese, grated
1 tablespoon paprika
1/2 teaspoon garlic powder

Beat together the egg whites and the mustard. Set the mixture aside. Combine the bread crumbs, grated cheese, paprika and garlic powder. Brush the chicken pieces with the egg white mixture and dip them into the crumb mixture. Set the chicken pieces in a buttered 12x16-inch roasting pan, in one layer. Bake at 350° for 45 minutes. Pour Herbed Tomato Wine Sauce over the top and continue baking for 40 minutes or until chicken is tender. Serve with some crusty Italian bread. Serves 6.

Herbed Tomato Wine Sauce

1 onion, finely chopped
1/2 pound mushrooms, cleaned and thinly sliced. Use the stems.
4 tablespoons butter
1 teaspoon Italian Herb Seasoning
1/2 cup dry white wine
salt and pepper to taste
1 can (1 pound) stewed tomatoes, finely chopped

Saute onions and mushrooms in butter until onions are soft. Add the Italian Herb Seasoning and the wine and cook for 10 minutes, uncovered. Add the remaining ingredients and simmer for 20 minutes. Makes about 3 cups sauce.

Note— You can substitute 6 whole chicken breasts for the chicken pieces. Proceed in very much the same way, except shorten the baking time to 1 hour, instead of 1 hour and 25 minutes.

Chicken with Garlic & Herbs in Mushroom Wine Sauce

2 frying chickens, cut up (about 2-1/2 to 3 pounds, each), dust lightly in
    flour
2 tablespoons butter
3 cloves garlic, mashed
3 tablespoons finely minced onion (about 1/2 onion)

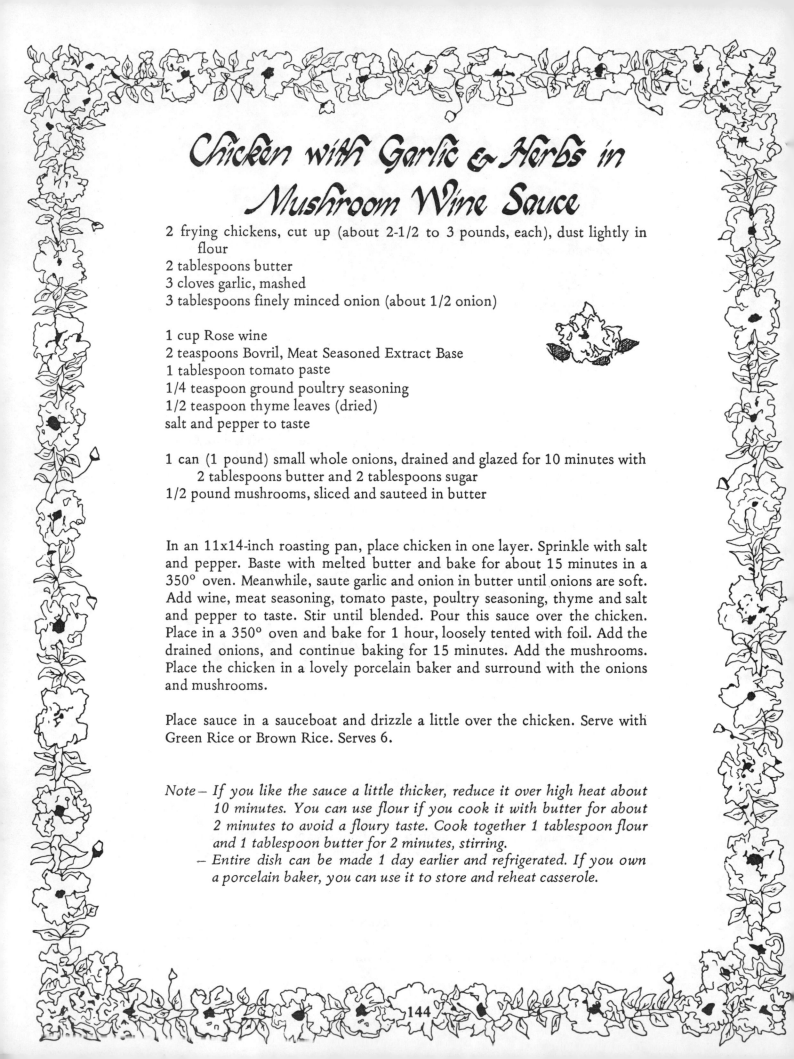

1 cup Rose wine
2 teaspoons Bovril, Meat Seasoned Extract Base
1 tablespoon tomato paste
1/4 teaspoon ground poultry seasoning
1/2 teaspoon thyme leaves (dried)
salt and pepper to taste

1 can (1 pound) small whole onions, drained and glazed for 10 minutes with
    2 tablespoons butter and 2 tablespoons sugar
1/2 pound mushrooms, sliced and sauteed in butter

In an 11x14-inch roasting pan, place chicken in one layer. Sprinkle with salt
and pepper. Baste with melted butter and bake for about 15 minutes in a
350° oven. Meanwhile, saute garlic and onion in butter until onions are soft.
Add wine, meat seasoning, tomato paste, poultry seasoning, thyme and salt
and pepper to taste. Stir until blended. Pour this sauce over the chicken.
Place in a 350° oven and bake for 1 hour, loosely tented with foil. Add the
drained onions, and continue baking for 15 minutes. Add the mushrooms.
Place the chicken in a lovely porcelain baker and surround with the onions
and mushrooms.

Place sauce in a sauceboat and drizzle a little over the chicken. Serve with
Green Rice or Brown Rice. Serves 6.

Note – If you like the sauce a little thicker, reduce it over high heat about
    10 minutes. You can use flour if you cook it with butter for about
    2 minutes to avoid a floury taste. Cook together 1 tablespoon flour
    and 1 tablespoon butter for 2 minutes, stirring.
   – Entire dish can be made 1 day earlier and refrigerated. If you own
    a porcelain baker, you can use it to store and reheat casserole.

Chicken Stroganoff with Buttered Noodles

4 chicken breasts. Ask your butcher to bone and cut them in 1-inch cubes.
    Sprinkle them with salt, pepper, garlic powder and paprika. Dust them
    lightly in flour.
4 tablespoons butter

1 onion, chopped
2 tablespoons butter
1/2 pound mushrooms, sliced

2 tablespoons flour

1/4 cup dry white wine
2 tablespoons paprika
1 can (10-1/2 ounces) chicken broth
1 teaspoon chicken seasoned stock base
salt and pepper to taste

1 cup cream

Saute chicken pieces in 4 tablespoons butter until chicken is cooked. Do not
overcook. Remove chicken with a slotted spoon and set aside.

In same skillet, saute onions in 2 tablespoons butter until onions are soft.
Add mushrooms and saute until mushrooms are tender. Add flour and cook
for two minutes, stirring.

Add wine, paprika, chicken broth, stock base, salt and pepper and cook for a
few minutes until sauce has thickened. Add cream and chicken and heat
through. Serve on a bed of buttered noodles that have been sprinkled with
paprika. Serves 4 or 5.

Chicken in Mustard Wine Sauce

2 fryer chickens (about 2-1/2 pounds each), cut up. Sprinkle with salt and
    pepper to taste and 1 teaspoon paprika.
4 tablespoons Dijon-style mustard
1/4 cup dry white wine
1 clove garlic, put through a press
1/4 cup butter, melted
1/2 cup bread crumbs

Combine mustard, wine and garlic and baste chicken with this mixture. Place
chicken in roasting pan and drizzle it with the melted butter. (Lay chicken in
one layer in a 12x16-inch roasting pan.) Sprinkle with bread crumbs.

Bake chicken in a 350° oven for 1 hour 15 minutes, basting now and again
with the juices formed in the pan. Serve chicken "natural" with strained pan
juices on the side. Serves 6.

Turkey with Raisins & Apples

12 slices cooked breast of turkey (or enough leftover turkey to serve 6.)
    Sprinkle with salt and garlic powder to taste.

3 apples, peeled, cored and sliced in rings
2 tablespoons butter
1/2 cup brown sugar
1 cup apple juice
1/2 cup golden raisins
salt and pepper to taste

Butter a lovely heat and serve baker and layer bottom with cooked turkey.
In a skillet, saute apples in butter until they are tender. Add brown sugar,
apple juice and raisins and simmer until bubbly and thickened, about 5 minutes of vigorous bubbling.

Place apples over the turkey and pour the sauce evenly over all. Heat in a
350° oven until heated through. Serves 6.

Turkey Cutlets Parmigiana with Marinara Tomato Sauce & Mozzarella

Many stores are now featuring turkey cutlets which are cut from the turkey breast. They cook quickly and are a good substitute for veal.

8 turkey cutlets (about 6 ounces, each)

2 eggs, beaten
2 tablespoons water

CRUMB COATING

1/2 cup cracker crumbs
1/2 cup flour
1 cup grated Parmesan cheese
1/4 teaspoon garlic powder
2 tablespoons paprika
salt and pepper to taste

TOPPING

1/2 cup grated Parmesan
1 cup grated Mozzarella cheese

Beat eggs with water until blended. Set mixture aside. Combine the crumb coating ingredients and toss to mix.

In a large skillet, heat about 1/2-inch of oil. Dip turkey cutlets into the beaten eggs and then into the crumb mixture. Fry cutlets in oil until golden brown on both sides. Remove cutlets to a 9x13-inch roasting pan. Lay them in one layer in pan.

Pour Tomato Sauce over the cutlets and sprinkle them with Parmesan and Mozzarella cheeses. Heat them in a 350° oven for 30 minutes. Serves 8.

Marinara Tomato Sauce

1 can (1 pound) stewed tomatoes, finely chopped
1 can (8 ounces) tomato sauce
1 tablespoon onion flakes
1 tablespoon parsley
1 tablespoon sugar
1/4 teaspoon garlic powder
1 tablespoon oil

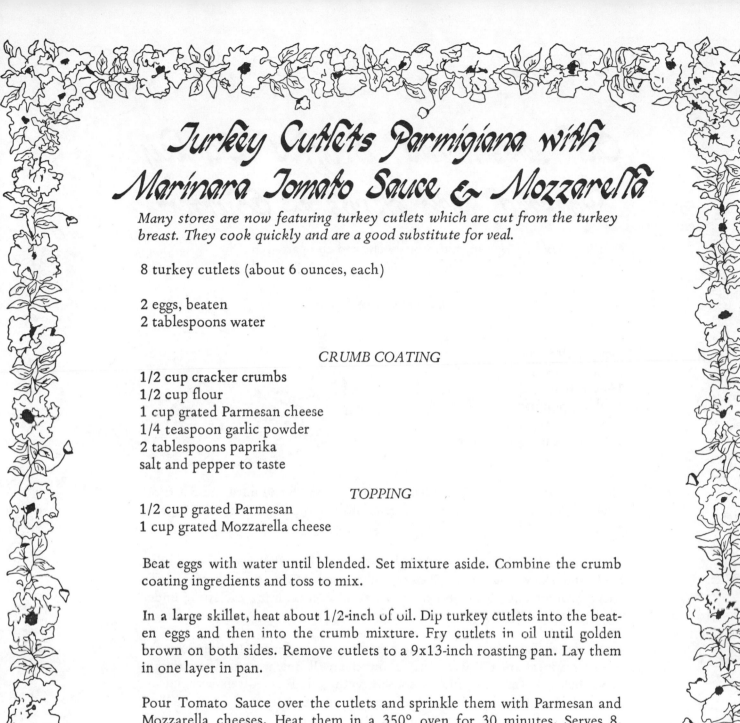

In a saucepan, simmer together all the ingredients for 5 minutes. Pour over the cutlets.

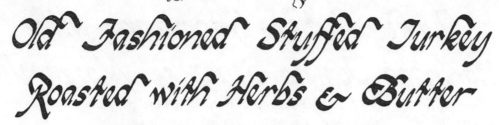

Old Fashioned Stuffed Turkey Roasted with Herbs & Butter

1 turkey, about 15 pounds, thorougly cleaned and patted dry

BASTING MIXTURE

1 cup melted butter
1 teaspoon salt
1/4 teaspoon pepper
1 tablespoon paprika
4 large cloves garlic
1/4 teaspoon onion powder

Place all the ingredients in a blender container and blend until garlic is thoroughly ground. Baste turkey very generously, inside and out, with basting mixture.

Pack stuffing loosely into neck and body of turkey. Pull neck skin over to back and skewer it down. Skewer body opening with poultry pins. Lace string around pins, back and forth. At the last turn, bring the string under the legs and tie them together. Baste turkey again.

Place turkey on a rack in roasting pan, breast side down. (If directions for roasting appear on the wrapper, follow them. If not, use the approximate chart below.) Tent the turkey loosely with foil. Baste often with juices. About 1 hour before turkey is cooked, turn it breast up, and continue baking, uncovered, until turkey is finished. Remove skewers and set on a platter. Let turkey rest for 20 minutes, so that it will be easier to carve. Remove any fat from gravy. Gravy is very flavorful and does not need to be thickened.

ROASTING CHART

| Under 12 pounds | 300° | 25 minutes per pound |
| Over 12 pounds | 300° | 20 minutes per pound |

Roasting times are approximate. If you are using a meat thermometer, turkey should reach 190° in the center of the inside thigh muscle. Insert thermometer during the last hour of roasting. Or you can test for doneness by moving the drumstick up and down. If it gives easily, turkey is done.

Old Fashioned Herb Stuffing

1 cup butter (2 sticks)
2 cups onions, finely chopped
1 cup celery, finely chopped
1/2 pound mushrooms, thinly sliced

2 eggs
1/4 cup finely chopped parsley
2 teaspoons poultry seasoning
2 teaspoons chicken seasoned stock base
2 cans (10-1/2 ounces, each) chicken broth
salt and pepper to taste

2 packages (8 ounces, each) herbed seasoned stuffing mix

Saute onions and celery in butter until they are soft. Add mushrooms and saute until mushrooms are tender. Add remaining ingredients, using only enough chicken broth to hold stuffing together.

Note— If you have any leftover stuffing, bake it during the last 30 minutes before serving.

Important: *Do not stuff turkey in advance. Remove stuffing before storing leftover turkey. Improper handling of stuffing can lead to growth of harmful bacteria. So please take care to stuff turkey shortly before roasting and remove stuffing from turkey right after serving.*

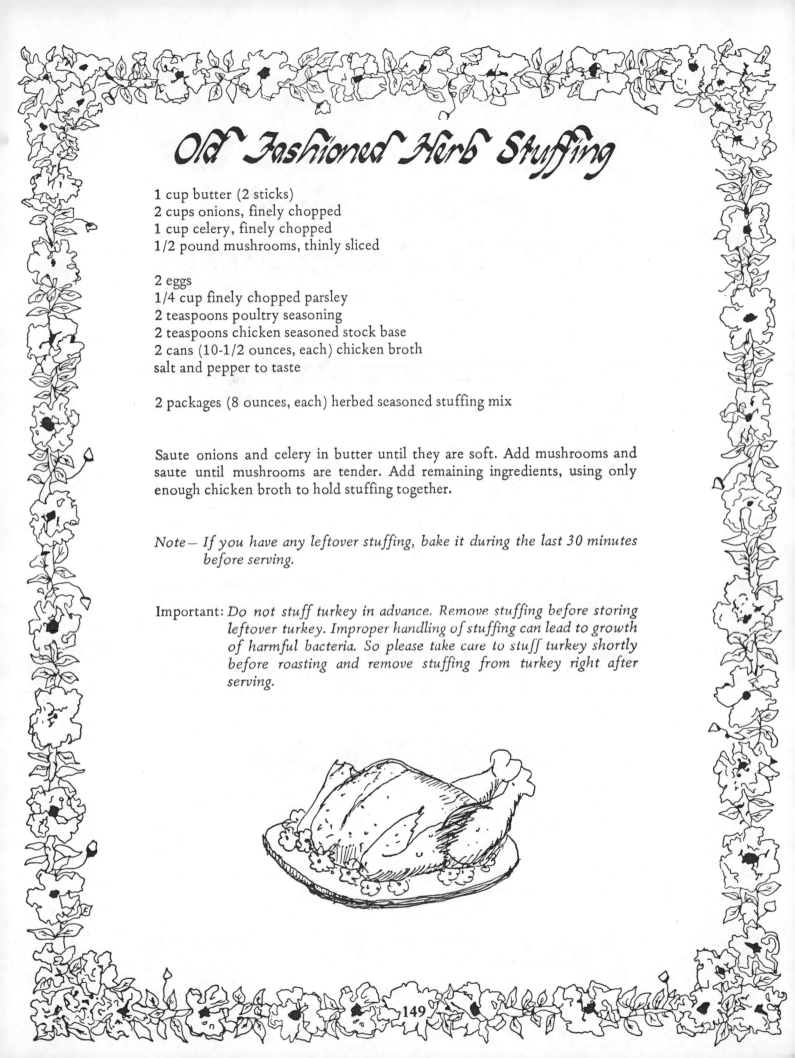

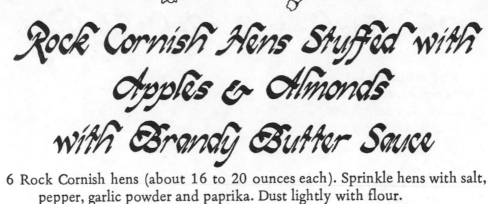

Rock Cornish Hens Stuffed with Apples & Almonds with Brandy Butter Sauce

6 Rock Cornish hens (about 16 to 20 ounces each). Sprinkle hens with salt, pepper, garlic powder and paprika. Dust lightly with flour.

Apple Almond Stuffing

1 package, 8 ounces, herb seasoned stuffing mix
1 apple, peeled and grated
1/2 cup butter, melted
2 teaspoons chicken seasoned stock base
1 cup apple juice, more or less as needed
3/4 cup sliced almonds, lightly toasted in a 350° oven for 8 minutes
1/8 teaspoon poultry seasoning
salt and pepper to taste

Combine all the ingredients, adding only enough apple juice to hold stuffing together. Stuff hen cavities about 3/4 full and skewer them with toothpicks or skewers.

Baste hens generously with Brandy Butter mixture and bake in a 325° oven for 1 hour 10 minutes. Baste often during baking time, turning once or twice. Hens will turn a lovely golden color. Remove skewers and decorate platter with lots of parsley, crab apples and orange slices. Serves 6.

Brandy Butter Sauce

1/2 cup butter (1 stick)
2 tablespoons apricot flavored brandy
2 tablespoons honey

Combine butter, brandy and honey in a saucepan and heat until butter melts and mixture is blended.

Note — If hens are browning too rapidly, tent the roasting pan loosely with aluminum foil.

Rock Cornish Hens Stuffed with Fruit & Apricot Wine Glazed

6 Rock Cornish hens (about 16 to 20 ounces, each). Sprinkle hens with salt, pepper, garlic powder and paprika.

Prune Apple Stuffing

2 apples, peeled and grated
12 prunes, pitted and coarsely chopped
1 tablespoon grated orange peel
1 cup orange juice
1/2 cup butter
1/2 cup golden raisins

1 package (8 ounces) herb seasoned stuffing mix
chicken broth

Combine first 6 ingredients in a saucepan and simmer the mixture for 10 minutes. Add the stuffing mix and enough chicken broth to hold the stuffing together. Stuff hen cavities about 3/4 full and skewer them with toothpicks or skewers.

Brush the hens generously with melted butter and roast them in a 325° oven for 45 minutes, basting them every 15 minutes. Now baste with Apricot Wine Glaze and continue baking and basting for an additional 30 minutes. Hens will turn a lovely golden color.

Remove skewers and place hens on a bed of parsley. Serves 6.

Apricot Wine Glaze

1 cup apricot jam
1/2 cup melted butter
1/4 cup dry white wine

Combine jam, butter and wine in a saucepan and heat until butter melts and mixture is blended.

Seasoned Salt for Poultry & Meats

I know I have given this to you before, but it is such a good combination of herbs and spices that I felt I should include it. It is excellent on chicken and turkey and produces the finest tasting gravy.

1-1/2 cups salt
1 whole garlic, peeled
1 tablespoon poultry seasoning
1 tablespoon paprika
1/4 teaspoon ginger
1 teaspoon seasoned pepper
1/4 teaspoon powdered mustard
1 teaspoon chili powder
1 teaspoon toasted onion powder
1-1/2 teaspoons MSG

Place salt and garlic cloves in blender container and blend at high speed until garlic is thoroughly mashed. Remove salt and garlic mixture and place in a quart jar with a tight lid. Add the remaining ingredients and shake to thoroughly mix. Refrigerate. (Sprinkle over your buttered turkey or chicken as you would salt. Use a little less at first until you find the right amount for your taste.) Makes about 2 cups of heavenly seasoning.

Note — Transfer some of the seasoned salt to a small shaker jar with large sprinkling holes. This makes it easier to use.
* — I like to store this seasoning in the refrigerator, but it isn't mandatory.*
* — In a lovely amber glass jar, this seasoning makes an unforgettable gift from your kitchen.*

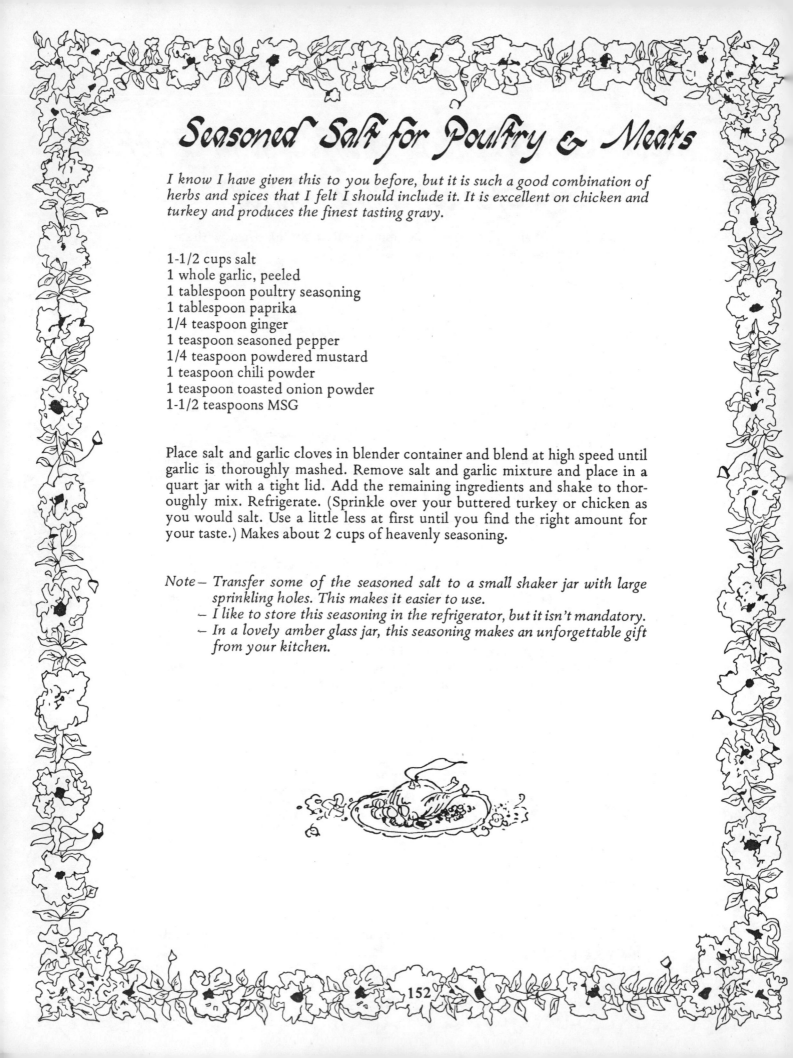

Molds

Spiced Peach Cream Mold

1 package (6 ounces) peach gelatin

1 can (1 pound 12 ounces) spiced peaches, slice and remove seeds. Reserve
     syrup.
Water and reserved peach syrup to equal 1-1/2 cups liquid

1 pint cream

Place gelatin in large bowl of your electric mixer. In a saucepan, heat water
and reserved syrup to boiling point. Pour syrup mixture into the bowl with
the gelatin and stir until gelatin is dissolved. Chill gelatin until it is partially
congealed, but not firm set. Whip gelatin until it is light and frothy.

Beat cream until it is stiff. Beat together gelatin and whipped cream until
mixture is blended. Fold in the sliced peaches.

Pour mixture into a 2-quart mold and refrigerate it until firm. Unmold by
placing mold into warm water for a few seconds until it is loosened and in-
verting it on a serving platter. Serves 12.

Spicy Applesauce Raisin Mold

1 package (6 ounces) lemon gelatin
2 cups apple juice
1/8 teaspoon cinnamon
1 cup yellow raisins
1 cup applesauce

Cook together the lemon gelatin, apple juice, cinnamon and raisins until
gelatin is dissolved. Stir in the applesauce. Pour mixture into a pretty glass
bowl and refrigerate until firm. Serve directly from the bowl; no need to
unmold. Serves 10.

Apricot Mold with Yogurt, Bananas & Coconut

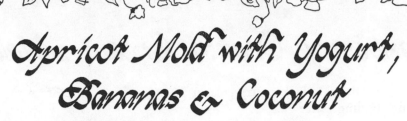

1 package (6 ounces) apricot gelatin
1 can (1 pound 12 ounces) apricots, drained (reserve juice). Remove seeds
    and chop.
Water and reserved apricot juice to equal 1-1/2 cups liquid
2 cups yogurt, unflavored
2 bananas, sliced
6 tablespoons coconut flakes

Place gelatin in a large bowl. Heat to boiling the water and apricot juice
and add it to the gelatin. Stir until gelatin is dissolved. Add yogurt and stir
until blended. Add remaining ingredients and stir to mix well.

Pour mixture into a 2-quart mold and refrigerate until firm. Unmold on a
lovely platter and decorate with banana slices that were dipped in sour cream
and then in coconut flakes. Serves 10 or 12.

Lemon Mold with Strawberries & Sherbet

1 package (6 ounces) lemon gelatin
1-1/2 cups boiling water

2 cups lemon sherbet
1 pint strawberries (fresh or frozen)

In a large bowl, dissolve gelatin in boiling water. Add sherbet and stir until
sherbet is dissolved. Stir in the strawberries. Pour mixture into a 2-quart
mold and chill in the refrigerator until firm.

Unmold on a footed platter and decorate with strawberries and green leaves.
Serves 10 or 12.

*Note— Molds can be made a day earlier. Can also be unmolded earlier in the
day, decorated and then refrigerated until serving time.*

Cranberry Orange Cream Mold

1 package (6 ounces) black cherry gelatin
1-1/2 cups boiling water

1 can (16 ounces) whole berry cranberry sauce
1 can (8 ounces) mandarin orange sections
1 tablespoon grated orange zest
1 pint sour cream
1/2 cup toasted chopped walnuts

Dissolve gelatin in boiling water. Add the cranberry sauce and stir until the sauce is melted and the berries float separately. Add the remaining ingredients and stir until they are well blended. Pour mixture into a 2-quart mold and refrigerate until firm.

Unmold by placing mold in warm water for a few seconds or until it is loosened and invert it on a pretty platter.

Decorate with halved orange slices and pretty green leaves around the edge. Serves 12.

Black Cherry Cream Parfait

1 package (6 ounces) black cherry gelatin
2 cups boiling water

2 cups cream, whipped stiff

Dissolve gelatin in boiling water. Whip cream until stiff. Beat together the hot gelatin and the whipped cream. Beat until thoroughly blended.

Pour mixture into a glass bowl or 2-quart mold. Refrigerate until firm. When gelatin is firm, it will have separated into 3 distinct layers, which is very festive. Each layer has its distinct taste which makes it quite exciting.

Unmold on a footed platter or serve directly from the glass bowl. Serves 10.

Mixed Fruit Peach Mold

1 package (12 ounces) dried mix fruits, coarsely chopped
2 cups orange juice
1/2 lemon, thinly sliced
1/2 cup yellow raisins
1/2 cup sugar
1 teaspoon vanilla

1 package (6 ounces) peach gelatin
2 cups boiling water

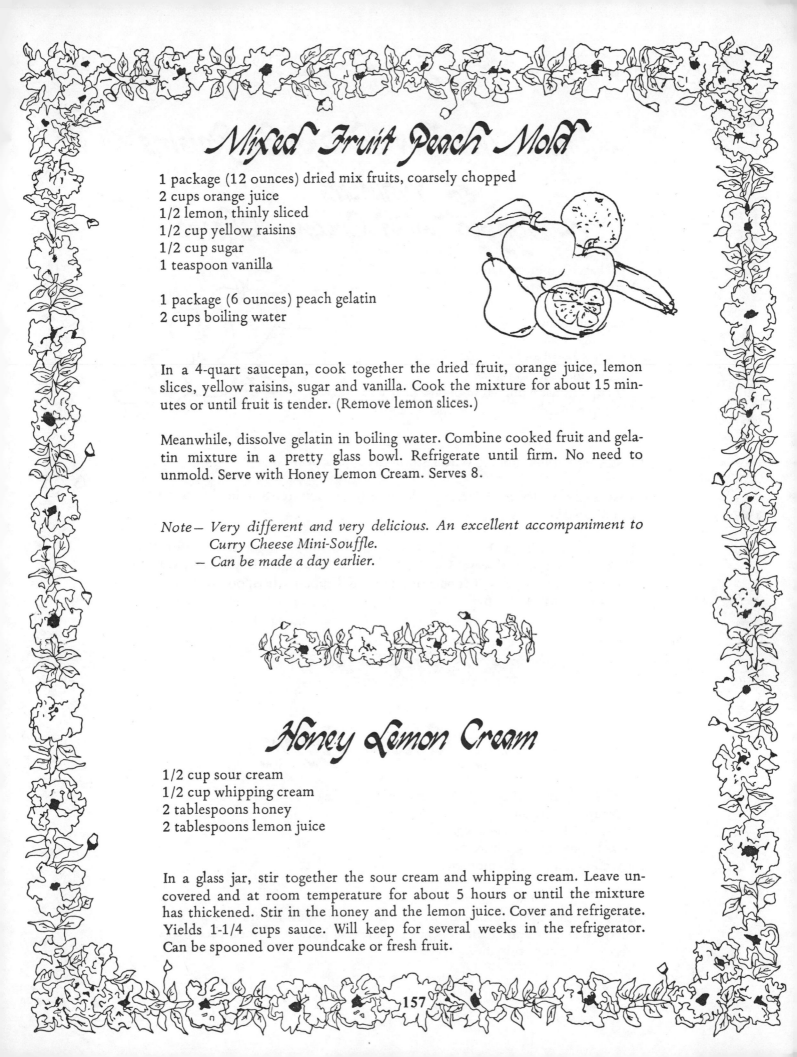

In a 4-quart saucepan, cook together the dried fruit, orange juice, lemon slices, yellow raisins, sugar and vanilla. Cook the mixture for about 15 minutes or until fruit is tender. (Remove lemon slices.)

Meanwhile, dissolve gelatin in boiling water. Combine cooked fruit and gelatin mixture in a pretty glass bowl. Refrigerate until firm. No need to unmold. Serve with Honey Lemon Cream. Serves 8.

Note — Very different and very delicious. An excellent accompaniment to Curry Cheese Mini-Souffle.
— Can be made a day earlier.

Honey Lemon Cream

1/2 cup sour cream
1/2 cup whipping cream
2 tablespoons honey
2 tablespoons lemon juice

In a glass jar, stir together the sour cream and whipping cream. Leave uncovered and at room temperature for about 5 hours or until the mixture has thickened. Stir in the honey and the lemon juice. Cover and refrigerate. Yields 1-1/4 cups sauce. Will keep for several weeks in the refrigerator. Can be spooned over poundcake or fresh fruit.

Lemon Mold with Apples, Raisins & Walnuts & Topped with Creamy Cheese

1 package (3 ounces) lemon gelatin
1 cup boiling water

1 cup applesauce

2 apples, cored and diced. Do not peel.
2 tablespoons lemon juice
1/2 cup raisins, plumped in orange juice and drained
1/2 cup toasted walnuts, chopped coarsely

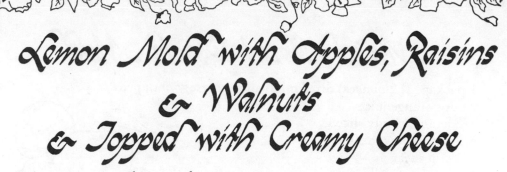

Dissolve gelatin in boiling water. Stir in the applesauce.

Toss apples in lemon juice and add to gelatin mixture. Stir in the raisins and toasted walnuts.

Pour mixture into a 9 or 10-inch glass pie plate and refrigerate until firm. Frost with Creamy Cheese Topping and serve in wedges. If you like, you could place the Cheese Topping in a bowl and spoon a teaspoon or two at time of serving. Serves 6.

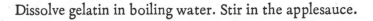

Creamy Cheese Topping

1/4 pound cream cheese (1/2 of an 8 ounce package)
1/2 cup sour cream
1/2 cup sifted powdered sugar
2 tablespoons lemon juice
1 tablespoon grated lemon peel

Beat together the cream cheese, sour cream and powdered sugar until the mixture is light and creamy. Beat in the lemon juice and lemon peel. Makes about 1-1/2 cups topping.

Noodles

&

Rice

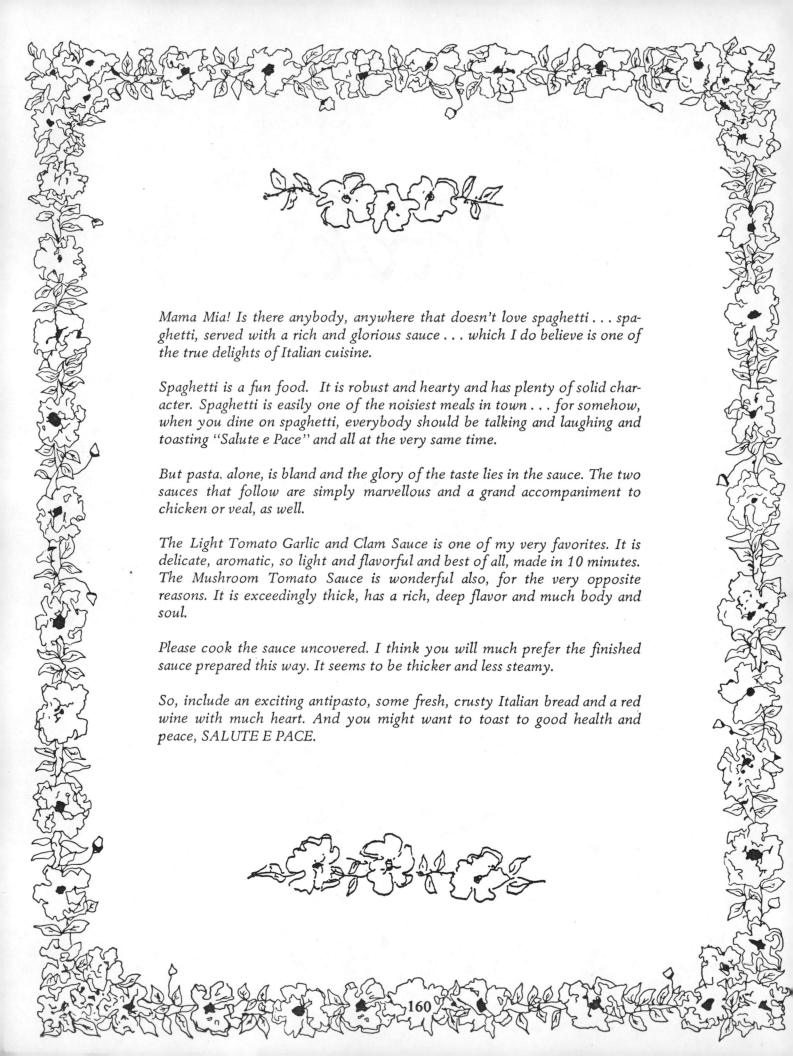

Mama Mia! Is there anybody, anywhere that doesn't love spaghetti . . . spaghetti, served with a rich and glorious sauce . . . which I do believe is one of the true delights of Italian cuisine.

Spaghetti is a fun food. It is robust and hearty and has plenty of solid character. Spaghetti is easily one of the noisiest meals in town . . . for somehow, when you dine on spaghetti, everybody should be talking and laughing and toasting "Salute e Pace" and all at the very same time.

But pasta, alone, is bland and the glory of the taste lies in the sauce. The two sauces that follow are simply marvellous and a grand accompaniment to chicken or veal, as well.

The Light Tomato Garlic and Clam Sauce is one of my very favorites. It is delicate, aromatic, so light and flavorful and best of all, made in 10 minutes. The Mushroom Tomato Sauce is wonderful also, for the very opposite reasons. It is exceedingly thick, has a rich, deep flavor and much body and soul.

Please cook the sauce uncovered. I think you will much prefer the finished sauce prepared this way. It seems to be thicker and less steamy.

So, include an exciting antipasto, some fresh, crusty Italian bread and a red wine with much heart. And you might want to toast to good health and peace, SALUTE E PACE.

Spaghetti in a Light Tomato Garlic & Clam Sauce

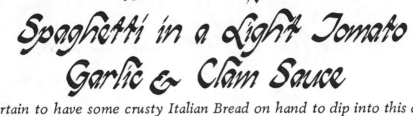

Be certain to have some crusty Italian Bread on hand to dip into this delectable sauce.

1 pound spaghetti, cooked al dente (tender but firm) and drained. Toss spaghetti in a little olive oil.

Light Tomato Garlic & Clam Sauce

3 cloves garlic, mashed
3 tablespoons oil

2 cans (1 pound, each) stewed tomatoes, finely chopped
2 cans (8 ounces, each) tomato sauce
2 cans (7 ounces, each) chopped clams
2 teaspoons sugar
2 teaspoon Italian Herb Seasoning
1 teaspoon dried thyme leaves
1/2 teaspoon crushed red hot peppers
Salt and freshly ground pepper to taste

Saute garlic in olive oil in pan you will be making the sauce. Now add the remaining ingredients (except the spaghetti) and simmer sauce, uncovered, for about 10 to 15 minutes. Sauce is now ready to serve. Yields enough sauce for 1 pound of spaghetti.

Note — Sauce can be made earlier in the day and refrigerated. Reheat before serving.
— This red clam sauce is delicate and aromatic. Although I doubt you will have any sauce left over, you can freeze it.
— If you wish to substitute another pasta for the spaghetti, of course do.
— If you enjoy grated Parmesan or Romano cheese with your pastas, go sparingly so that the flavor of the sauce is not lost.

Spaghetti with Mushroom Tomato Sauce

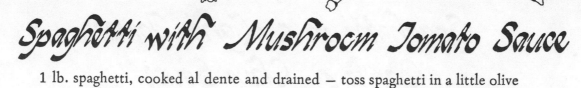

1 lb. spaghetti, cooked al dente and drained — toss spaghetti in a little olive
    oil.

4 tablespoons olive oil
2 cloves garlic, mashed
2 cups chopped onions
1 carrot, finely grated

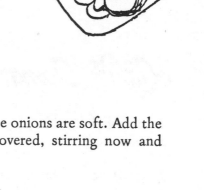

2 cans (1 pound, each) stewed tomatoes, finely chopped
2 cans (8 ounces, each) tomato sauce
1 can (6 ounces) tomato paste
1 teaspoon Italian Herb Seasoning
2 tablespoons sugar
2 bay leaves
salt and freshly ground pepper

Saute garlic, onions and carrot in olive oil until the onions are soft. Add the
remaining ingredients and simmer mixture, uncovered, stirring now and
again, for about 30 minutes. Now add:

1/2 pound mushrooms, sliced and sauteed in butter

Heat through and serve. Yields enough sauce for 1 pound of spaghetti.

Noodle & Broccoli Mold

1 package (8 ounces) medium noodles, cooked and drained. Do not over-
    cook.
2 packages (10 ounces, each) chopped broccoli, defrosted and drained

1/2 cup butter, melted
1/2 pound mushrooms, sliced
2 eggs, well beaten
1 cup sour cream
1/2 cup grated Parmesan cheese
salt and pepper to taste

Cook noodles and set aside. Defrost broccoli and drain. Saute mushrooms
in 1/2 cup butter until mushrooms are tender. Combine all the ingredients
and mix well.

Butter and sprinkle with crumbs a 2-quart ring mold. Place mixture into
mold, cover with foil and bake in a 350° oven for 45 minutes. Remove from
oven, loosen sides and invert on a lovely platter immediately. Serves 8.

Noodles with Bacon, Tomatoes & Mushrooms

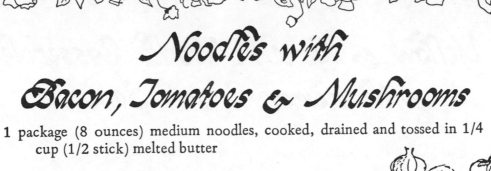

1 package (8 ounces) medium noodles, cooked, drained and tossed in 1/4
    cup (1/2 stick) melted butter

1/4 pound bacon, cooked crisp and crumbled
1/2 pound mushrooms, sliced and sauteed in butter until tender
1/2 cup finely minced green onions
1/4 teaspoon thyme flakes
1 can (16 ounces) stewed tomatoes, finely chopped and drained
1 cup sour cream
salt and pepper to taste

Combine all the ingredients and toss to mix well. Turn mixture into a buttered oval baking dish and heat in a 350° oven until heated through, about 20 minutes. Serves 5 or 6.

Note – Entire dish can be assembled earlier in the day and reheated at time
    of serving.
   – Drain the tomatoes fairly dry to avoid getting the noodles soupy.

Noodle Pudding with Onions & Cheese

1 package (8 ounces) medium noodles, cooked and drained, salt to taste
3/4 pound Ricotta cheese
1-1/2 cups sour cream
4 eggs, beaten
3 green onions, finely chopped
1/4 cup minced parsley or 1 heaping tablespoon dried parsley flakes
3/4 cup Parmesan cheese, grated

Combine all the ingredients and place in a heavily buttered 9x13-inch pan. Bake at 350° until top is golden and cheese is set, about 50 minutes to 1 hour. Serves 8.

Yellow & Green Noodle Casserole with Lemon Cream Sauce

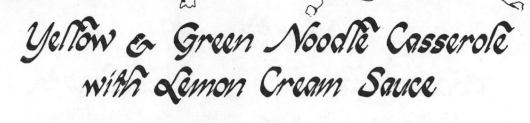

Yellow and green noodles in a delicate sauce are especially good.

1 package (8 ounces) green noodles (spinach noodles), cooked and drained
1 package (8 ounces) egg noodles, cooked and drained

salt and pepper to taste
1 stick butter (1/2 cup)

1/2 cup sour cream
1/2 cup cream
3 tablespoons lemon juice
1 tablespoon dried parsley flakes
1 teaspoon Italian Herb Seasoning

1/2 cup grated Parmesan cheese
1/2 cup toasted pine nuts (or slivered almonds)

Cook noodles separately until tender firm. Toss hot, cooked noodles with salt, pepper and butter, in a 9x13-inch pan. In a bowl, stir in sour cream, cream, lemon juice, parsley flakes and Italian seasoning until the mixture is blended. Pour mixture over cooked noodles and toss until evenly mixed. Toss in grated Parmesan cheese.

Now, if you have a pretty cook and serve casserole, place noodles and sprinkle top with pine nuts or almonds. If you do not, sprinkle the almonds and place noodles in a serving dish.

If you are planning to reheat, cover the pan with foil and heat in a 325° oven until just heated through. Serves 10 to 12.

Molded Noodle Ring with Cinnamon & Pecans

3 tablespoons butter, melted
3 tablespoons cinnamon sugar
1 cup pecan halves

1 package (8 ounces) wide noodles, cooked tender but firm, according to the directions on the package. Sprinkle lightly with salt.
1/4 cup butter (1/2 stick), melted
4 tablespoons cinnamon sugar

2 eggs
1/2 cup sour cream
1/2 cup sugar
1/2 teaspoon vanilla

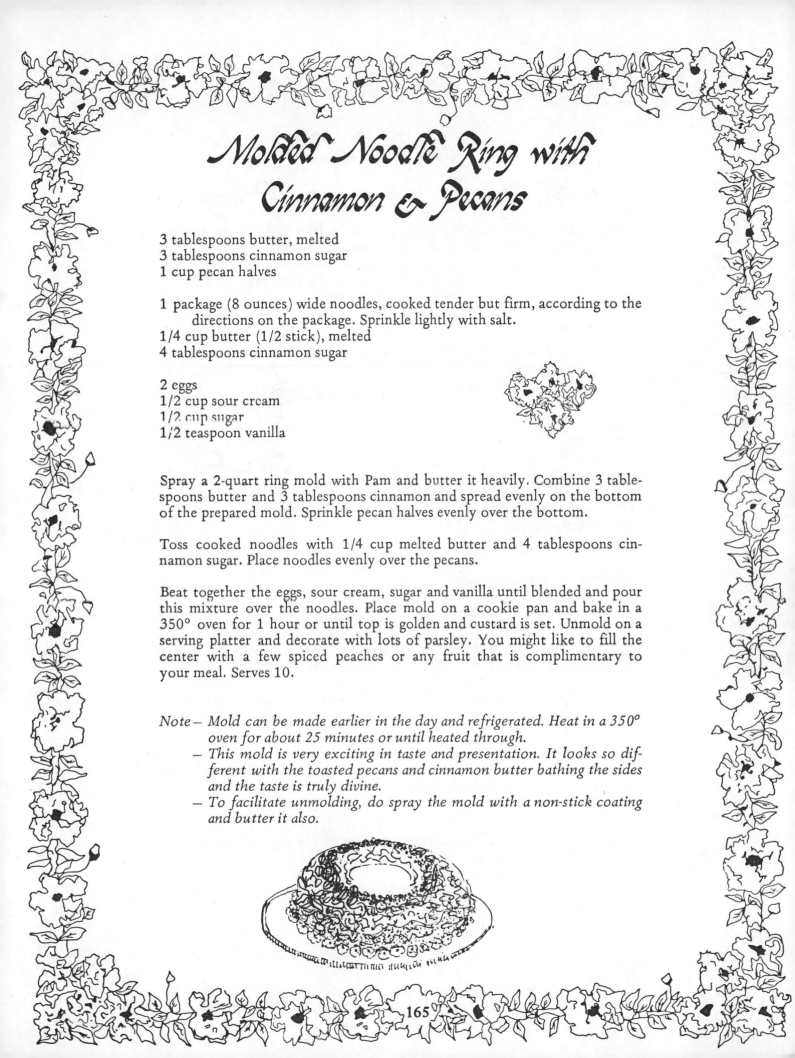

Spray a 2-quart ring mold with Pam and butter it heavily. Combine 3 tablespoons butter and 3 tablespoons cinnamon and spread evenly on the bottom of the prepared mold. Sprinkle pecan halves evenly over the bottom.

Toss cooked noodles with 1/4 cup melted butter and 4 tablespoons cinnamon sugar. Place noodles evenly over the pecans.

Beat together the eggs, sour cream, sugar and vanilla until blended and pour this mixture over the noodles. Place mold on a cookie pan and bake in a 350° oven for 1 hour or until top is golden and custard is set. Unmold on a serving platter and decorate with lots of parsley. You might like to fill the center with a few spiced peaches or any fruit that is complimentary to your meal. Serves 10.

Note— *Mold can be made earlier in the day and refrigerated. Heat in a 350° oven for about 25 minutes or until heated through.*
— This mold is very exciting in taste and presentation. It looks so different with the toasted pecans and cinnamon butter bathing the sides and the taste is truly divine.
— To facilitate unmolding, do spray the mold with a non-stick coating and butter it also.

Noodle Pudding
with Apples, Raisins & Orange

Grandma's incredible noodle pudding filled with fruit and almonds and lots of good things. The aroma of the orange and cinnamon baking will fill your home with friends and neighbors. For additional excitement, you might want to bake individual puddings in buttered muffin tins. Bake for about 30 minutes or until top is browned and custard is set.

8 ounces (1/2 pound) medium noodles, cooked nearly tender and drained.
    Sprinkle lightly with salt.
1/2 cup butter (1 stick), melted

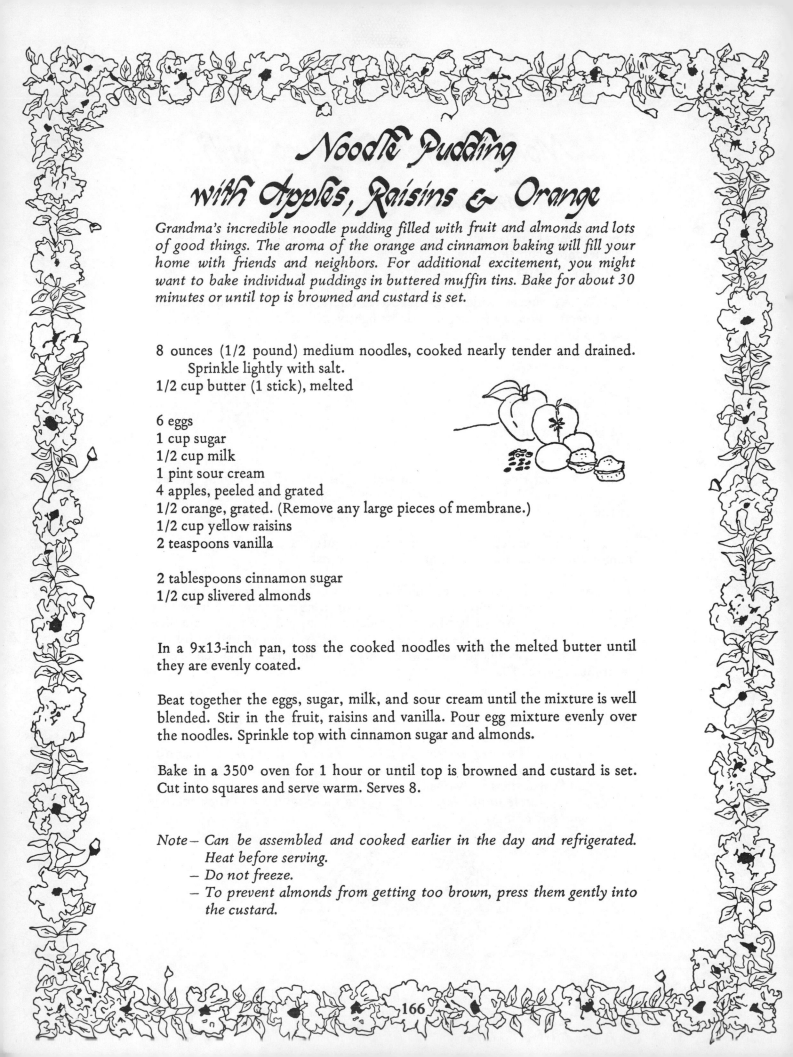

6 eggs
1 cup sugar
1/2 cup milk
1 pint sour cream
4 apples, peeled and grated
1/2 orange, grated. (Remove any large pieces of membrane.)
1/2 cup yellow raisins
2 teaspoons vanilla

2 tablespoons cinnamon sugar
1/2 cup slivered almonds

In a 9x13-inch pan, toss the cooked noodles with the melted butter until they are evenly coated.

Beat together the eggs, sugar, milk, and sour cream until the mixture is well blended. Stir in the fruit, raisins and vanilla. Pour egg mixture evenly over the noodles. Sprinkle top with cinnamon sugar and almonds.

Bake in a 350° oven for 1 hour or until top is browned and custard is set. Cut into squares and serve warm. Serves 8.

Note – Can be assembled and cooked earlier in the day and refrigerated. Heat before serving.
   – Do not freeze.
   – To prevent almonds from getting too brown, press them gently into the custard.

Noodle Pudding with Prunes & Pecans

Try this delicious dish when you next make Honey Roasted Chicken.

8 ounces (1/2 pound) medium noodles, cooked and drained

1/2 cup butter (1 stick)

1/2 cup milk
4 eggs
4 ounces cream cheese (1/2 of an 8 ounce package), softened
1-1/2 cups sour cream
1 cup sugar
1/2 teaspoon salt
1 teaspoon vanilla
1/2 cup finely chopped prunes
1/2 cup golden raisins, plumped in orange juice

1/2 cup chopped pecans
2 tablespoons cinnamon sugar

In a 9x13-inch roasting pan, melt butter and toss the cooked noodles to coat evenly.

Beat together the milk, eggs, cream cheese, sour cream, sugar, salt and vanilla until the mixture is well blended. Add the prunes and the raisins. Pour the egg mixture evenly over the noodles. Sprinkle top with pecans and cinnamon sugar.

Bake in a 350° oven for 1 hour. Cut into squares and serve warm. Serves 8.

Note — Can be made early in the day and refrigerated.
— Can be made 1 day early and refrigerated.
— I have not found it satisfactory to freeze.
— You can substitute apricots for the prunes.

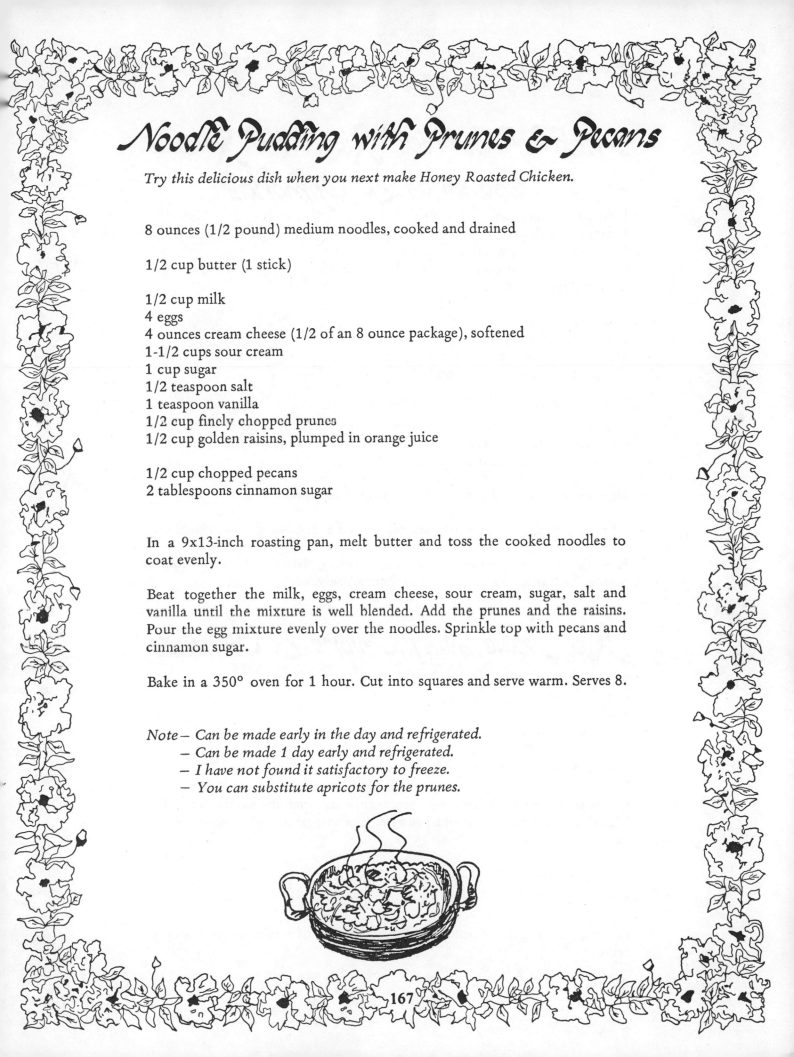

Mold of Curried Rice with Raisins, Bananas & Almonds

1 cup long grain rice
2 tablespoons butter
1/2 teaspoon curry powder
2 cups chicken broth (can use canned broth and water to equal 2 cups)
salt and pepper to taste

2 bananas, sliced
2 tablespoons orange juice
1/2 cup raisins, plumped in orange juice
1/2 cup toasted slivered almonds

Combine rice, butter, curry powder, chicken broth, salt and pepper in a sauce pan, stir, cover and simmer over low heat until the liquid is absorbed and rice is tender, about 30 minutes.

Meanwhile, toss sliced bananas in orange juice to prevent discoloring.

When rice is cooked, add bananas, raisins and almonds and toss to combine.

Press rice into a ring mold, invert on a serving platter and serve at once. (Can be held in a 200° oven for 15 minutes.) Serves 6.

Rice India with Onions & Almonds

1 can (10-1/2 ounces) chicken broth
3/4 cup water
2 tablespoons butter
1 cup long grain rice
1/4 teaspoon tumeric
salt and pepper to taste

Combine all the ingredients in a saucepan, stir, cover and simmer over low heat until the liquid is absorbed and rice is tender (about 30 minutes). When rice is cooked, add:

1 onion, sauteed in 2 tablespoons butter until soft
1/2 cup toasted slivered almonds.

Mix together and heat through. Decorate with lots of parsley or green leaves. Serves 6.

Cinnamon Rice with Onions

1 onion, very finely chopped
3 tablespoons butter
1 cup long-grain rice

1 can (10-1/2 ounces) chicken broth
3/4 cup water
salt and pepper to taste
1/8 teaspoon ground cinnamon

Saute onion in butter until onions are soft. Add rice and cook and stir for 5 minutes or until rice is very lightly browned. Add the remaining ingredients, stir rice, cover pan and simmer rice until liquid is absorbed and rice is tender. This is a delicious accompaniment to pork or lamb.

Brown Rice with Bacon & Green Onions

1-1/4 cups brown rice
3 tablespoons butter

1 can (10-1/2 ounces) beef broth
1 can (10-1/2 ounces) chicken broth
1 tablespoon soy sauce
salt and pepper to taste

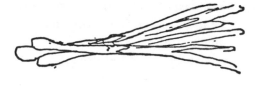

Saute rice in butter and cook and stir for 5 minutes. Add the remaining ingredients and stir. Cover rice and simmer it until liquid is absorbed and rice is tender. When rice is cooked, stir in:

6 strips bacon, cooked crisp, drained and crumbled
4 green onions, finely chopped

Toss rice to fluff up and serve. Serves 6.

Pink Rice with Tomatoes & Onions

1 onion, finely chopped
2 tablespoons butter
1 cup long-grain rice

1 can (10-1/2 ounces) chicken broth
3/4 cup water
1 tomato, peeled and chopped. (You can use a canned tomato.)
1 tablespoon tomato sauce
1 tablespoon chopped parsley
1 tablespoon dried chopped chives
salt and pepper to taste

Saute onion in butter until onion is soft. Add rice and saute until rice is just beginning to color. Add the remaining ingredients, cover and simmer rice slowly until liquid is absorbed and rice is tender, about 30 minutes. Serves 6.

Note — Rice can be made earlier in the day and reheated at time of serving. Sprinkle a few drops of water over the rice before reheating.

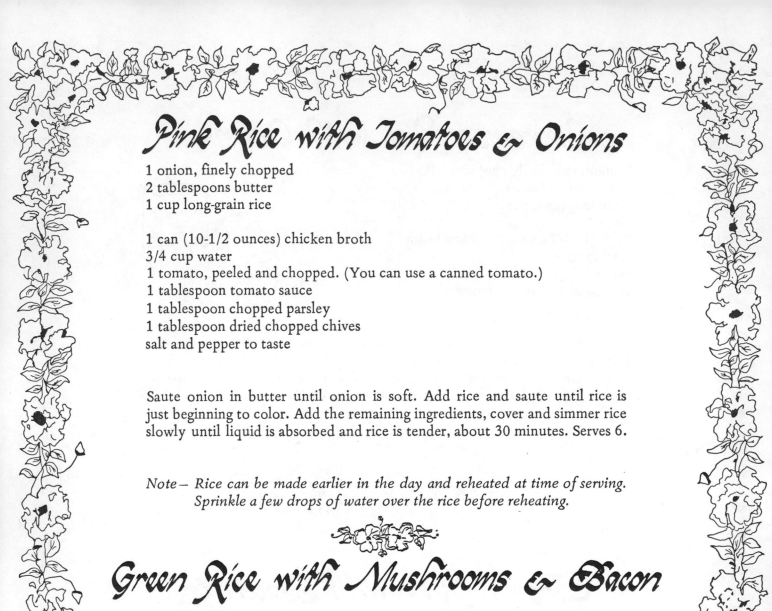

Green Rice with Mushrooms & Bacon

1 cup long grain rice
2 tablespoons butter
2 cups water
3 teaspoons chicken seasoned stock base
3 tablespoons finely minced parsley (or 1 tablespoon dried parsley)
1 tablespoon dried chopped chives
pinch poultry seasoning
salt and pepper to taste

Combine all the ingredients in a saucepan, stir, cover and simmer over low heat until the liquid is absorbed and rice is tender, about 30 minutes. When rice is cooked, add:

1/4 pound mushrooms, sauteed in 2 tablespoons butter
6 strips bacon, cooked crisp and crumbled

Mix well and heat through. Serves 6.

Fried Rice with Mushrooms & Green Onions

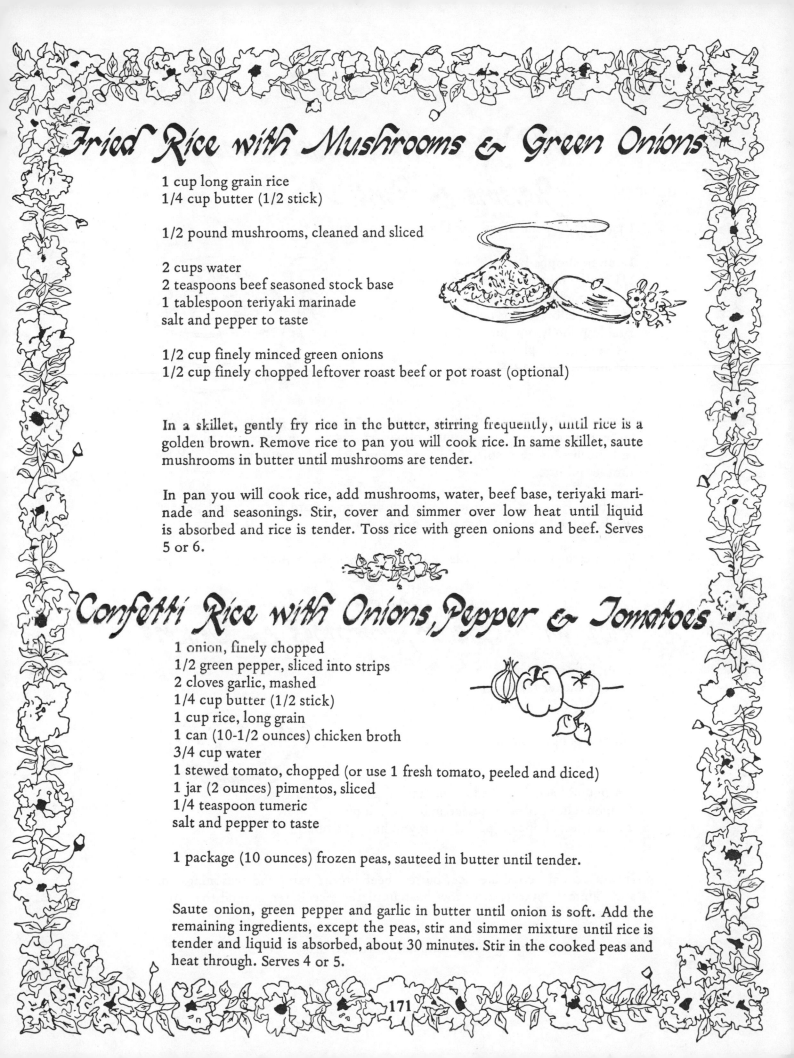

1 cup long grain rice
1/4 cup butter (1/2 stick)

1/2 pound mushrooms, cleaned and sliced

2 cups water
2 teaspoons beef seasoned stock base
1 tablespoon teriyaki marinade
salt and pepper to taste

1/2 cup finely minced green onions
1/2 cup finely chopped leftover roast beef or pot roast (optional)

In a skillet, gently fry rice in the butter, stirring frequently, until rice is a golden brown. Remove rice to pan you will cook rice. In same skillet, saute mushrooms in butter until mushrooms are tender.

In pan you will cook rice, add mushrooms, water, beef base, teriyaki marinade and seasonings. Stir, cover and simmer over low heat until liquid is absorbed and rice is tender. Toss rice with green onions and beef. Serves 5 or 6.

Confetti Rice with Onions, Pepper & Tomatoes

1 onion, finely chopped
1/2 green pepper, sliced into strips
2 cloves garlic, mashed
1/4 cup butter (1/2 stick)
1 cup rice, long grain
1 can (10-1/2 ounces) chicken broth
3/4 cup water
1 stewed tomato, chopped (or use 1 fresh tomato, peeled and diced)
1 jar (2 ounces) pimentos, sliced
1/4 teaspoon tumeric
salt and pepper to taste

1 package (10 ounces) frozen peas, sauteed in butter until tender.

Saute onion, green pepper and garlic in butter until onion is soft. Add the remaining ingredients, except the peas, stir and simmer mixture until rice is tender and liquid is absorbed, about 30 minutes. Stir in the cooked peas and heat through. Serves 4 or 5.

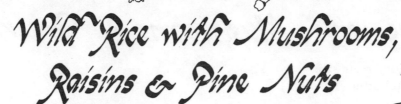

Wild Rice with Mushrooms, Raisins & Pine Nuts

1 package (6 ounces) wild and long-grain rice mix

1 onion, chopped
1/4 pound mushrooms, sliced
3 tablespoons butter
1/2 cup yellow raisins
1 tablespoon lemon juice
1/4 cup shelled pine nuts
salt and pepper to taste

Prepare wild rice according to the directions on the package. Meanwhile, saute together the onion, mushrooms, raisins in the butter, until onions and mushrooms are soft. Add the lemon juice and pine nuts and cook for another minute.

Combine rice and mushroom mixture and now taste for salt and pepper. (Packaged wild rice mix has salt added to it.)

Place rice in a lovely casserole and heat through. Serves 4 or 5.

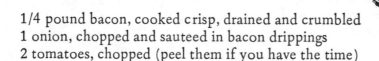

Rice with Bacon, Tomatoes & Onions

1 cup long-grain rice
1/4 cup butter (1/2 stick)
1 can (10-1/2 ounces) beef broth
3/4 cup water
salt and pepper to taste

1/4 pound bacon, cooked crisp, drained and crumbled
1 onion, chopped and sauteed in bacon drippings
2 tomatoes, chopped (peel them if you have the time)

In a saucepan, combine rice, butter, beef broth, water and seasonings and stir. Simmer mixture over low heat until the rice is tender and the liquid is absorbed.

Add the remaining ingredients and heat through. Serves 4 or 5.

Vegetables

Artichokes with Spinach Souffle & Cheese Sauce

This is an exciting vegetable and really quite simple to prepare. It takes advantage of the frozen spinach souffle you can purchase in a market and some instant cheese sauce that can be assembled in moments. It's showy but grand.

8 cooked artichoke bottoms (about 3 inches, each), canned or frozen. Brush
  with melted butter.
1 package (12 ounces) frozen spinach souffle, defrosted

2 cups grated Swiss cheese
1 cup sour cream
Grated Parmesan cheese

In a 6x12-inch baking dish, arrange artichoke bottoms in one layer. Mound spinach souffle evenly on each artichoke. Combine Swiss cheese and sour cream and arrange evenly over the spinach. Sprinkle top ever so lightly with grated Parmesan cheese.

Place pan in a 350° oven and bake for 40 to 45 minutes or until souffle is set. Serves 8.

Note— *Artichokes should lay side by side in the pan. If the artichoke bottoms are smaller, then you will need extras or use a smaller pan.*
— Entire dish can be assembled earlier in the day and refrigerated. Heat it before serving.
— Do not freeze.

Asparagus with Instant Hollandaise Sauce

2 packages (10 ounces, each) frozen asparagus spears, cooked firm. Season
with salt.

INSTANT HOLLANDAISE

3 egg yolks
1-1/2 tablespoons lemon juice
pinch of salt and white pepper
3/4 cup butter (1-1/2 sticks)

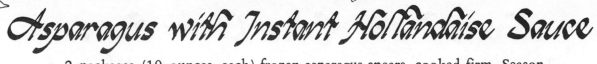

Place hot asparagus on serving dish. Place egg yolks, lemon juice, salt and
pepper in a blender container and blend for 10 seconds at high speed.

Heat butter until it is sizzling hot and bubbly, but be careful not to brown
it. Add the hot, sizzling butter very slowly and in a steady stream, while the
blender continues running at high speed. When the butter is completely incorporated, sauce is ready.

Pour warm sauce over hot asparagus and serve at once. Serves 6.

Asparagus with Instant Bearnaise Sauce

2 packages (10 ounces, each) frozen asparagus spears, cooked firm. Season
with salt.

INSTANT BEARNAISE

1 shallot
1 tablespoon tarragon vinegar
1 teaspoon Dijon-style mustard
3 egg yolks
1-1/2 tablespoons lemon juice
1 teaspoon chopped parsley
pinch of dried tarragon

3/4 cup butter, heated until it is sizzling hot but not brown

Place hot asparagus on serving platter and keep warm. Cook shallot with
vinegar until vinegar is evaporated. Place shallot in a blender container. Add
mustard, yolks, lemon, parsley and tarragon and blend for 10 seconds. Add
the hot sizzling butter very slowly and in a steady stream while the blender
continues running at high speed. When the butter is completely incorporated
sauce is ready. Pour sauce over asparagus and serve at once. Serves 6.

Broccoli with Lemon Cream Sauce

2 packages (10 ounces, each) frozen broccoli, defrosted and cooked over
very low heat for 5 minutes in 2 tablespoons butter. Season with salt.

1/2 cup sour cream
1/4 cup cream
1 tablespoon lemon juice

1/2 cup garlic croutons, rolled into crumbs

Lay drained broccoli in a lovely porcelain baker. Combine sour cream, cream
and lemon juice and stir to blend thoroughly. Cream will thicken in 10 minutes. Spoon this mixture over the broccoli and sprinkle garlic crouton
crumbs over all.

Bake in a 350° oven until heated through. Brown under the broiler until
crumbs are golden. (Watch carefully so that the crumbs do not burn.) Serves
6.

Broccoli with Instant Cheese Sauce

2 packages (10 ounces each) frozen broccoli, defrosted and cooked over low
heat for 5 minutes in 2 tablespoons butter. Season with salt.

1/2 cup sour cream
1/4 cup mayonnaise
1/2 cup grated Swiss cheese
1 tablespoon lemon juice

1/2 cup bread crumbs
2 tablespoons butter, melted
1/4 cup grated Parmesan cheese

Lay drained broccoli in a heat and serve porcelain baker. Combine sour
cream, mayonnaise, Swiss cheese and lemon juice and spread mixture over
the broccoli. Combine bread crumbs, butter and Parmesan cheese and toss
to blend thoroughly. Sprinkle crumb mixture over the top.

Bake in a 350° oven until heated through and cheese is melted.
Brown under the broiler for a few seconds until cheese and crumbs are
tinged with brown. Serves 6.

Red Cabbage with Apples & Currants

1 jar (1 pound) sweet and sour red cabbage
1 apple, peeled, cored and grated
2 tablespoons currant jelly
1/4 cup black currants
salt to taste

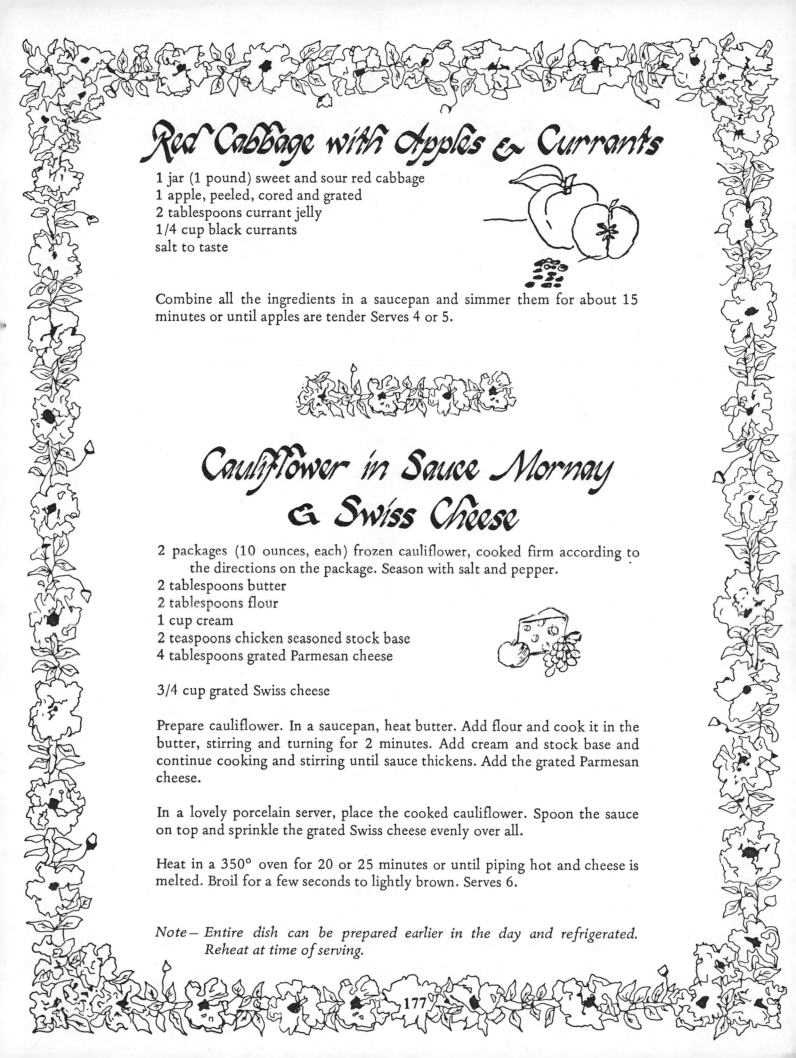

Combine all the ingredients in a saucepan and simmer them for about 15 minutes or until apples are tender Serves 4 or 5.

Cauliflower in Sauce Mornay & Swiss Cheese

2 packages (10 ounces, each) frozen cauliflower, cooked firm according to the directions on the package. Season with salt and pepper.
2 tablespoons butter
2 tablespoons flour
1 cup cream
2 teaspoons chicken seasoned stock base
4 tablespoons grated Parmesan cheese

3/4 cup grated Swiss cheese

Prepare cauliflower. In a saucepan, heat butter. Add flour and cook it in the butter, stirring and turning for 2 minutes. Add cream and stock base and continue cooking and stirring until sauce thickens. Add the grated Parmesan cheese.

In a lovely porcelain server, place the cooked cauliflower. Spoon the sauce on top and sprinkle the grated Swiss cheese evenly over all.

Heat in a 350° oven for 20 or 25 minutes or until piping hot and cheese is melted. Broil for a few seconds to lightly brown. Serves 6.

Note – Entire dish can be prepared earlier in the day and refrigerated. Reheat at time of serving.

Glazed Baby Carrots with Raisins

1 package (1 pound) frozen baby carrots
3 tablespoons sugar
3 tablespoons butter
1/2 cup yellow raisins
1 teaspoon dried parsley flakes
1/4 cup water
salt to taste

Combine all the ingredients in a skillet. Cover and cook carrots over low heat until carrots are tender, about 15 to 20 minutes. Uncover and continue cooking and stirring until the liquid is absorbed and carrots are glazed. Serves 6.

Orange Glazed Carrots & Onions

1 pound baby carrots, cooked until tender
1 can (16 ounces) small onions, drained
1/4 cup orange marmalade
2 tablespoons lemon juice
2 tablespoons orange juice

salt and pepper to taste

Place cooked carrots and drained onions in a 12-inch skillet. Combine marmalade, lemon juice, orange juice and salt and pepper to taste and stir to mix well. Pour mixture over the carrots and onions. Cook over low heat, stirring and turning until carrots and onions are glazed and glossy. Serves 6.

Honeyed Carrots with Prunes & Raisins

1 package frozen baby carrots (whole), 10 ounces

2 tablespoons butter
2 tablespoons honey
1/4 cup orange juice
1 tablespoon lemon juice

1/2 cup pitted prunes, coarsely chopped
1/4 cup golden raisins

sprinkle of cinnamon (optional)
salt to taste

Cook carrots in salted water until they are tender and drain. In a skillet, melt the butter and add the honey. Stir to mix. Add the carrots and the remaining ingredients to the skillet and continue cooking until the prunes are tender and the carrots are glazed. Excellent with pot roast. Serves 4 or 5.

Honey Glazed Buttered Carrots & Onions

1 package frozen baby carrots (whole), 10 ounces

4 tablespoons butter
4 tablespoons honey
2 tablespoons sugar
3 tablespoons lemon juice

1 can (16 ounces) small boiled onions

salt to taste

Cook carrots in salted water until they are tender and drain. In a 10-inch skillet, melt the butter. Add the honey, sugar and lemon juice and stir until the mixture is well combined. Add the carrots and the onions and cook and stir until they are evenly coated. Taste for salt. Serves 6.

Eggplant & Cheese Mini-Soufflé

2 eggplants, peeled and cut into 1/2-inch thick slices

4 eggs, beaten
2 cups cottage cheese
4 ounces cream cheese
1/2 cup grated Parmesan cheese
1/2 cup instant mashed potato flakes
salt and pepper to taste

Place eggplant slices in a greased 12x16-inch pan. Cover pan with foil and bake in a 400° oven for 15 to 20 minutes or until eggplant is soft.

In the large bowl of your electric mixer, beat together all the ingredients until the mixture is well blended. Place the mixture in a lightly greased 9x13-inch pan and spread evenly. Bake in a 350° oven for 40 or 45 minutes or until mixture is set and top is golden. Serves 8.

Eggplant Frittata with Tomatoes & Cheese

1 eggplant, peeled and cut into 1/2-inch thick slices

1 onion, finely chopped
1/4 cup butter (1/2 stick)
1 cut grated Swiss cheese
1 tomato, chopped and drained
4 eggs, beaten
1-1/2 cups cream (can use half and half)
1/2 cup grated Parmesan cheese
salt and pepper to taste

Place eggplant slices in a greased 12x16-inch pan. Cover pan with foil and bake in a 400° oven for 15 to 20 minutes or until eggplant is soft.

Saute onion in butter until onion is soft. Grease a 10-inch square pan and spread eggplant and onion in pan, evenly. Sprinkle with grated Swiss and chopped tomato. Beat eggs with cream until blended and pour mixture evenly into the pan. Sprinkle top with grated Parmesan. (Note: Go easy on the salt as cheese is salty.) Bake in a 350° oven until eggs are set and top is golden, about 40 minutes. Serves 6.

Eggplant with Tomato & Mozzarella

1 eggplant, about 1-1/2 pounds. Do not peel. Cut into 1/4-inch slices

1/2 cup bread crumbs
1/2 cup grated Parmesan cheese
1/4 teaspoon garlic powder
salt and pepper to taste

2 eggs, lightly beaten

1 cup grated Mozzarella cheese
1 cup grated Parmesan cheese
Thick Meat Sauce

Combine bread crumbs, 1/2 cup Parmesan cheese, garlic powder and salt and pepper to taste. Dip eggplant slices in beaten egg and then in crumb mixture. Saute eggplant slices in hot oil until brown on both sides.

Now make alternate layers of the eggplant, Mozzarella, Parmesan and Thick Meat Sauce in a 9x13-inch pan.

Heat casserole in a 350° oven until it is piping hot and cheese is melted, about 20 minutes. Serves 4 or 5.

Thick Meat Sauce

2 tablespoons olive oil
2 cloves garlic, mashed
1 cup onions, chopped
1 pound lean ground beef

1 can (1 pound 12 ounces) Italian tomatoes, finely chopped
1 can (6 ounces) tomato paste
2 tablespoons sugar
1 teaspoon Italian Herb Seasoning
1 bay leaf
Salt and freshly ground pepper to taste

Saute garlic and onion in olive oil until onions are soft. Add meat and saute until meat loses its pinkness. Now add the remaining ingredients and simmer sauce uncovered, for about 20 to 30 minutes.

Green Beans with Tomatoes & Garlic

2 packages (10 ounces, each) frozen green beans, defrosted
3 tablespoons butter
2 cloves garlic
2 canned tomatoes, seeded and chopped (or fresh)
1 teaspoon chicken seasoned stock base
2 tablespoons chopped parsley (or 2 teaspoons dried parsley flakes)

salt and pepper to taste

Saute green beans in butter with garlic until green beans are half cooked. Add the remaining ingredients and simmer them, covered for 10 minutes or until vegetable is tender. Serves 6.

Note— If you are using fresh tomatoes, I'm afraid you are going to have to peel them to avoid the skin specks spoiling the appearance of the dish.

French Style Green Beans & Mushrooms in Cream

1 package frozen French-style green beans (10 ounces), defrosted
1/2 pound mushrooms, thinly sliced
4 green onions, finely chopped
3 tablespoons butter
1 teaspoon chicken seasoned stock base

1/2 cup cream
salt and pepper to taste

Saute green beans, mushrooms and onions in butter and stock base until mushroom liquid is almost evaporated. Add cream and turn heat to high. Mixture will bubble briskly and cream will evaporate into a shiny sauce. Season with salt and pepper. Serves 6.

Note— Entire dish can be assembled earlier in the day and refrigerated. Reheat at time of serving.

Glazed Onions in Raisin Cream Sauce

1 can (1 pound) small whole onions, drained
1 tablespoon brown sugar
2 tablespoons butter
1/2 cup yellow raisins

1 tablespoon butter
1 tablespoon flour
1 teaspoon beef seasoned stock base
3/4 cup cream
salt to taste

Saute together the onions, brown sugar, butter and raisins until the onions are nicely glazed and browned, about 15 minutes. Do this over low heat and stir now and again so that the onions are well coated.

Meanwhile, cook together the butter and the flour for about 1 minute (flour should not brown). Add the beef stock base, cream and salt and continue stirring until the sauce has thickened. Add the onions to the sauce and heat through. Serves 4.

Buttered Peas with Tiny White Onions

1/4 pound tiny white onions
1 teaspoon sugar
2 packages (10 ounces, each) frozen peas
1/4 cup butter
1 teaspoon chicken seasoned stock base
1 tablespoon minced parsley
salt and pepper to taste

Boil onion in boiling water for 5 minutes and drain. Place onions, sugar, peas, butter, stock base, parsley, salt and pepper in a sauce pan. Cover and cook peas until they are tender but firm, about 10 minutes. Serves 6 to 8.

French Style Green Peas with Shredded Lettuce

1/4 cup butter
1 shallot or green onion, finely chopped
2 packages (10 ounces, each) frozen petite peas, defrosted
1 cup shredded iceberg lettuce
1 teaspoon chicken seasoned stock base
1 teaspoon sugar
2 tablespoons chopped parsley
salt and pepper to taste

In a large skillet, saute shallot or green onion in butter for 2 minutes. Add the remaining ingredients and continue sauteing until peas are tender. Serves 6.

Peas, Mushrooms & Onions in Cream

1/4 cup butter
1/2 pound mushrooms, sliced
2 or 3 green onions, finely chopped
2 packages (10 ounces, each) frozen peas, defrosted

3/4 cup cream

Saute mushrooms in butter until mushrooms are tender. Add the green onions and peas and continue sauteing until peas are tender. Stir and baste often.

Increase the heat and add the cream. Let mixture bubble and evaporate. Sauce will thicken. Serves 6.

Potato Pancakes with Sour Cream & Lingonberries

3 potatoes, peeled and grated
1 onion, grated

1 egg, beaten
1/4 cup cracker meal
salt and pepper to taste

Combine all the ingredients and stir until well mixed. Heat a 12-inch skillet with 1/2-inch oil. When a drop of water skitters around, start making the pancakes. Pour 1/4 cup batter for each pancake, but do not crowd them in the pan.

Fry one side until golden brown; turn and brown other side. Serve warm with a dollup of sour cream and lingonberry preserves. Serves 6.

Note — Grate the potatoes just before using so that the batter does not darken. If you grate the potatoes earlier, cover them with cold water and drain them before using.

Creamed Potatoes with Mushrooms

2 pounds potatoes, peeled and cut into 1/2-inch slices
1 can (10-1/2 ounces) beef broth

1/4 pound mushrooms, cleaned and sliced
1 onion, chopped
3 tablespoons butter

1/2 cup cream
salt and pepper to taste
1 tablespoon dried parsley flakes

In a saucepan, cook the potatoes in the beef broth until the potatoes are tender, but not mushy.

Meanwhile, in a skillet, saute the mushrooms and onions in the butter until the onions are tender. Add the cream, parsley, salt and pepper and continue cooking until the cream is reduced to half. Mix together the potatoes and the mushroom mixture.

Place this mixture in a 2-quart souffle dish and place in a 350° oven until heated through. Serves 6.

Potato & Chive Cake
with Sour Cream & Apple Sauce

3 potatotes, peeled and grated
1/4 cup chopped chives

2 eggs
2 tablespoons flour
1/2 teaspoon baking powder
salt and pepper to taste

Combine all the ingredients and stir until well mixed. Pour mixture into a heavily oiled 8x8-inch pan. Bake in a 350° oven until potatotes are tender and crust is a golden brown, about 45 minutes. Cut into squares and serve with a spoonful of sour cream and applesauce. Serves 5 or 6.

Note — Grate the potatoes just before using so that the batter does not darken. If you grate the potatoes earlier, cover them with cold water and drain them before using. Pat them dry with paper towelling.
— For a little added excitement why not try a sparkled applesauce?

Applesauce with Prunes & Raisins

1 jar (1 pound) applesauce
3 pitted prunes, finely chopped
1/4 cup golden raisins

Combine all the ingredients and refrigerate overnight in a covered jar.

Applesauce with Apricots & Currants

1 jar (1 pound) applesauce
6 dried apricots, finely chopped
1/4 cup black currants, dried

Combine all the ingredients and refrigerate them overnight in a covered jar.

German Style Potatoes with Apples & Bacon

2 pounds potatoes, peeled and cut into 1/2-inch slices
1 can (10-1/2 ounces) beef broth

3 apples, peeled, cored and cut into 1/2-inch slices
1 onion, cut into 1/4-inch slices
1 tablespoon brown sugar
1 teaspoon vinegar
1/4 cup butter (1/2 stick)

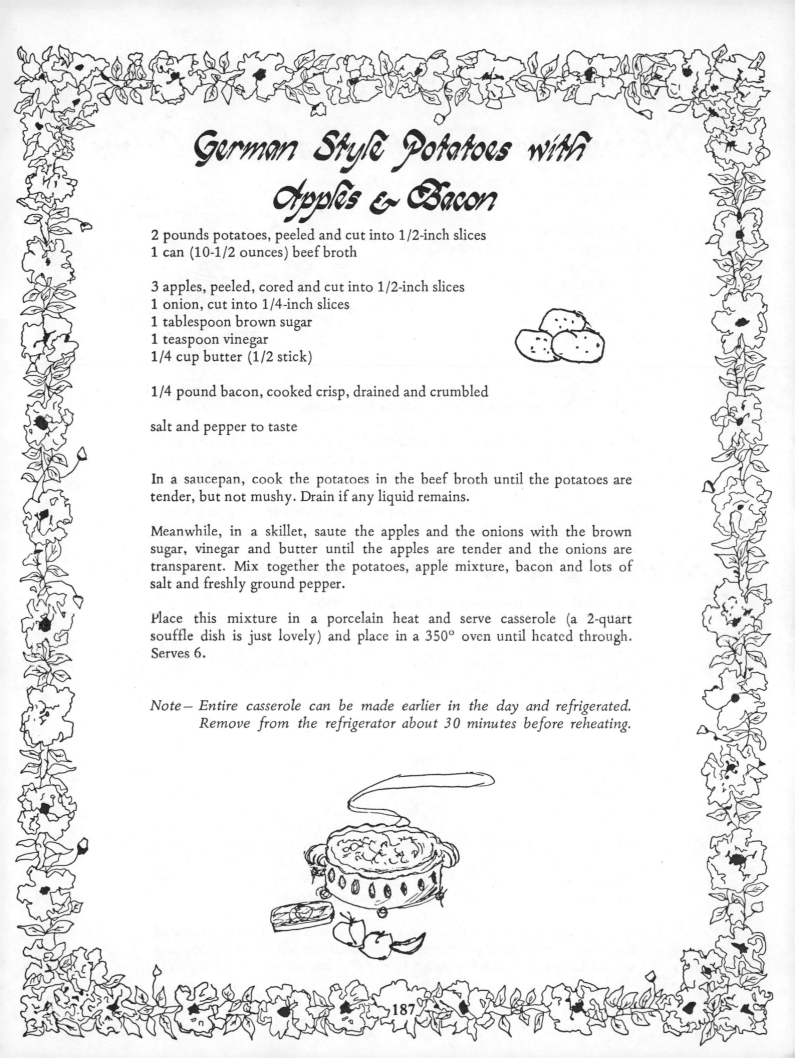

1/4 pound bacon, cooked crisp, drained and crumbled

salt and pepper to taste

In a saucepan, cook the potatoes in the beef broth until the potatoes are tender, but not mushy. Drain if any liquid remains.

Meanwhile, in a skillet, saute the apples and the onions with the brown sugar, vinegar and butter until the apples are tender and the onions are transparent. Mix together the potatoes, apple mixture, bacon and lots of salt and freshly ground pepper.

Place this mixture in a porcelain heat and serve casserole (a 2-quart souffle dish is just lovely) and place in a 350° oven until heated through. Serves 6.

Note — Entire casserole can be made earlier in the day and refrigerated. Remove from the refrigerator about 30 minutes before reheating.

Potatoes Paprikas with Tomatoes & Onions

2 pounds potatoes, peeled and cut into 1/2-inch slices
1 can (10-1/2 ounces) chicken broth

1 onion, chopped
1 tomato, peeled, seeded and chopped
2 tablespoons butter
1 clove garlic, mashed

1 tablespoon paprika
salt and pepper to taste

In a saucepan, cook the potatoes in the chicken broth until the potatoes are tender, but not mushy. Drain if any liquid remains.

Meanwhile, in a skillet, saute the onion and the tomato with the butter and the garlic until the onions are soft. Add the paprika, salt and pepper and cook for a minute or two. Mix together the potatoes and the onion mixture.

Place this mixture in a lovely heat and serve casserole and place in a 350° oven until heated through. Serves 6.

Potatoes Stuffed with Gruyere & Sour Cream

6 large baking potatoes, rubbed, tubbed and scrubbed

6 tablespoons butter
1/2 cup sour cream
2 eggs
1/2 cup grated Gruyere cheese
1/2 teaspoon onion powder
salt and pepper to taste

6 teaspoons grated Parmesan cheese
paprika
parsley

Bake potatoes in a 400° oven until cooked through. Slice 1/2 inch off the tops and scoop out the potatoes carefully to keep skins intact. Mash the potatoes while they are still hot. Add butter, sour cream, eggs, Gruyere, onion powder and lots of salt and pepper and mix until blended.

Spoon potatoes back into their shells. Sprinkle each with 1 teaspoon grated Parmesan, a sprinkle of paprika and a few parsley flakes. Cover the potatoes and refrigerate them. Heat through in a 350° oven before serving. Serves 6.

Potato Fans
Roasted in Butter with Herbs

6 medium-sized baking potatoes, peeled
salt to taste
4 tablespoons butter, 1/2 stick, melted

1 teaspoon dried parsley flakes
1 teaspoon dried chopped chives
1/4 teaspoon paprika

Cut potatoes in 1/4-inch slices, crosswise, but only cutting down to 1/4-inch from the bottom. Place butter in pan you will be baking potatoes. Baste the potatotes thoroughly with the butter. Sprinkle with salt and bake in a 350° oven for about 20 minutes, basting now and again.

Sprinkle potatoes with parsley, chive and paprika and continue baking until potatotes are tender, about 25 minutes. Baste two or three times more. Potatoes should be golden, crisped on the outside and fanned out. Keep warm in a low oven until ready to serve. Can be held for 20 minutes. Serves 6.

Note — To facilitate slicing the potatoes, insert a metal skewer, lengthwise, about 1/4-inch from the bottom of the potato. This will prevent the knife from cutting through to the bottom.

Potatoes Roasted in
Butter with Onions & Cheese

4 large baking potatoes, peeled and cut into 1-inch slices
4 tablespoons butter, 1/2 stick, melted
salt to taste

2 tablespoons grated Parmesan cheese
1 teaspoon dried onion flakes

Place the sliced potatoes in a shallow roasting pan. Baste potatoes on all sides with the melted butter. Drizzle remaining butter over the top. Bake in a 350° oven for 30 minutes, basting now and again. Sprinkle potatoes with cheese and onions and continue baking and basting until potatoes are tender and crusty brown. Serves 6.

Candied Sweet Potatoes with Caramel & Pecans

When I made these lovely sweet potatoes last Thanksgiving, I was asked for the recipe. My friend raved so much about their candied taste, I was almost embarrassed to tell her how easily this was achieved.

1 can (1 pound 12 ounces) sweet potatoes, drained and cut into 3/4-inch thick slices

1/4 cup butter, salted (1/2 stick)
1/4 cup Caramel Ice Cream Topping
1/2 cup chopped pecans

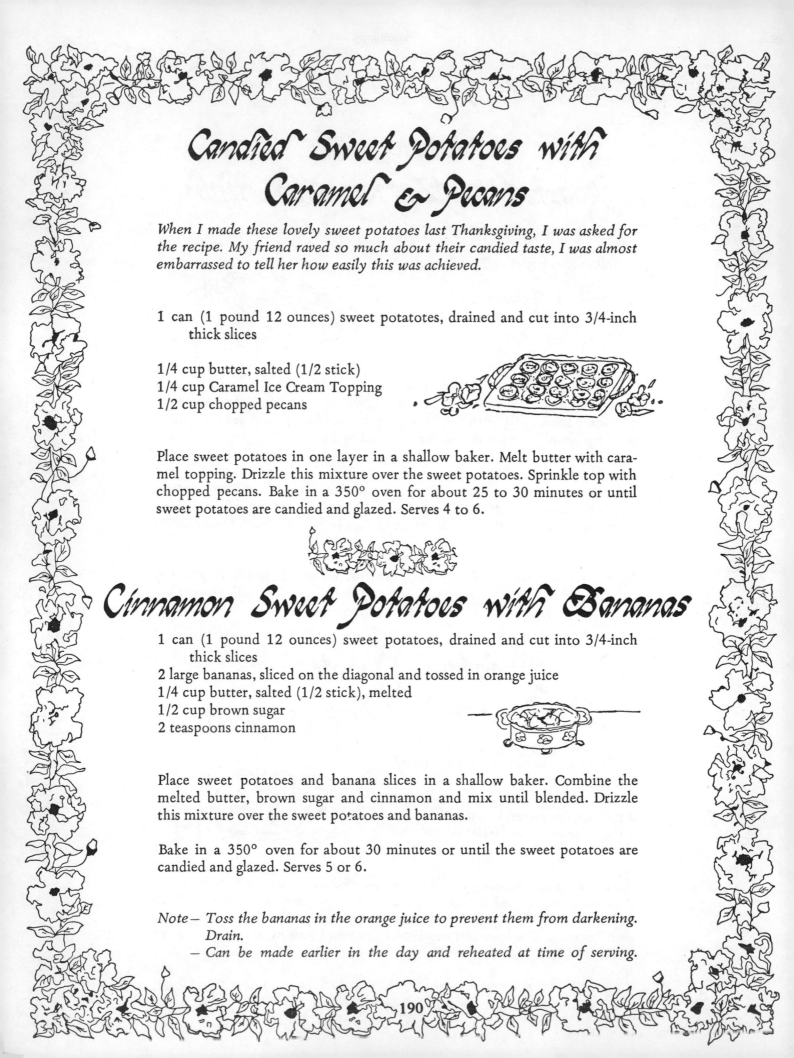

Place sweet potatoes in one layer in a shallow baker. Melt butter with caramel topping. Drizzle this mixture over the sweet potatoes. Sprinkle top with chopped pecans. Bake in a 350° oven for about 25 to 30 minutes or until sweet potatoes are candied and glazed. Serves 4 to 6.

Cinnamon Sweet Potatoes with Bananas

1 can (1 pound 12 ounces) sweet potatoes, drained and cut into 3/4-inch thick slices
2 large bananas, sliced on the diagonal and tossed in orange juice
1/4 cup butter, salted (1/2 stick), melted
1/2 cup brown sugar
2 teaspoons cinnamon

Place sweet potatoes and banana slices in a shallow baker. Combine the melted butter, brown sugar and cinnamon and mix until blended. Drizzle this mixture over the sweet potatoes and bananas.

Bake in a 350° oven for about 30 minutes or until the sweet potatoes are candied and glazed. Serves 5 or 6.

Note— Toss the bananas in the orange juice to prevent them from darkening. Drain.
— Can be made earlier in the day and reheated at time of serving.

Sweet Potato Pudding with Orange Gingersnaps

1 can sweet potatoes (1 pound, 13 ounces) drained and mashed. Sprinkle lightly with salt.

3 eggs, beaten
1/2 cup orange juice concentrate
1/2 cup sugar

1 tablespoon grated orange peel
1 teaspoon grated lemon peel
1 cup gingersnap cookie crumbs
2 teaspoons pumpkin pie spice

Beat eggs with orange juice. Add remaining ingredients and beat until blended. Pour mixture into a lovely low baking dish and bake in a 350° oven for about 45 minutes. Sprinkle top with Walnut Cinnamon Topping and continue baking for 15 minutes. Serves 6 or 8.

Walnut Cinnamon Topping

3/4 cup chopped walnuts
6 tablespoons cinnamon sugar

Combine the walnuts and the sugar and mix them together until they are blended.

Broiled Tomatoes
with Herb Crumb Topping

4 medium tomatoes, sliced in half, crosswise

1 cup bread crumbs
3 cloves garlic, put through a press
2 tablespoons parsley, finely chopped
1/2 teaspoon basil
1/4 teaspoon dried thyme flakes
1 teaspoon dried chive flakes
salt and pepper to taste
1/3 cup melted butter

Combine all the ingredients except the tomatoes and mix them until they are blended. Divide the mixture on the cut side of the tomatoes and pat it on evenly. Bake them in a 350° oven for about 20 minutes, or until they are cooked. Just before serving, place tomatoes under the broiler for a few seconds until they are lightly browned. Serves 4.

Broiled Tomatoes
with Cheese Crumb Topping

1/2 cup Ritz cracker crumbs
1/2 cup grated Parmesan cheese

3 tablespoons mayonnaise
1 teaspoon lemon juice
1 teaspoon chopped chives

8 slices tomatoes, cut 1-inch thick
salt and pepper to taste

Combine cracker crumbs and cheese and set aside. Combine mayonnaise, lemon juice and chopped chives. Sprinkle tomatoes with salt and pepper and brush with mayonnaise mixture. Sprinkle top of tomatoes generously with cracker-crumb mixture.

Broil tomatoes for a minute or so until top is golden brown. Serves 4.

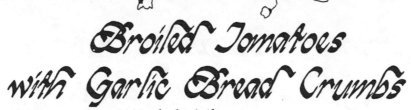

Broiled Tomatoes with Garlic Bread Crumbs

6 tomatoes, cut into 1/2-inch thick slices

1 cup bread crumbs
2 tablespoons dried parsley flakes
1 clove garlic, put through a press
salt and pepper to taste

mayonnaise
2 to 3 tablespoons melted butter

Place tomato slices on a buttered cookie sheet. Combine crumbs, parsley, garlic and salt and pepper.

Brush tops of tomato slices with mayonnaise and sprinkle with crumb mixture. Pat crumb mixture gently over the tomatoes. Drizzle tops with melted butter.

Broil for a few minutes until crumbs are lightly browned. Serves 6.

Creamed Spinach with Mushrooms & Shallots

2 tablespoons butter
2 shallots, minced
1/4 pound mushrooms, sliced

2 packages (10 ounces, each) frozen chopped spinach, defrosted.
1 package (8 ounces) cream cheese, at room temperature
salt and pepper to taste
pinch of nutmeg

Saute mushrooms and shallots in butter until mushrooms are tender. Add the remaining ingredients and heat over a low flame until cream cheese is melted and all the ingredients are blended.

Place in a lovely vegetable dish and serve immediately. Serves 6 to 8.

Spinach Dumplings with a Light Marinara Sauce

1 package (10 ounces) frozen chopped spinach. Defrost and place in a
  strainer and press very dry.
2 eggs
1 cup cottage cheese
1/4 cup bread crumbs
1/2 cup grated Parmesan cheese
salt and pepper to taste
pinch of nutmeg.

Combine all the ingredients and stir until they are thoroughly blended.
Shape mixture into 1-inch balls. Roll them in flour and flatten them gently
to about 1/2 inch thickness.

Place about 1/2-inch oil in a skillet and heat it until it is sizzling hot. Place a
few dumplings in the skillet at a time and saute them until they are golden
brown. Turn and saute other side until golden brown. Remove to a paper
towel and drain.

Serve the dumplings warm as a side dish or a main dish. Spoon Light Mari-
nara Sauce over the top and sprinkle with additional grated Parmesan cheese,
if desired. Yields about 28 dumplings.

Note— Dumplings can be served without the sauce. In that case, sprinkle
with grated Parmesan cheese and broil for a few seconds until cheese
melts.

Light Marinara Sauce

1 can (16 ounces) stewed tomatoes, finely chopped
3 ounces (1/2 can) tomato paste
1 tablespoon sugar
1 teaspoon parsley flakes
1 clove garlic, mashed
1 teaspoon Italian Herb Seasoning
1 tablespoon olive oil
salt and pepper to taste

Combine all the ingredients in a saucepan and simmer sauce for 15 minutes,
uncovered.

Zucchini with Tomatoes, Onion & Garlic

1 pound zucchini, sliced thinly, do not peel.
1 onion, finely chopped
2 cloves garlic, put through a press
2 shallots, finely chopped
4 tablespoons butter
salt and pepper to taste

2 canned tomatoes, seeded and chopped
1/2 cup tomato sauce
2 tablespoons chopped parsley
1 teaspoon sugar

Saute zucchini, onion, garlic, shallots, in butter with seasonings until zucchini are half cooked. Now add the remaining ingredients and simmer mixture for 15 minutes. Serves 4 or 5.

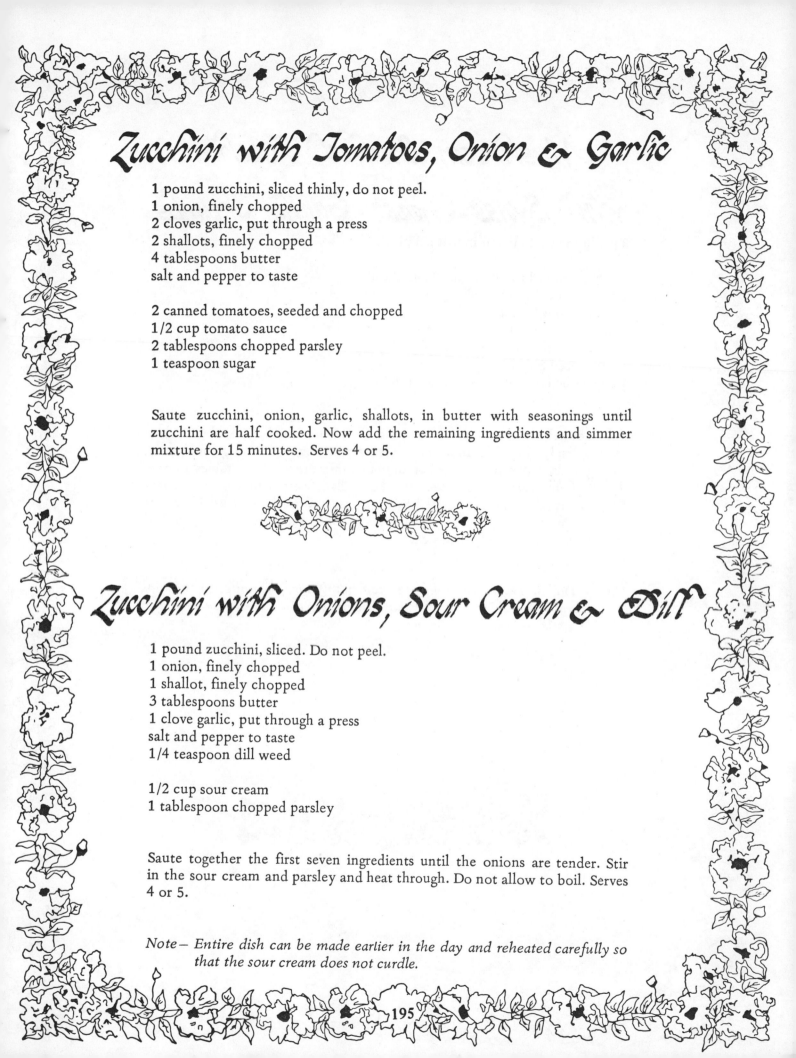

Zucchini with Onions, Sour Cream & Dill

1 pound zucchini, sliced. Do not peel.
1 onion, finely chopped
1 shallot, finely chopped
3 tablespoons butter
1 clove garlic, put through a press
salt and pepper to taste
1/4 teaspoon dill weed

1/2 cup sour cream
1 tablespoon chopped parsley

Saute together the first seven ingredients until the onions are tender. Stir in the sour cream and parsley and heat through. Do not allow to boil. Serves 4 or 5.

Note— Entire dish can be made earlier in the day and reheated carefully so that the sour cream does not curdle.

Mushroom Stuffed Zucchini with Swiss Cheese Garlic Crumbs

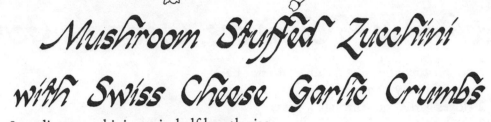

8 medium zucchini, cut in half lengthwise

1/2 pound mushrooms, cleaned and sliced
1 clove garlic, put through a press
4 tablespoons butter
2 tablespoons finely chopped parsley
salt and pepper to taste
1 cup grated Swiss cheese
1 cup garlic croutons, rolled into crumbs

Scoop out the zucchini pulp, leaving a shell 1/8-inch thick. Chop the zucchini pulp coarsely and place in a large skillet. Add the mushrooms, garlic, butter, parsley, salt and pepper to skillet and saute mixture until vegetables are tender. Stuff mixture into the zucchini shells. Place stuffed zucchini in shallow baker. Sprinkle tops with grated Swiss cheese and garlic crumbs. Bake in a 350° oven for about 20 or 25 minutes or until piping hot and cheese is melted and top is lightly browned.

Note— This dish can be simplified if you simply slice the unpeeled zucchini and saute them with the mushrooms. Layer them in a shallow casserole and proceed as above.

Desserts

Okay kids! It's your turn now. When it gets around this time of year. . . you know what that means. It's the day for pink carnations and red roses and lots of pretty bows made with shiny ribbons.

Of course, you know, I mean the day reserved for dear, dear Mom. And you know, I was thinking, wouldn't it be nice to give Mom, on this very special day, some candies made especially for her, by YOU.

When visions of sugar plums dance in my head, they are usually made of chocolate. So, I am sharing with you, a recipe that I think your Mom will like and which Dad and you might enjoy a taste (or two) as well.

However, one word of warning. Please have dear, old Dad around to help with the heating and to kinda' watch over things.

Wrap the candies in a pretty box or a lovely glass jar and write your feelings on a card. And, I know, Mom will sure be glad that kids were invented.

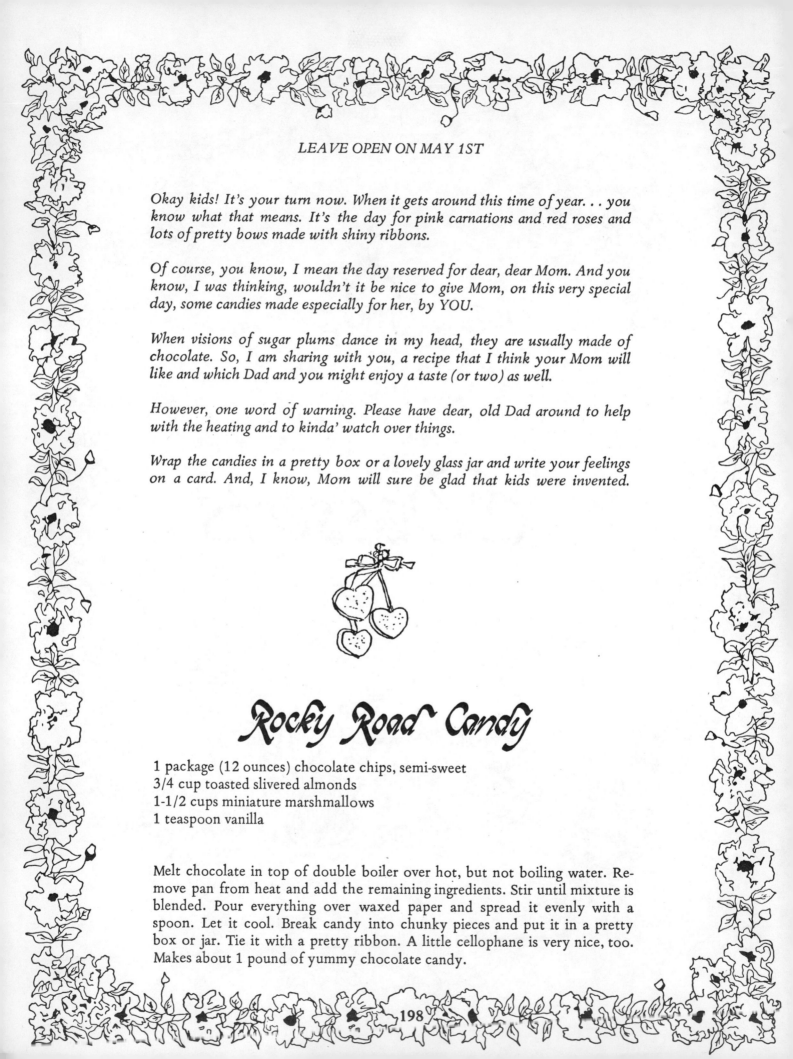

Rocky Road Candy

1 package (12 ounces) chocolate chips, semi-sweet
3/4 cup toasted slivered almonds
1-1/2 cups miniature marshmallows
1 teaspoon vanilla

Melt chocolate in top of double boiler over hot, but not boiling water. Remove pan from heat and add the remaining ingredients. Stir until mixture is blended. Pour everything over waxed paper and spread it evenly with a spoon. Let it cool. Break candy into chunky pieces and put it in a pretty box or jar. Tie it with a pretty ribbon. A little cellophane is very nice, too. Makes about 1 pound of yummy chocolate candy.

Easiest & Best Chocolate Cake with Heavenly Chocolate Frosting

(Makes 1 layer)

4 extra large eggs
1 cup walnuts or pecans
7/8 cup sugar
1 teaspoon vanilla
2 tablespoons dry bread crumbs
2 tablespoons cocoa
2 teaspoons baking powder

Place eggs in blender container and whip for a few seconds. While the blender continues running, add the remaining ingredients in the order listed and blend for 30 seconds.

Pour the batter into a greased and floured 10-inch layer pan with a removable bottom. Repeat this for second layer. Bake the 2 layers at one time in a 350° oven for 20 minutes or until a cake tester inserted in center comes out clean.

Fill with whipped cream between the layers and frost with Heavenly Chocolate Frosting. Serves 8 very lucky people.

WHIPPED CREAM FILLING

Beat 3/4 cup cream with 1 tablespoon sugar and 1 teaspoon vanilla until cream is stiff.

Heavenly Chocolate Frosting

6 ounces semi-sweet chocolate chips
1/4 cup butter
1/2 cup cream
1 teaspoon vanilla

Place chocolate chips in blender container. Heat together the butter and cream until it comes to a boil. Pour hot mixture into blender container and whip for 30 seconds or until frosting is smooth and chocolate is melted. Allow to cool and spread on cake. Will frost the top and sides of 1 10-inch cake.

Apple Walnut Honey Cake

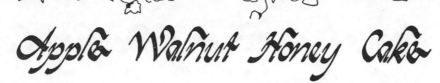

2 cups flour
2 cups sugar
1 teaspoon baking soda
2 teaspoons cinnamon
1/4 teaspoon salt

3 eggs
1/2 cup oil
1/2 cup honey
2 teaspoons vanilla

3 large apples (about 4 cups) peeled, cored and thinly sliced
2 cups walnuts, coarsely chopped

Combine first five dry ingredients. Beat together the eggs, oil, honey and vanilla. Add the dry ingredients all at once and beat until blended, about 1 minute. Stir in the apples and the walnuts. Pour mixture into a buttered 9-inch tube pan. Bake in a preheated 350° oven for about 60 to 65 minutes or until a cake tester inserted in center comes out clean. Cool in pan. Frost with Cream Cheese Butter Frosting. Serves 12.

Cream Cheese Butter Frosting

1/4 pound cream cheese (4 ounces)
1/4 cup butter (1/2 stick)
1 teaspoon vanilla
2 cups sifted powdered sugar

Beat together the butter and the cream cheese until the mixture is well blended. Add the vanilla and the sugar and beat until smooth. Will frost one 9-inch cake.

Chocolate Chip Velvet Cheesecake with Chocolate Cream

2 packages cream cheese (8 ounces, each), softened
1-1/4 cups sugar
3 eggs
1 pint sour cream
2 tablespoons cocoa
2 teaspoons vanilla
1/4 cup cream

1 9-inch Chocolate Chip Wafer Crust

Chocolate Cream

In the large bowl of an electric mixer, beat together the first seven ingredients until the mixture is thoroughly blended. Pour mixture into prepared 9-inch crust.

Bake in a 350° oven for about 50 minutes or until a cake tester inserted in center comes out clean. Cool in pan and refrigerate 4 to 6 hours or overnight. Remove ring from springform pan and spread Chocolate Cream over the top. Serves 10 or 12.

CHOCOLATE CHIP WAFER CRUST

1-1/2 cups vanilla wafer crumbs
3/4 stick butter (3 ounces), melted
2 teaspoons cocoa
4 tablespoons sugar
1/4 cup crushed chocolate chips

Combine all the ingredients and mix until blended. Pat crumb mixture on the bottom of a 9-inch springform pan. Bake crust in a 350° oven for about 7 minutes. Set aside to cool.

CHOCOLATE CREAM

3/4 cup cream
1/2 cup sour cream
1/2 cup chocolate syrup

Combine cream and sour cream in a glass jar and stir until blended. Leave jar at room temperature for about 4 hours, stirring now and again. Stir in chocolate syrup and refrigerate until ready to use. Chocolate cream will last for 2 weeks in the refrigerator.

Carrot Cake with Chocolate Cream Cheese Frosting

1 cup butter
2 cups sugar

4 eggs

2-1/2 cups flour
1/4 teaspoon salt
2 teaspoons cinnamon
2 teaspoons soda

2 teaspoons vanilla
2 cups grated carrots (finely grated)
1 cup crushed pineapple, drained
1-1/2 cups chopped walnuts

Cream together the butter and the sugar until mixture is light. Add eggs, one at a time, beating well after each addition. Add flour, salt, cinnamon and soda and beat until blended, about 1 minute. Add the remaining ingredients and beat until blended.

Pour mixture evenly into 2 buttered 10-inch layer pans with removable bottoms. Bake in a 325° oven for about 45 to 50 minutes or until a cake tester inserted in center comes out clean. Remove rings and let layers cool. With a sharp knife remove cake layers. Frost with Chocolate Cream Cheese Frosting. Serves 10.

Chocolate Cream Cheese Frosting

1/2 cup cream cheese (1/2 of an 8 ounce package)
1/4 cup butter (1/2 stick)
1/2 orange, grated. Use peel and juice, (or 1/2 cup chopped walnuts).
2 tablespoons cocoa
2 to 3 cups sifted powdered sugar

Cream together the butter and the cream cheese until mixture is blended. Beat in the orange (or the walnuts). Beat in the cocoa. Now, beat in the sifted powdered sugar until the frosting is of spreading consistency. Will frost a 2-layer cake.

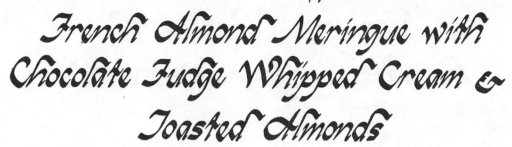

French Almond Meringue with Chocolate Fudge Whipped Cream & Toasted Almonds

6 egg whites, at room temperature
1-1/2 cups sugar
1-1/2 cups almond meal (ground almonds purchased at health food store)
2 teaspoons lemon juice
1 teaspoon vanilla

Grease and flour 2 10-inch layer pans with removable bottoms. Line them with parchment paper and grease and flour the parchment.

Beat whites until stiff. Add the remaining ingredients and fold them in gently. Divide the batter between the prepared pans. Bake at 350° for about 20 or 25 minutes or until the top is golden. Place a rack over the layer pan and invert the layer onto the rack. Carefully remove the rim and bottom of pan. Peel off the parchment paper. Allow layers to cool.

Fill and frost with Chocolate Fudge Whipped Cream and sprinkle top with sliced toasted almonds to taste. Serves 8 or 10 with pride.

Chocolate Fudge Whipped Cream

1-1/2 cups whipping cream
1/2 cup Fudge Ice Cream Topping

Whip cream until foamy. Add the fudge topping and beat until cream is stiff. Will fill and frost a 10-inch layer cake.

Note – Cake should be made 1 day before serving to allow meringue to softens.
– Sprinkle top with some shaved chocolate as an optional.
– Torte layers are very thin, about 1/2-inch thick. Don't feel that something went wrong. Entire cake is about 1-1/2-inches high.
– Torte can be frozen.

Meringue Clouds with Chocolate Fudge & Almonds

8 egg whites, at room temperature
pinch of salt
pinch of cream of tartar
2 cups sugar

Beat egg whites until foamy. Beat in salt and cream of tartar. Beat in sugar, a little at a time, beating all the while until the meringue is stiff and glossy.

Divide the meringue between 2 heavily greased 10-inch layer pans with a removable bottom. Smoothen the meringue with a spatula and bake the layers together in a 275° oven for 50 minutes. Remove metal rims and cool. Remove layers with a very sharp knife.

Fill and frost with Chocolate Whipped Cream. Drizzle top with Chocolate Fudge Sauce and sprinkle with toasted sliced almonds. Serves 10.

Chocolate Whipped Cream

1-1/2 cup cream
1 tablespoon rum
3/4 cup chocolate syrup

Beat cream until foamy. Beat in rum. Slowly add the chocolate syrup, beating, until cream is stiff. Will fill and frost a 10-inch cake.

Chocolate Fudge Sauce

6 tablespoons prepared Fudge Flavored Iced Cream Topping

In the top of a double boiler, heat fudge topping until it is melted. Drizzle over the frosted cake. (You can heat the sauce in a small pyrex dessert dish, set in a pan of hot water.)

Note — Dessert can be completely assembled and frozen. Place on a doily and freeze. Wrap in double thicknesses of plastic wrap. Defrost in refrigerator.

Chocolate Cream Fudge Cake with Chocolate Chips

1 package chocolate cake mix (18-1/2 ounces)
1 cup cream
1/2 cup sour cream
2 eggs

1 cup semi-sweet chocolate chips

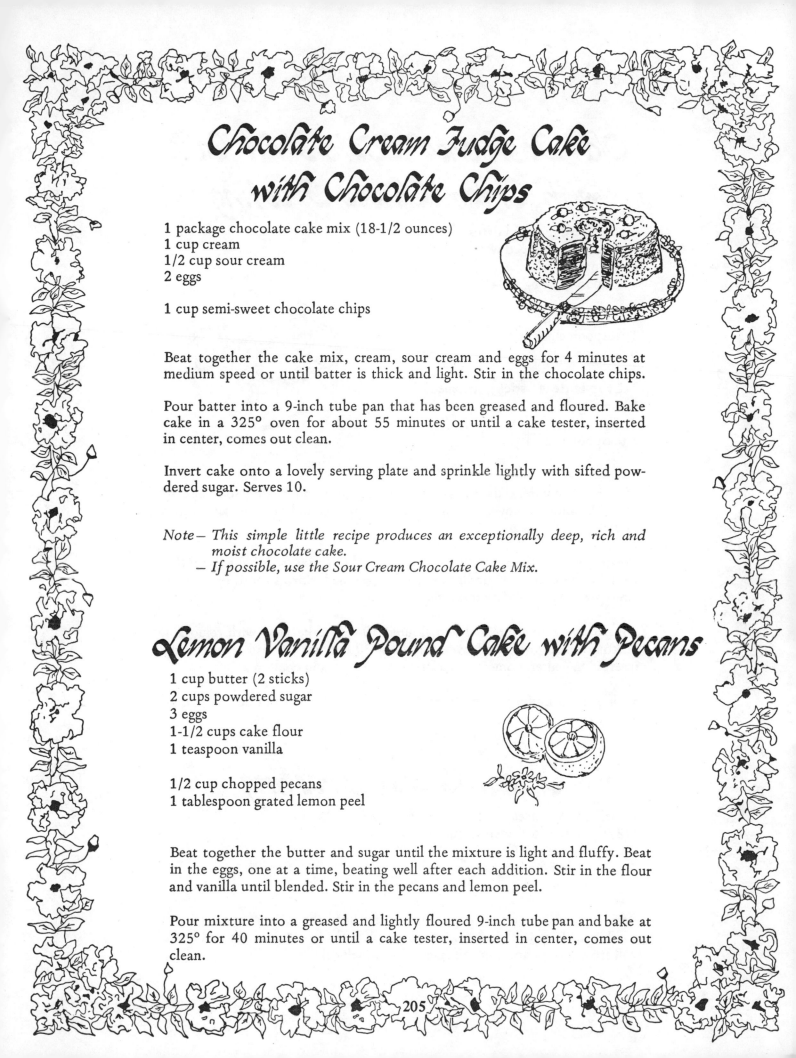

Beat together the cake mix, cream, sour cream and eggs for 4 minutes at medium speed or until batter is thick and light. Stir in the chocolate chips.

Pour batter into a 9-inch tube pan that has been greased and floured. Bake cake in a 325° oven for about 55 minutes or until a cake tester, inserted in center, comes out clean.

Invert cake onto a lovely serving plate and sprinkle lightly with sifted powdered sugar. Serves 10.

Note – *This simple little recipe produces an exceptionally deep, rich and moist chocolate cake.*
   – *If possible, use the Sour Cream Chocolate Cake Mix.*

Lemon Vanilla Pound Cake with Pecans

1 cup butter (2 sticks)
2 cups powdered sugar
3 eggs
1-1/2 cups cake flour
1 teaspoon vanilla

1/2 cup chopped pecans
1 tablespoon grated lemon peel

Beat together the butter and sugar until the mixture is light and fluffy. Beat in the eggs, one at a time, beating well after each addition. Stir in the flour and vanilla until blended. Stir in the pecans and lemon peel.

Pour mixture into a greased and lightly floured 9-inch tube pan and bake at 325° for 40 minutes or until a cake tester, inserted in center, comes out clean.

Old Fashioned Date Nut Cake with Cream Cheese Frosting

1 cup finely chopped dates
1 cup finely chopped walnuts
1 cup orange juice
1 teaspoon baking soda

1-1/2 cups flour
1 teaspoon cinnamon
pinch of salt

1/2 cup butter (1 stick), softened
1 cup sugar
2 eggs
1 teaspoon vanilla

In a bowl, combine dates, walnuts, orange juice and baking soda and set aside. In another bowl, combine flour, cinnamon and salt and set mixture aside.

Cream together the butter and the sugar until the mixture is light and fluffy. Beat in the eggs and vanilla until well combined. Stir in the flour mixture alternately with the date mixture.

Pour batter into 2 greased and floured 10-inch cake pans with removable bottoms. Bake in a 350° oven for about 30 minutes or until a cake tester, inserted in center, comes out clean. Remove rings and cool on a rack.

With a sharp knife, loosen layers. Fill and frost with Cream Cheese Frosting. Serves 10.

Cream Cheese Frosting

1 package (8 ounces) cream cheese, softened
1/2 cup butter, softened (1 stick)
2 teaspoons vanilla
3 cups sifted powdered sugar

Beat together the cream cheese and butter until the mixture is thoroughly combined. Beat in the vanilla and sugar until the frosting is light and fluffy. Will frost 1 layer and top and sides of a 10-inch cake.

Grandma's Old Fashioned Prune & Walnut Cake

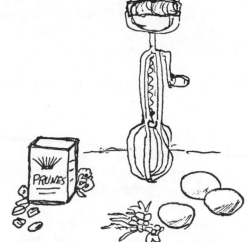

3 eggs
2 cups sugar
1 cup oil
1 cup sour cream

2 cups flour
1 teaspoon baking powder
1 teaspoon baking soda
1 teaspoon cinnamon
2 teaspoons pumpkin pie spice

1 cup finely chopped soft pitted prunes
1 cup finely chopped walnuts

Beat together the eggs, sugar, oil and sour cream until the mixture is well blended. Stir in the dry ingredients until thoroughly combined. Stir in the prunes and walnuts.

Pour mixture into 2 greased and floured 10-inch cake pans with removable bottoms. Bake in a 350° oven for about 30 minutes or until a cake tester inserted in center comes out clean. Remove rings and cool layers on a rack.

With a sharp knife, loosen layers. Fill and frost with Fluffy Vanilla Frosting. Serves 10 or 12.

Fluffy Vanilla Frosting

2 egg whites
3/4 cup sugar
pinch of salt
pinch cream of tartar
1 teaspoon vanilla

Place all the ingredients in the top of a double boiler and beat until blended. Place top over simmering water and beat with a rotary beater or electric hand mixer until mixture stands in stiff peaks. Swirl frosting between cake layers and on the top and sides of cake. Will fill and frost a 10-inch cake.

Velvet Chocolate Chip Cake with Fluffy Chocolate Frosting

1 package (18-1/2 ounces) chocolate cake mix
2 eggs
1-1/4 cups sour cream

1/2 cup semi-sweet chocolate chips

In the large bowl of your electric mixer, beat together all the ingredients for 4 minutes at medium speed. (Chocolate chips will break up in the beating process.) Pour the batter into 2 10-inch layer pans with removable bottoms that have been greased and lightly floured.

Bake in a 350° oven for 25 to 30 minutes or until a cake tester, inserted in center, comes out clean. Allow to cool for 5 minutes, remove the metal rings and continue cooling the layers on a rack.

Fill and frost with Fluffy Chocolate Frosting. Serves 8.

Fluffy Chocolate Frosting

1 cup milk
3 cups miniature marshmallows
8 ounces semi-sweet chocolate chips
1 teaspoon vanilla
1 tablespoon orange liqueur

In a saucepan, heat the milk, marshmallows and chocolate chips, stirring until the marshmallows and chocolate are melted and the mixture is thoroughly blended. Add the vanilla and orange liqueur. Allow to come to room temperature and spread on cake layers. Will fill and frost a 2-layer cake.

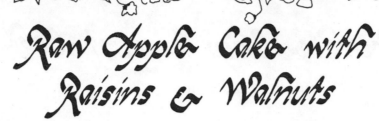

Raw Apple Cake with Raisins & Walnuts

2 cups flour
2 cups sugar
2 teaspoons cinnamon
1/2 teaspoon salt
2 teaspoons baking soda

1/2 cup oil
2 teaspoons vanilla
2 eggs
1 cup chopped walnuts
1 cup yellow raisins
4 apples, chopped or grated

Combine flour, sugar, cinnamon, salt and soda and set aside.

Beat together the oil, vanilla and eggs. Stir in the walnuts, raisins and apples. Add dry ingredients all at once and stir until blended.

Place batter in a buttered 9-inch tube pan and bake in a 350° oven for about 50 minutes, or until a cake tester inserted in center comes out clean. You can use a 9x13-inch pan, in which case you will bake the cake for 40 to 45 minutes. In either case, test for doneness. Frost with Cream Cheese Frosting.

Cream Cheese Frosting

1/4 cup butter (1/2 stick), softened
4 ounces cream cheese, softened
1 teaspoon vanilla
pinch of salt
1-1/2 cups sifted powdered sugar

Beat together the cream cheese and butter until mixture is blended. Beat in remaining ingredients until frosting is smooth.

Chocolate Chip Yogurt Cake

1 package (18-1/2 ounces) yellow cake mix
1 cup yogurt
2 eggs
5 tablespoons water

1 cup chocolate chips, semi-sweet
3 tablespoons chocolate flavored Nestle's Quik

In your electric mixer, beat together the cake mix, yogurt, eggs and water. Beat for 4 minutes at medium speed. Add the chocolate chips and stir until they are mixed into the batter.

Pour half the batter into a greased and floured 9-inch tube pan. Sprinkle the chocolate powder evenly over the batter. Pour the remaining batter evenly over the chocolate powder. With your scraper, cut into the batter at 2-inch intervals.

Bake in a 325° oven for about 50 minutes or until a cake tester, inserted in center, comes out clean. Drizzle with Chocolate Glaze when cool.

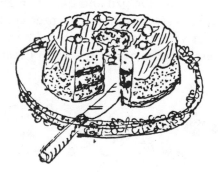

Instant Chocolate Glaze

1/4 pound (4 ounces) sweet or semi-sweet chocolate chips
1/2 cup whipping cream

Place chocolate pieces in blender container. Heat cream to boiling point and pour into the blender. Blend for about 30 seconds or until the chocolate is melted and the mixture is smooth. Swirl over the cake and let a little run down the sides.

Apple Cobbler with Apricots & Pecans

Tart fruit between two pastry layers and topped with crunchy pecans and coconut make this easy apple cake a bounty for those busy days.

3/4 stick butter (3 ounces) melted
1 package yellow cake mix (18-1/2 ounces)
1 can apple pie filling (1 pound 5 ounces)
1 cup apricot jam, chop the large pieces of fruit

1 cup orange juice
3/4 stick butter (3 ounces) melted

1 cup chopped pecans
1/2 cup coconut flakes

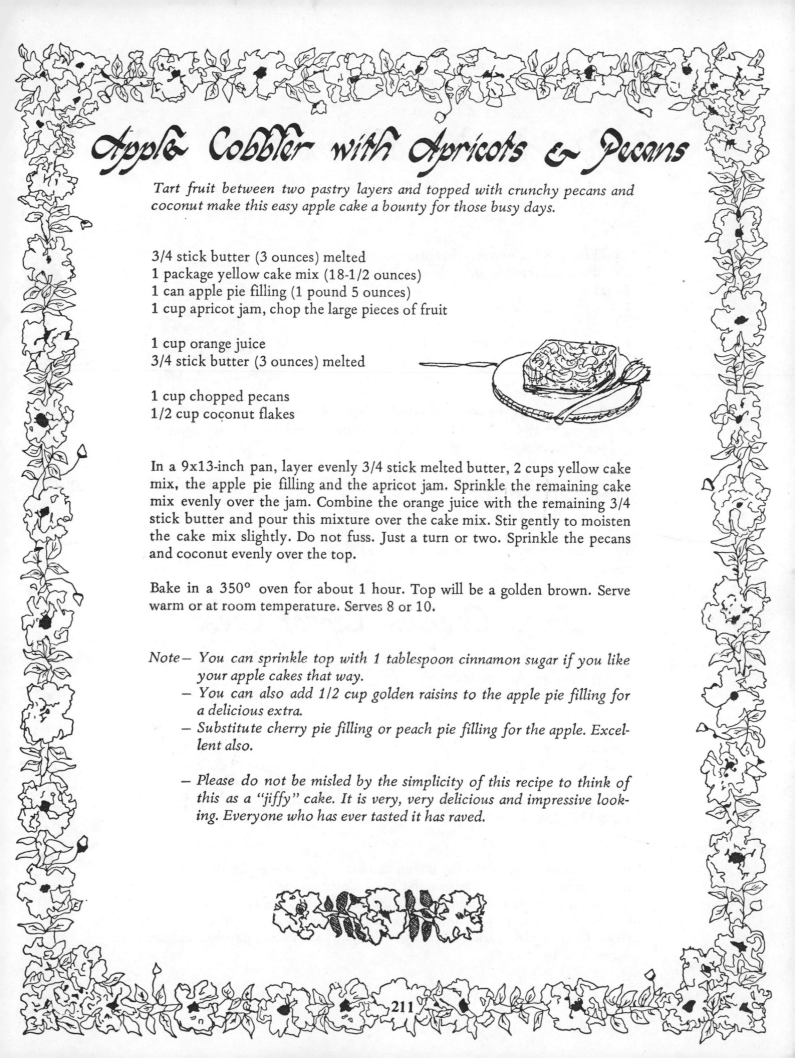

In a 9x13-inch pan, layer evenly 3/4 stick melted butter, 2 cups yellow cake mix, the apple pie filling and the apricot jam. Sprinkle the remaining cake mix evenly over the jam. Combine the orange juice with the remaining 3/4 stick butter and pour this mixture over the cake mix. Stir gently to moisten the cake mix slightly. Do not fuss. Just a turn or two. Sprinkle the pecans and coconut evenly over the top.

Bake in a 350° oven for about 1 hour. Top will be a golden brown. Serve warm or at room temperature. Serves 8 or 10.

Note — *You can sprinkle top with 1 tablespoon cinnamon sugar if you like your apple cakes that way.*
  — *You can also add 1/2 cup golden raisins to the apple pie filling for a delicious extra.*
  — *Substitute cherry pie filling or peach pie filling for the apple. Excellent also.*

  — *Please do not be misled by the simplicity of this recipe to think of this as a "jiffy" cake. It is very, very delicious and impressive looking. Everyone who has ever tasted it has raved.*

Fudgy Chocolate Banana Nut Cake

I think you will just love this absolutely fantastic cake. It is moist and delicious and takes seconds to assemble. The cake tastes like pure fudge.

1 package (18-1/2 ounces) chocolate sour cream cake mix
3 medium bananas, mashed (about 1-1/2 cups)
2 eggs
1/4 cup orange juice

1 cup chocolate chips, semi-sweet
1 cup chopped walnuts

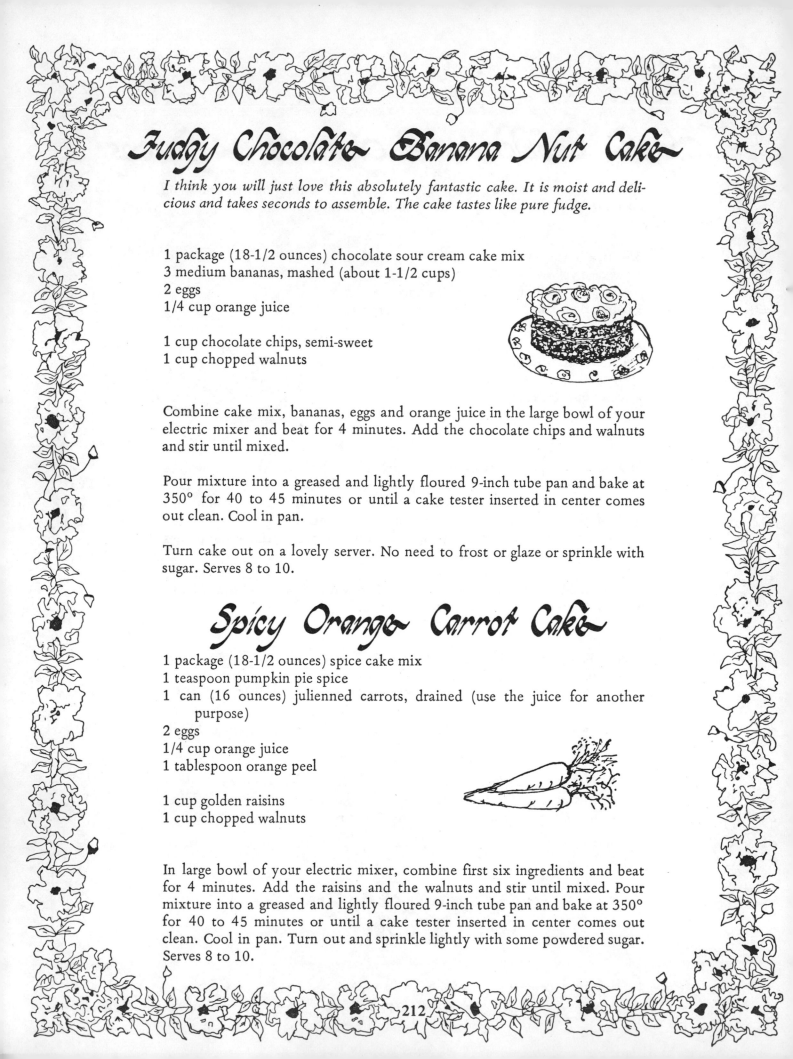

Combine cake mix, bananas, eggs and orange juice in the large bowl of your electric mixer and beat for 4 minutes. Add the chocolate chips and walnuts and stir until mixed.

Pour mixture into a greased and lightly floured 9-inch tube pan and bake at 350° for 40 to 45 minutes or until a cake tester inserted in center comes out clean. Cool in pan.

Turn cake out on a lovely server. No need to frost or glaze or sprinkle with sugar. Serves 8 to 10.

Spicy Orange Carrot Cake

1 package (18-1/2 ounces) spice cake mix
1 teaspoon pumpkin pie spice
1 can (16 ounces) julienned carrots, drained (use the juice for another
   purpose)
2 eggs
1/4 cup orange juice
1 tablespoon orange peel

1 cup golden raisins
1 cup chopped walnuts

In large bowl of your electric mixer, combine first six ingredients and beat for 4 minutes. Add the raisins and the walnuts and stir until mixed. Pour mixture into a greased and lightly floured 9-inch tube pan and bake at 350° for 40 to 45 minutes or until a cake tester inserted in center comes out clean. Cool in pan. Turn out and sprinkle lightly with some powdered sugar. Serves 8 to 10.

Velvet Almond Chocolate Cheesecake

CHOCOLATE COOKIE CRUST

1-1/2 cups chocolate cookie crumbs
3 ounces butter (3/4 stick), melted
1/4 cup sliced almonds, toasted
4 tablespoons sugar

Combine the crumbs, melted butter, almonds and sugar and mix until they are blended. With your fingers, press the mixture on the bottom and up the sides of a 9-inch pie plate. Bake in a 350° oven for 5 minutes.

Pour Chocolate Almond Cheese Filling into prepared crust and bake in a 325° oven for 35 minutes. Cool and then refrigerate for several hours. Remove from the refrigerator about 20 minutes before serving. Serve "natural" without sauce or topping for it is incredibly rich and delicious. Serves 6.

Chocolate Almond Cheese Filling

1 package (8 ounces) cream cheese
1/2 cup sugar
2 eggs
1-1/2 cups sour cream
1 teaspoon vanilla
1 teaspoon almond extract

6 ounces melted semi-sweet chocolate

Beat cream cheese until light and fluffy. Add sugar, eggs, sour cream, vanilla and almond extract and beat until blended. Beat in the melted chocolate.

French Orange Almond Wafers

3 egg whites
1/2 cup sugar
1/2 teaspoon vanilla

1/3 cup flour
1/2 cup almond meal (ground almonds that can be purchased at any health
    food store)
1/2 cup sliced almonds (purchased at any market)
1 tablespoon finely grated orange peel
1/4 cup melted butter

Beat together the egg whites, sugar and vanilla until mixture is creamy, about
1 minute at high speed. Beat in the flour, almond meal, sliced almonds and
orange peel until the mixture is blended. Beat in the melted butter.

Heavily butter a 12x16-inch cookie sheet and drop batter by the teaspoonful
onto the pan, leaving plenty of space between the cookies. Do not make
more than 16 cookies for that size pan. Bake in a 325° oven for about 10 to
12 minutes or until the edges of cookies are golden brown.

Immediately remove cookies onto a brown paper bag and allow to cool.
Store in a tightly covered cookie tin. Makes 32 heavenly wafers.

Note — *If cookies are not removed immediately from the pan, they will
    harden and be difficult to remove. Then, you must return them to
    the oven for about 30 seconds to soften them.*
   — *You can substitute grated tangerine peel for the orange peel for a
    slightly different and incredibly delicious variation.*

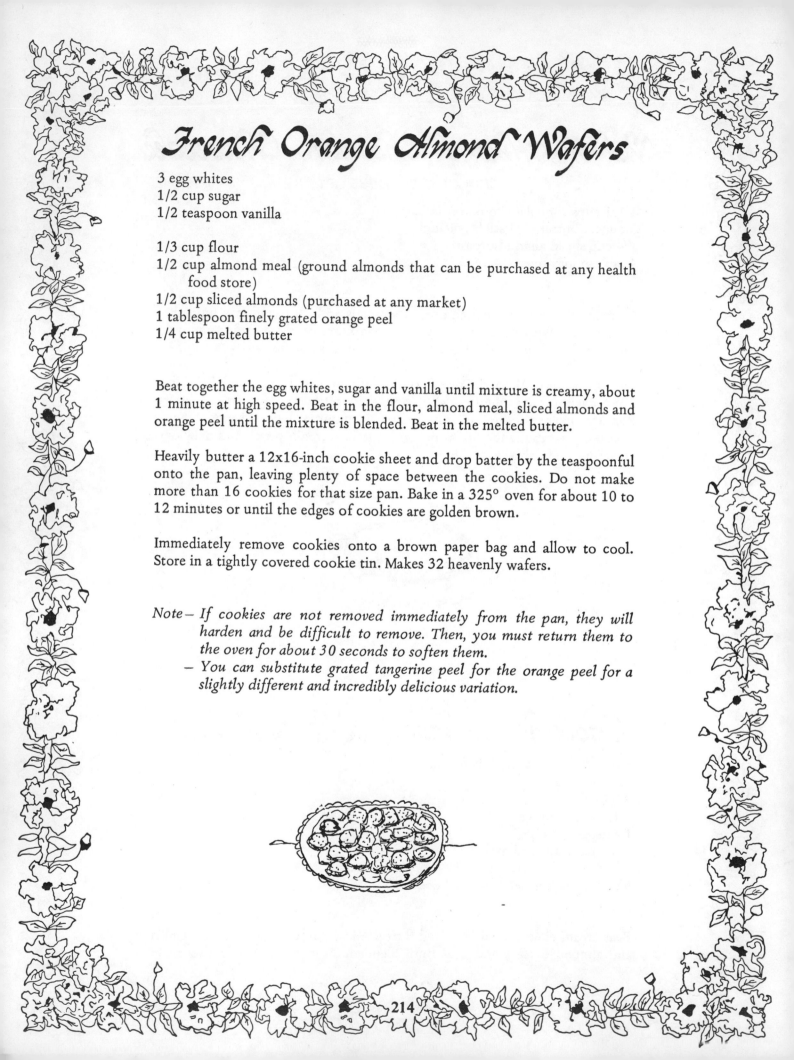

Chocolate Chip Walnut Chewies

Incredibly easy and incredibly delicious, these heavenly cookies will quickly become a part of your repertoire.

1/2 cup butter (1 stick), melted
2 cups yellow cake mix
1/2 cup coconut flakes
1-1/2 cup walnuts, coarsely chopped
1 package (6 ounces) semi-sweet chocolate chips (or more to taste)

1 can (14 ounces) condensed milk

In a 9x13-inch pan, melt the butter and spread it evenly over the bottom. Now layer and sprinkle *evenly*, the cake mix, coconut flakes, walnuts and chocolate chips. Drizzle the condensed milk evenly over all. Bake in a 350° oven for about 25 to 30 minutes, or until the top is golden brown.

Allow to cool in the pan for about 25 minutes. When still warm, but can be handled easily, cut into 1-1/2-inch squares and remove from pan. Place cookies on a brown paper bag. When cool, sprinkle ever so lightly with some powdered sugar. Yields 48 chewies.

Note — Cookies freeze beautifully. Freeze in double plastic bags. Remove from bag when defrosting.
— Store cookies in an airtight container.

Cherry Walnut Chewies

Prepare the cookies above with the following considerations. Instead of the chocolate chips use 1 cup of candied cherries. Slice the cherries and sprinkle them evenly over the walnuts. Proceed as above for baking, slicing and storing. These cookies freeze also.

French Chocolate Chip Macaroons

3 egg whites
1/2 cup sugar
1/2 teaspoon vanilla

1/3 cup flour
1/2 cup macaroon coconut (can be purchased at any health food store)
1/2 cup chocolate chips
1/4 cup melted butter

Beat together the egg whites, sugar and vanilla until the mixture is creamy, about 1 minute at high speed. Beat in the flour, coconut and chocolate chips. Beat in the melted butter.

Heavily butter a 12x16-inch cookie sheet and drop batter by the teaspoonful onto the pan, leaving plenty of space between the cookies. Do not make more than 16 cookies at a time for that size pan. Bake in a 325° oven for about 10 to 12 minutes or until edges look a little dry. Do not overcook.

Immediately remove cookies onto a brown paper bag and allow to cool. Store in a tightly covered cookie tin. Makes 32 never-to-be-forgotten cookies.

Note – If cookies are not removed immediately from the pan, they will harden and be difficult to remove. Then, you must return them to the oven for about 30 seconds to soften them.

Chocolate Cheese Cake Cookies

1/2 cup butter (1 stick)
1/2 cup light brown sugar, pack firmly
1 cup flour
1/2 cup finely chopped pecans
2 tablespoons grated orange peel

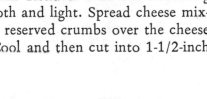

1 package (8 ounces) cream cheese
3/8 cup sugar
1 egg
2 tablespoons cream
2 tablespoons orange juice concentrate
1/2 teaspoon vanilla
1 tablespoon cocoa

Cream butter and brown sugar. Add flour, pecans and orange peel and blend until mixture forms crumbs. Set aside 1 cup of crumb mixture. Press remaining crumbs into an 8-inch square pan. Bake at 350° for 12 minutes.

Beat together cream cheese and sugar until blended. Add the remaining ingredients and beat until mixture is smooth and light. Spread cheese mixture evenly over the baked crust. Sprinkle reserved crumbs over the cheese mixture. Bake at 350° for 25 minutes. Cool and then cut into 1-1/2-inch squares. Makes 25 cookies.

Lemon Cookies with Pecans & Cherries

1 cup butter
1 cup sugar
1 egg yolk
2 cups cake flour
4 tablespoons grated lemon peel

1 egg white, beaten
1 cup finely chopped pecans
1/2 cup maraschino cherries, finely chopped

Cream together the butter and sugar. Add the egg yolk and cake flour and blend thoroughly. Mix in the lemon peel. Pat the mixture evenly into a 10x15-inch cookie pan. Brush top lightly with beaten egg white and sprinkle with chopped pecans and chopped cherries. Pat nuts and cherries gently into the dough.

Bake in a 350° oven until golden brown, about 25 minutes. Remove from the oven and cut into 1-1/2-inch squares or diamonds while still warm. Remove from the pan and finish cooling on a brown paper bag. Makes about 60 cookies.

Apricot Bar Delice Cookies

1-1/2 cups flour
1 teaspoon baking powder
1-1/2 cups quick cooking oats
1 cup brown sugar
3/4 cup butter

1 cup coconut flakes
1 cup apricot jam
1 tablespoon lemon juice
1 cup chopped walnuts

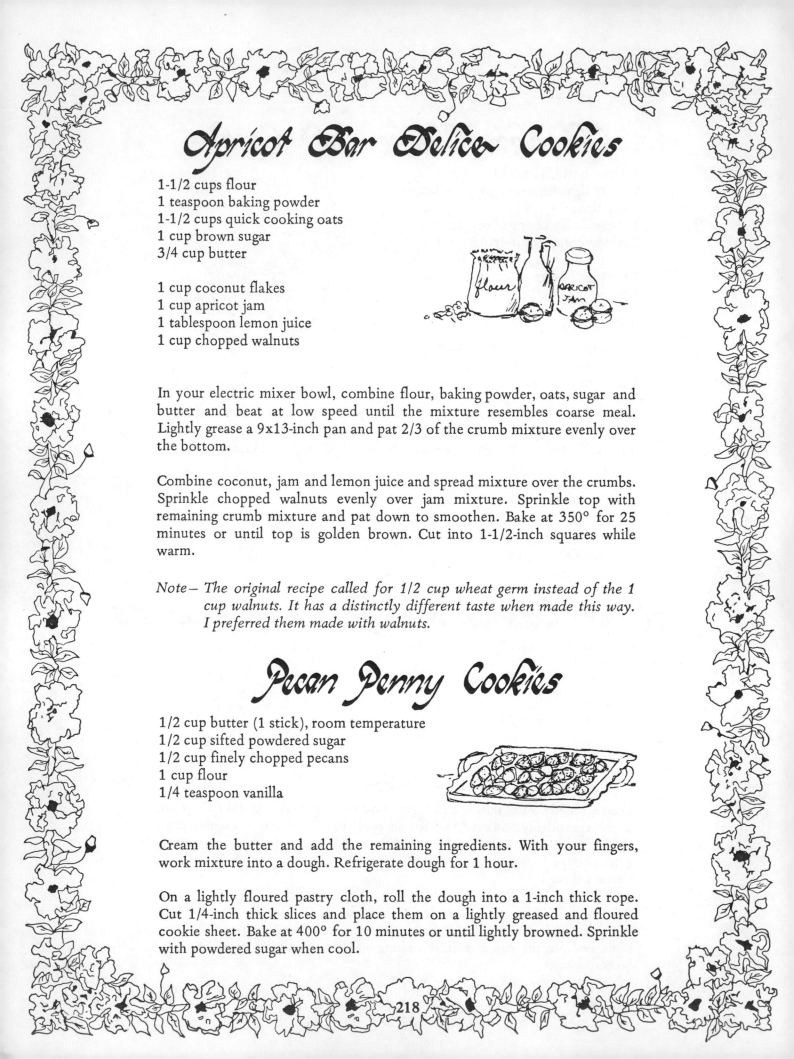

In your electric mixer bowl, combine flour, baking powder, oats, sugar and butter and beat at low speed until the mixture resembles coarse meal. Lightly grease a 9x13-inch pan and pat 2/3 of the crumb mixture evenly over the bottom.

Combine coconut, jam and lemon juice and spread mixture over the crumbs. Sprinkle chopped walnuts evenly over jam mixture. Sprinkle top with remaining crumb mixture and pat down to smoothen. Bake at 350° for 25 minutes or until top is golden brown. Cut into 1-1/2-inch squares while warm.

Note— The original recipe called for 1/2 cup wheat germ instead of the 1 cup walnuts. It has a distinctly different taste when made this way. I preferred them made with walnuts.

Pecan Penny Cookies

1/2 cup butter (1 stick), room temperature
1/2 cup sifted powdered sugar
1/2 cup finely chopped pecans
1 cup flour
1/4 teaspoon vanilla

Cream the butter and add the remaining ingredients. With your fingers, work mixture into a dough. Refrigerate dough for 1 hour.

On a lightly floured pastry cloth, roll the dough into a 1-inch thick rope. Cut 1/4-inch thick slices and place them on a lightly greased and floured cookie sheet. Bake at 400° for 10 minutes or until lightly browned. Sprinkle with powdered sugar when cool.

Coeur a la Creme with Strawberry Raspberry Sauce

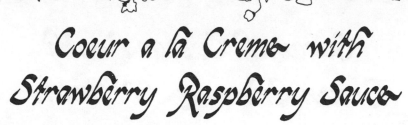

1 package (8 ounces) cream cheese
1/2 cup sifted powdered sugar
1 teaspoon vanilla
1/2 cup sour cream
1/2 cup cream, whipped
1/4 lemon, grated

Beat together the cream cheese, sugar and vanilla until the mixture is light and fluffy. Beat in the sour cream and whipped cream until the mixture is blended. Stir in the lemon.

Line a 4-cup heart-shaped mold with a dampened piece of double thickness cheesecloth, extended 4 inches extra on the sides. Pour in the cheese mixture and cover with the extra cheesecloth. Refrigerate overnight...2 days is better.

Unmold creme on a lovely platter and remove cheesecloth. Decorate with a rim of halved strawberries. Serve with Strawberry Raspberry Sauce. Serves 4.

Strawberry Raspberry Sauce

1 package (10 ounces) frozen sliced strawberries in heavy syrup
1 package (10 ounces) frozen raspberries in heavy syrup
1 tablespoon lemon juice

Combine all the ingredients and stir until blended. Refrigerate until serving time.

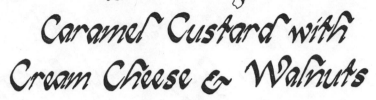

Caramel Custard with Cream Cheese & Walnuts

3/4 cup sugar
1 tablespoon water
2 tablespoons coarsely chopped walnuts

4 eggs
1 cup cream
1 package (8 ounces) cream cheese
1 can (14 ounces) condensed milk
1 teaspoon almond extract
1 teaspoon vanilla

In a saucepan, cook together the sugar, water and walnuts. Let the mixture bubble for about 3 minutes over medium low heat until sugar is a golden, caramel color, but do not let it brown. Coat bottom and sides of a 1-quart ring mold with caramel nut mixture.

Beat together the remaining ingredients until they are thoroughly blended. Pour the mixture into the prepared mold and set the mold in a pan with 1 inch of water. Bake at 350° for about 1 hour, or until a cake tester inserted in center comes out clean. Allow to cool and then refrigerate.

To serve, unmold onto a platter and spoon a little of the caramel on each slice. Serves 6.

Note— Custard can be made in individual ramekins, in which case, divide the caramel in the souffle dishes and pour the custard evenly into each dish. Reduce baking time to 30 minutes. Serve in the ramekins.

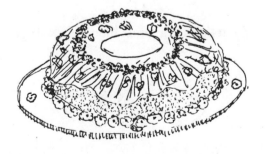

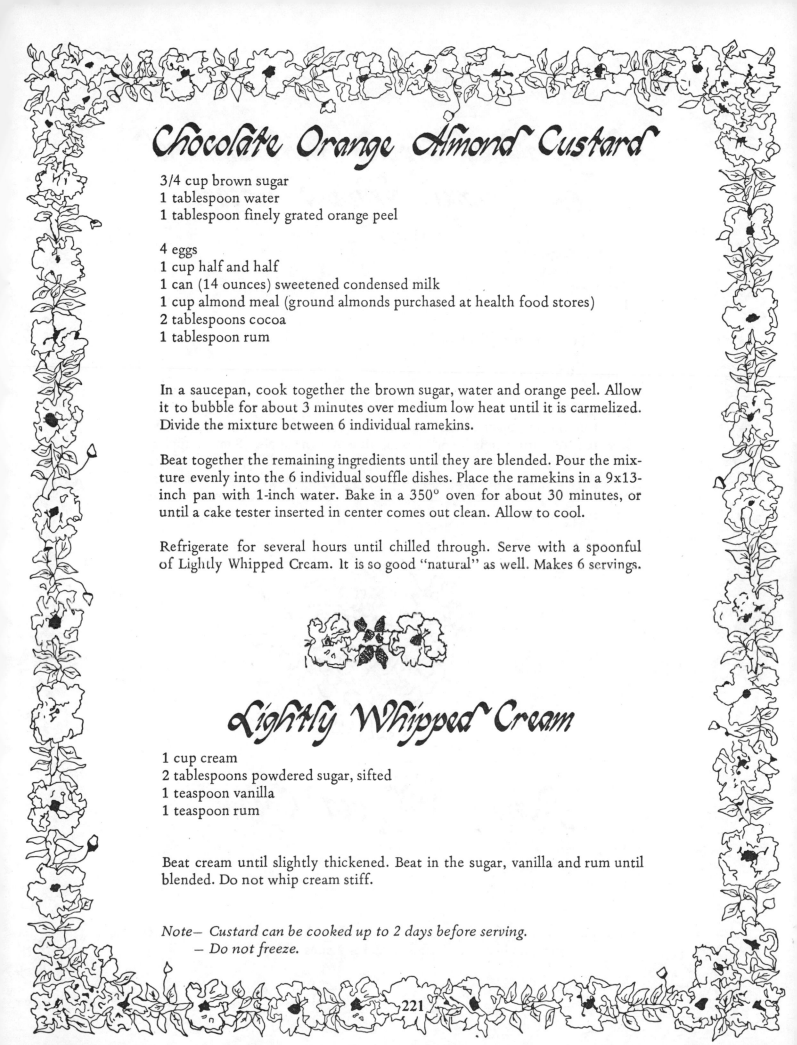

Chocolate Orange Almond Custard

3/4 cup brown sugar
1 tablespoon water
1 tablespoon finely grated orange peel

4 eggs
1 cup half and half
1 can (14 ounces) sweetened condensed milk
1 cup almond meal (ground almonds purchased at health food stores)
2 tablespoons cocoa
1 tablespoon rum

In a saucepan, cook together the brown sugar, water and orange peel. Allow it to bubble for about 3 minutes over medium low heat until it is carmelized. Divide the mixture between 6 individual ramekins.

Beat together the remaining ingredients until they are blended. Pour the mixture evenly into the 6 individual souffle dishes. Place the ramekins in a 9x13-inch pan with 1-inch water. Bake in a 350° oven for about 30 minutes, or until a cake tester inserted in center comes out clean. Allow to cool.

Refrigerate for several hours until chilled through. Serve with a spoonful of Lightly Whipped Cream. It is so good "natural" as well. Makes 6 servings.

Lightly Whipped Cream

1 cup cream
2 tablespoons powdered sugar, sifted
1 teaspoon vanilla
1 teaspoon rum

Beat cream until slightly thickened. Beat in the sugar, vanilla and rum until blended. Do not whip cream stiff.

Note— *Custard can be cooked up to 2 days before serving.*
    — Do not freeze.

Honey Glazed Apples with Almonds & Rummy Whipped Cream

8 apples, peeled, cored and cut in halves
1/2 cup butter, melted
1/2 cup honey
1 cup sugar
1 tablespoon grated orange zest

1/2 cup toasted slivered almonds

Rummy Whipped Cream

In a Dutch oven, place apples. Combine the butter, honey, sugar and orange zest and stir until blended. Pour this mixture over the apples. Simmer apples, uncovered, over medium low heat until syrup is golden and apple juices have evaporated, about 45 minutes. Sprinkle apples with toasted slivered almonds. Serve 1/2 apple in a lovely stemmed glass topped with Rummy Whipped Cream. Serves 8.

Rummy Whipped Cream

1 cup cream
2 tablespoons sugar
1 tablespoon rum

Beat cream until foamy. Add sugar and continue beating until the cream is stiff. Add rum and beat until blended. Makes 2 cups whipped cream.

Cranberry Ambrosia with Pineapple & Coconut

1 can (1 pound) whole cranberry sauce, broken up
1 can (1 pound 4 ounces) pineapple chunks. Pat dry with paper towels and
    reserve juice for another use.
1 cup shredded coconut
4 cups miniature marshmallows
1 tablespoon grated orange zest
1/2 cup toasted slivered almonds
1 pint sour cream

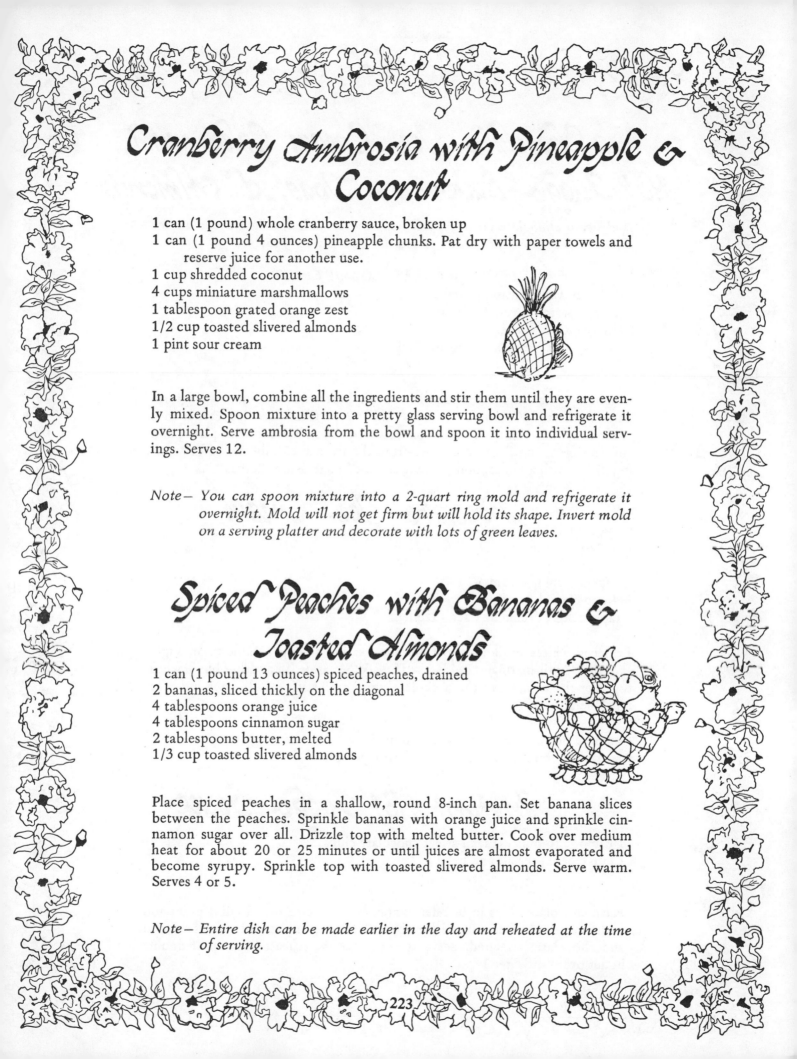

In a large bowl, combine all the ingredients and stir them until they are evenly mixed. Spoon mixture into a pretty glass serving bowl and refrigerate it
overnight. Serve ambrosia from the bowl and spoon it into individual servings. Serves 12.

*Note— You can spoon mixture into a 2-quart ring mold and refrigerate it
overnight. Mold will not get firm but will hold its shape. Invert mold
on a serving platter and decorate with lots of green leaves.*

Spiced Peaches with Bananas & Toasted Almonds

1 can (1 pound 13 ounces) spiced peaches, drained
2 bananas, sliced thickly on the diagonal
4 tablespoons orange juice
4 tablespoons cinnamon sugar
2 tablespoons butter, melted
1/3 cup toasted slivered almonds

Place spiced peaches in a shallow, round 8-inch pan. Set banana slices
between the peaches. Sprinkle bananas with orange juice and sprinkle cinnamon sugar over all. Drizzle top with melted butter. Cook over medium
heat for about 20 or 25 minutes or until juices are almost evaporated and
become syrupy. Sprinkle top with toasted slivered almonds. Serve warm.
Serves 4 or 5.

*Note— Entire dish can be made earlier in the day and reheated at the time
of serving.*

Chocolate Ice Cream Cake with Hot Fudge Sauce & Toasted Almonds

A delicate chocolate crust topped with the creamiest, velvet chocolate ice cream. It is spectacular to look at and the taste is simply divine.

CHOCOLATE COOKIE CRUST

1-1/4 cups vanilla wafer crumbs
1/2 cup toasted slivered almonds
1/3 cup melted butter
4 tablespoons Nestle's Chocolate Quik

Combine all the ingredients and pat on the bottom of a 10-inch springform pan. Bake at 350° for 7 minutes. Chill. Pour Chocolate Ice Cream into cooled shell. Sprinkle with additional toasted almonds, wrap with plastic and foil and freeze until firm. Remove from the freezer 15 minutes before serving. Serve with a tablespoon (or two) of Hot Fudge Sauce. Serves 10.

Chocolate Ice Cream

6 egg whites
8 tablespoons sugar

2 cups whipping cream
3/4 cup chocolate syrup
2 tablespoons Creme de Cacao Liqueur

Beat egg whites until foamy. Continue beating adding 1 tablespoon sugar at a time until meringue holds a stiff peak. Set aside. In another bowl, whip together the cream and the chocolate syrup until stiff. Add liqueur and beat until blended.

Combine beaten egg whites and whipped cream and beat together on lowest speed of your mixer until they are thoroughly blended.

Instant Hot Fudge Sauce

1 package (6 ounces) semi-sweet chocolate chips
1 cup cream (or half and half)

Place chocolate chips in blender container. Heat cream to boiling point and pour into the blender. Blend for about 1 minute or until mixture is smooth and chocolate is melted. Serve at once. (Can be reheated in top of double boiler over hot water.)

Light Lemon Cloud Sherbet

1 quart lemon sherbet, softened

4 egg whites
6 tablespoons sugar
pinch of cream of tartar
1/2 lemon, grated, use peel, fruit and juice. Remove any large pieces of
    membrane.

Soften sherbet in refrigerator for about 30 minutes. Beat egg whites until foamy. Continue beating and add cream of tartar and 1 tablespoon sugar at a time until all the sugar is incorporated and meringue is stiff and glossy.

Combine sherbet, meringue and grated lemon and stir until the mixture is well blended. Spoon into 12 freezer proof individual dessert dishes. (If you have stemware that can take freezing, it would be lovely.)

Serve with a tablespoon or two of champagne and a fresh raspberry on top. Makes 12 servings.

Creamy Dreamy Orange Sherbet

1 quart orange sherbet, softened

1 cup whipping cream
2 tablespoons sugar
3 tablespoons orange juice concentrate
1 tablespoon grated orange peel

Soften sherbet in refrigerator for about 30 minutes. Beat cream with sugar until stiff. Beat in orange juice concentrate and orange peel.

Stir together the whipped cream mixture and the orange sherbet until it is well blended. Spoon mixture into 12 freezer-proof individual dessert dishes. (If you have the time, you might want to scoop out the fruit of 12 oranges and fill them with the sherbet.) Serve with a dollup of whipped cream and a cherry on top.

Note— You can divide the mixture into a 12 cup paper-lined muffin pan.

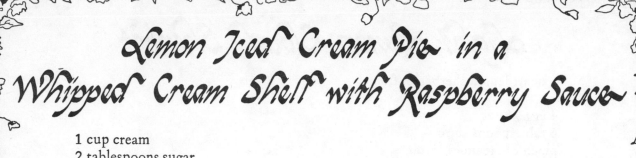

Lemon Iced Cream Pie in a Whipped Cream Shell with Raspberry Sauce

1 cup cream
2 tablespoons sugar
1 teaspoon vanilla
1 tablespoon orange liqueur

2 cups cream
1 lemon, grated (remove any large pieces of membrane)
1 cup sugar

1 package (10 ounces) frozen raspberries in syrup

Whip cream with sugar, vanilla and orange liqueur until cream is stiff. Spread cream on bottom and sides of a 9-inch deep dish pie plate. Freeze until firm.

When cream shell is frozen firm, prepare the lemon iced cream by stirring together the 2 cups cream, the grated lemon and the sugar. Do not beat, but simply stir until the sugar is dissolved. Pour lemon cream into frozen shell and return to the freezer. When pie is frozen, wrap in double thicknesses of plastic wrap, then foil.

Remove from the freezer about 10 minutes before serving. Slice in wedges and serve with a tablespoon or two of raspberries in syrup. Serves 6 or 7.

Note— Don't be misled by the simplicity of this recipe. It produces an elegant dessert. The lemon cream is delicate and the whipped cream shell is easier than "pie."
— Can be stored 1 week in the freezer.
— Use a little more lemon juice if you like it especially tart.

Iced Lemon Cream

This is a glorious dessert...light, tangy, and refreshing. It is excellent for lunch and dinner dessert as well. When you consider that it takes literally seconds to prepare (this dessert needs only to be stirred) you will want to keep some available in your freezer at all times.

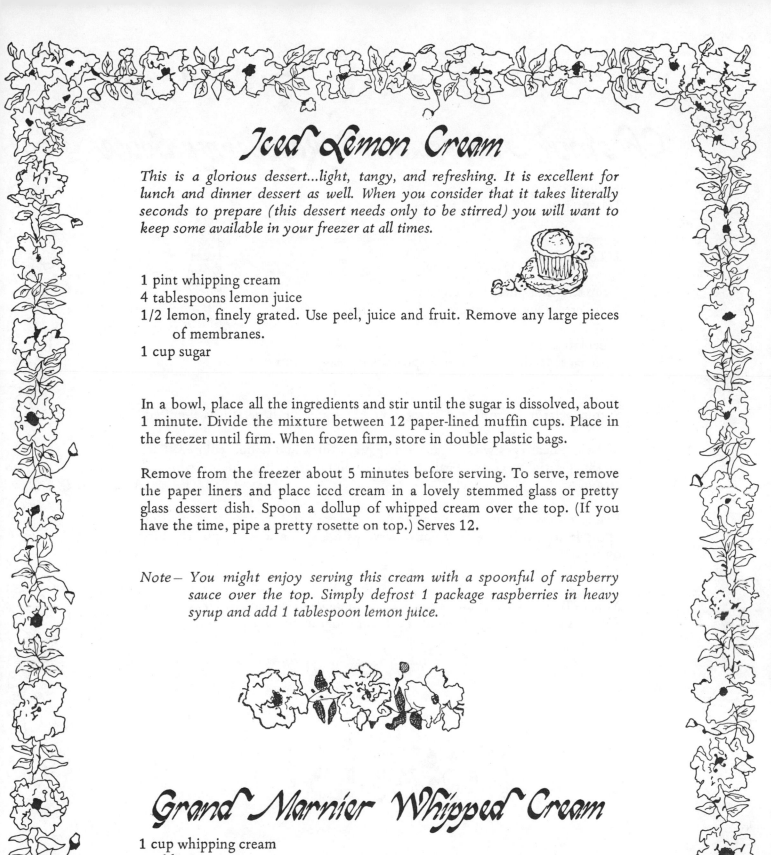

1 pint whipping cream
4 tablespoons lemon juice
1/2 lemon, finely grated. Use peel, juice and fruit. Remove any large pieces
    of membranes.
1 cup sugar

In a bowl, place all the ingredients and stir until the sugar is dissolved, about 1 minute. Divide the mixture between 12 paper-lined muffin cups. Place in the freezer until firm. When frozen firm, store in double plastic bags.

Remove from the freezer about 5 minutes before serving. To serve, remove the paper liners and place iced cream in a lovely stemmed glass or pretty glass dessert dish. Spoon a dollup of whipped cream over the top. (If you have the time, pipe a pretty rosette on top.) Serves 12.

Note— You might enjoy serving this cream with a spoonful of raspberry sauce over the top. Simply defrost 1 package raspberries in heavy syrup and add 1 tablespoon lemon juice.

Grand Marnier Whipped Cream

1 cup whipping cream
1 tablespoon sugar
1 tablespoon Grand Marnier liqueur

Whip cream until soft peaks form. Continue beating as you add the sugar and liqueur. Beat cream until stiff.

Chestnut Mousse with Raspberry Sauce

1 tablespoon gelatin
1/4 cup rum

4 eggs
1/2 cup sugar

1 cup chestnut puree, sweetened
1 cup cream, beaten until stiff

chocolate curls
1 package, 10 ounces, frozen raspberries in heavy syrup

Soften gelatin in rum and place over hot water until gelatin is liquified.

Meawhile beat eggs with sugar until eggs are thick and lemon colored. Beat in the gelatin mixture. Beat in the chestnut puree. Beat in the whipped cream.

Divide mousse between 6 lovely stemmed glasses and refrigerate until firm. Sprinkle top with chocolate curls. Serve with a spoonful of raspberry sauce on top. Serves 6.

Note – *To make chocolate curls, take a vegetable peeler and run it down the side of a bar of chocolate that is at room temperature.*

Cheese Pie
with Strawberry Orange Sauce

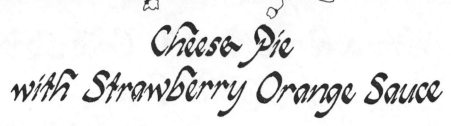

1 graham cracker pie shell, 9-inch

1/2 pound cream cheese
3/4 cup powdered sugar, sifted
1 tablespoon lemon juice
1 teaspoon lemon peel
1 cup whipping cream

1 recipe Strawberry Orange Sauce

Cream together cream cheese, sugar, lemon juice and lemon peel until light. Whip cream until stiff and add to the cream cheese mixture. Mix together on low setting of electric mixer. Pour into baked and cooled pie shell. Refrigerate.

Serve with Strawberry Orange Sauce spooned over the top. Serves 6 to 8.

Cracker Pie Shell

1/3 cup butter, melted
1-1/4 cups graham cracker crumbs
1/2 cup coarsely chopped walnuts
1 teaspoon orange zest
3 tablespoons cinnamon sugar

In a 9-inch pie pan, combine all the ingredients and mix to thoroughly combine. Press crumbs evenly along the bottom and the sides of the pie pan. Bake in a 350° oven for about 8 minutes. Cool before filling.

Strawberry Orange Sauce

Perhaps one of the simplest of sauces, but one of the best. Use it over ice cream, sponge cake, puddings, etc.

1 package (1 pound) frozen sliced strawberries in syrup
3 ounces (1/2 package) frozen orange juice concentrate. Do not dilute.
1 tablespoon Grand Marnier or Orange Liqueur

Thaw orange juice and mix with the other ingredients. Refrigerate until ready to use. Ladle over cream cheese pie when serving.

Nutcracker Chocolate Chip Torte
with Kahlua Cream

3 eggs
3/4 cup sugar

2 cups Ritz cracker crumbs (about 42 crackers, crushed into crumbs)
3/4 cup sugar
1 teaspoon baking powder
1 teaspoon vanilla
1 cup chocolate chips, semi-sweet
1 cup coarsely chopped walnuts (or pecans)

Beat eggs with 3/4 cup sugar until eggs are light and very pale, about 5 minutes, at high speed. Stir in the remaining ingredients until they are blended.

Lightly grease a 9-inch pie plate. Pour mixture into pie plate and bake at 350° for 30 minutes. Frost torte with Kahlua Cream and refrigerate it overnight. Serves 8.

Kahlua Cream

1 cup cream
1 tablespoon sugar
1 tablespoon Kahlua liqueur

Beat cream with sugar and liqueur until cream is stiff.

Note— *These very simple ingredients produce a superb tasting torte. Lavished with the Kahlua flavored whipped cream makes it elegant enough for the most discriminating party. Of course, it is simple enough to be part of your every day repertoire as well.*
  — Torte freezes beautifully. Wrap in double plastic wrap and then foil. Remove wrappers and defrost in the refrigerator.

Old Fashioned Apple Pie with Streusel Topping

Making a freshly baked apple pie is simplified by using the prepared frozen pie crust shells. I use the prepared shells often. They are very good and do allow you the option of making a yummy pie when you do not have the time to fuss. Outside of peeling and grating the apples there is little left to do except assembling and stirring the ingredients.

1 9-inch deep dish frozen pie crust shell. Brush sides and bottom with apricot jam.

6 apples, peeled, cored and thinly sliced
1/2 cup apricot jam
1 cup sugar
2 tablespoons flour
1/2 lemon, grated (remove any large pieces of membrane)
2 tablespoons orange liqueur
1/2 cup chopped toasted pecans
1/2 cup yellow raisins
2 teaspoons cinnamon

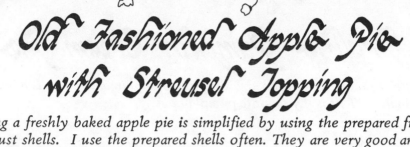

Combine all the ingredients and place them into the unbaked pie shell. Sprinkle Streusel Topping over the apple mixture. Bake in a 400° oven for 45 minutes. (To prevent edges from burning, place a 2-inch strip of aluminum foil around the edges.) Serves 6.

Streusel Topping

1/2 cup flour
1/2 cup sugar
1 teaspoon cinnamon
6 tablespoons butter, at room temperature

With your fingers, work the butter into the rest of the ingredients until mixture is combined.

Note— Baked pie can be frozen. Defrost and then warm in a 300° oven before serving.

Praline Pumpkin Cream Pie

A crunchy praline layer topped with spiced pumpkin and cream is a heavenly combination. This is my favorite pumpkin pie.

2 frozen 9-inch pie shells. Defrost them for 10 minutes and then bake them at 400° for 8 minutes or until very lightly browned.

2/3 cup butter, softened
1 cup brown sugar
1 cup chopped pecans

Combine butter and sugar and divide mixture into 2 prepared shells. Return shells to oven and bake them at 425° for about 5 minutes or until the praline is bubbling vigorously. Sprinkle pecans over the praline and let cool.

Pour Pumpkin Cream Filling into cooled shell and refrigerate until firm. You might want to decorate it with a little additional whipped cream, but just a few rosettes, no more. Yields two 9-inch pies. Serves 12-14.

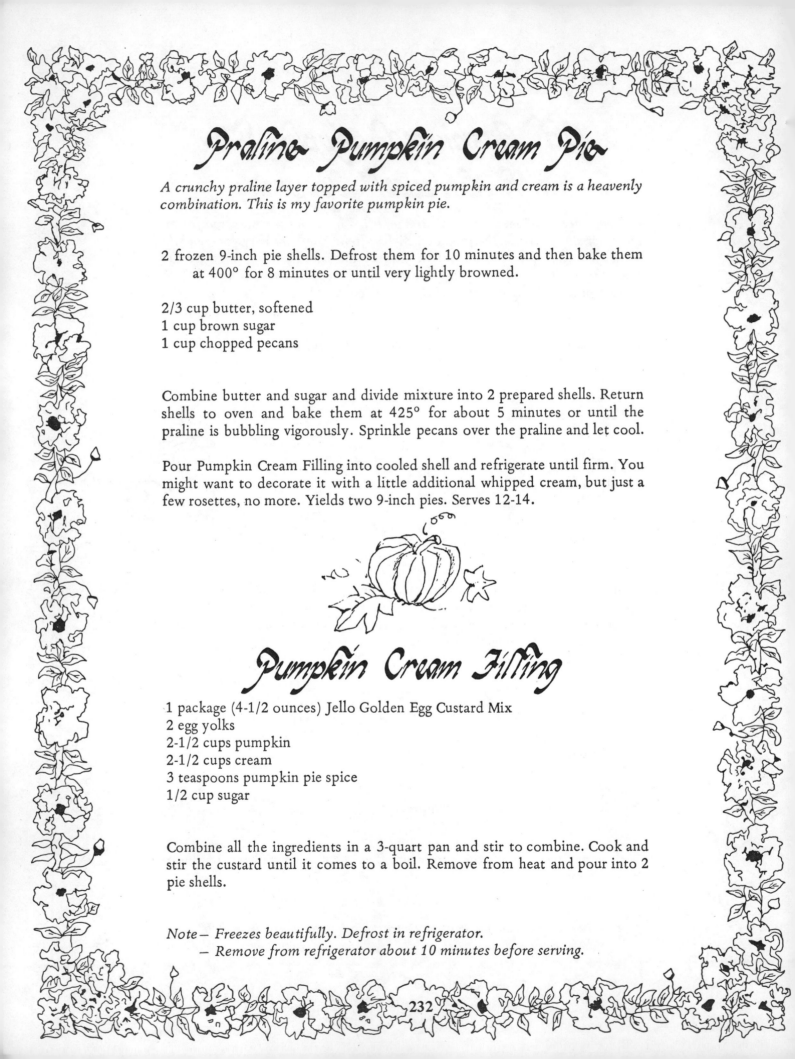

Pumpkin Cream Filling

1 package (4-1/2 ounces) Jello Golden Egg Custard Mix
2 egg yolks
2-1/2 cups pumpkin
2-1/2 cups cream
3 teaspoons pumpkin pie spice
1/2 cup sugar

Combine all the ingredients in a 3-quart pan and stir to combine. Cook and stir the custard until it comes to a boil. Remove from heat and pour into 2 pie shells.

Note — Freezes beautifully. Defrost in refrigerator.
 — Remove from refrigerator about 10 minutes before serving.

The Easiest & Best Old Fashioned Apple Pie

A good apple pie is the stuff legends are made of. Somehow the memories of warm, juicy apples in a flaky crust linger long after childhood is over. And of course, sprinkle some sugar on the crust so that it adds a little crunch and crispness.

2 9-inch deep-dish frozen pie shells. Brush bottom of 1 shell with 2 tablespoons apricot jam.

8 cups peeled, cored and thinly sliced green apples (about 2 1/2 pounds)
3/4 cup yellow raisins
1/2 cup brown sugar
1/2 cup granulated sugar
2 tablespoons flour
1 teaspoon cinnamon
pinch of nutmeg (I like a *good* pinch)
pinch of salt

Prepare bottom crust with apricot jam. Toss together the remaining ingredients and pile them into the prepared crust. Moisten the edges of the bottom crust with water.

Now, second pie shell should be slightly thawed and pliable. Invert over the
bottom shell and remove the pan. Carefully press the edges together to seal.
Flute the edges or pinch them. Cut numerous vents on the top pastry, brush
it with milk and sprinkle with sugar.

Place pie on a cookie sheet (important! it is easier to handle, will catch drippings and crust will bake more evenly) and bake in a 375° oven for about 1
hour or until crust is a golden brown. Serve warm or at room temperature.
And while you are at it, why not scoop a little ice cream on the top. Serves
6 very fortunate people (or 4 hungry kids).

Chocolate Pie Andy with Chocolate Cream Frosting

Incredibly rich and delicious, this pie is dedicated to Andy, chocolate lover "rara avis."

1 cup sugar
1/2 cup butter (1 stick)

2 eggs

1/2 cup flour
3 heaping tablespoons cocoa
1 teaspoon vanilla

1/2 cup miniature marshmallows
1/2 cup chopped walnuts

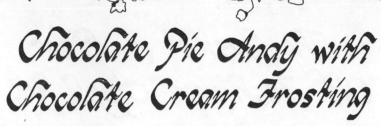

Beat together the sugar and butter until the mixture is blended. Beat in the eggs, flour, cocoa and vanilla and continue beating for 5 minutes. Stir in the marshmallows and walnuts.

Spread batter into a buttered and floured 9-inch pie pan and bake in a 350° oven for about 25 minutes or until a cake tester inserted in center comes out clean. Allow to cool.

Spread Chocolate Cream Frosting on the top and serve warm or at room temperature. Keep the portions small. Serves 8.

Note — The secret of this pie's chewy, fudgy quality is the miniature marsh-mallows that melt during baking.

CHOCOLATE CREAM FROSTING

3/4 cup semi-sweet chocolate chips
3/8 cup cream
1/2 teaspoon vanilla

Place chocolate chips in blender container. Heat cream to the boiling point and pour into container. Blend until chocolate is melted and frosting is smooth and glossy. Beat in vanilla. Makes about 1 cup frosting.

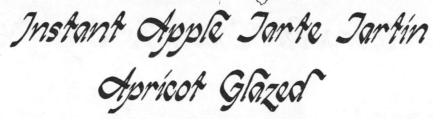

Instant Apple Tarte Tartin
Apricot Glazed

This instant variation of the exquisite Tarte Tartin is a great help for those days or nights when you don't have the time to carmelize the apples or make the puff pastry. Using the frozen patty shells and glazing with apricot jam is an alternative that is incredibly delicious and very, very easy.

3 patty shells, defrosted

2 apples, peeled, cored and cut in half vertically. Place cut ends down and
    cut apple halves into very thin slices, horizontally

4 tablespoons sugar mixed with 1/8 teaspoon cinnamon

Stack the patty shells and roll them out into an 8-inch circle. Scallop the edges and prick the bottom of the shell about 12 times with the tines of a fork. Paint bottom of shell with a thin coating of Apricot Glaze. Place shell on a teflon-coated cookie pan.

Fan apple slices around the shell in a decorative fashion. Sprinkle cinnamon sugar over the top and bake in a 400° oven for 20 minutes. Paint apples and crust generously with additional Apricot Glaze and continue baking for another 20 minutes, or until glaze is a rich golden color. Serve warm or at room temperature. Serves 4.

Apricot Glaze

1/2 cup apricot jam, mash up any large pieces of fruit
1 tablespoon sugar
1 teaspoon orange liqueur

Combine all the ingredients in a saucepan and simmer the mixture for 5 minutes. Spread on tart while still warm.

Note — Frozen patty shells usually come in a package of 6. You can easily
    double the recipe and bake 2 tarts at the same time.

Nutcracker Chocolate Chip Pie

3 egg whites
1 cup sugar
1 teaspoon vanilla

20 Ritz crackers, crushed into crumbs
1 cup chopped walnuts
1/2 cup semi-sweet chocolate chips

Beat egg whites until stiff. On low setting of electric mixer beat in the remaining ingredients just until blended. Pour mixture into a 9-inch pie plate which has been lightly greased. Bake pie at 350° for 30 minutes. When pie has cooled, frost with Whipped Cream de Cacao. Refrigerate overnight. Decorate with chocolate curls or shaved chocolate. Serves 8.

Note – Pie must refrigerate for at least 6 hours so that the meringue shell softens.
   – Entire pie can be frozen. Defrost in the refrigerator.

Whipped Cream de Cacao

1 cup cream
1/2 teaspoon vanilla
1 tablespoon sugar
1 tablespoon Creme de Cacao Liqueur

Whip cream until soft peaks form. Beat in the remaining ingredients until cream is stiff.

The Easiest & Best Southern Pecan Pie

This is an absolutely extravagant and rich pie. Using the frozen pie shells makes it availble to you in a moment's notice. No need to add anything to it, but a dollup of whipped cream is very good.

3 eggs
1 cup maple syrup
1 cup dark brown sugar
2 tablespoons flour
1/8 cup melted butter (1/4 stick)
1 teaspoon vanilla

1 9-inch frozen pie shell. Use the shallow shell, not the deep-dish kind.
1 cup shelled pecans

Beat together the eggs, syrup, sugar, flour, melted butter and vanilla until the mixture is blended. Place pecans evenly into pie shell. Pour egg mixture into the crust. Place pie on a cookie sheet and bake it in a 350° oven for about 45 minutes or until pie is set. Serve at room temperature with a dollup of whipped cream. Serves 6.

Instant Lemon Soufflé with Strawberry Sauce

4 eggs
3 tablespoons lemon juice
6 tablespoons sugar
1 package (8 ounces) cream cheese

1 tablespoon finely grated lemon rind (about 1 lemon)
1 package (10 ounces) frozen strawberries in heavy syrup

In a blender container, place eggs, lemon juice, sugar and cream cheese. Blend for 5 minutes. Stir in the grated lemon peel.

Pour mixture into 4 small souffle dishes (ramekins) that have been buttered and coated with sugar. Bake ramekins in a 400° oven for 15 minutes. Centers should be a little soft. Serve with a spoonful of strawberries in syrup. Serves 4.

Note— Souffle can be whipped up several hours earlier and refrigerated. Add another 4 or 5 minutes baking time if you are using them straight from the refrigerator.

Steamed Holiday Orange
Date Nut Pudding with Rum Cream Sauce

1 package (18-1/2 ounces) yellow cake mix
1/3 cup oil
4 eggs
2 tablespoons rum
1 teaspoon baking soda
2 cups finely chopped dates
1-1/2 cups coarsely chopped walnuts
2 tablespoons grated orange peel

Beat together the cake mix, oil, eggs, rum and soda at medium speed, in the large bowl of your electric mixer for about 2 minutes. Stir in the dates, walnuts and peel until mixture is well combined.

Divide batter between 2 souffle dishes (1-1/2 quart size) that have been heavily buttered and floured. Cover each with heavy-duty aluminum foil and place a thick rubber band around the rim to seal the pudding.

Place pudding on a rack in a pan with 1-1/2 inches of water. (You will need 2 pans.) Cover and steam over medium heat for about 2 hours or until a cake tester inserted in center comes out clean. Add boiling water to pan as needed.

Allow to cool in pan and unmold onto a platter while still warm. Drizzle Rum Cream Sauce over the top in a decorative fashion. Serve warm or at room temperature. Each pudding serves 6.

Rum Cream Sauce

1 teaspoon rum
1 tablespoon cream
sifted powdered sugar

Combine rum and cream. Add enough powdered sugar to make sauce thick enough to drizzle (about 3/4 cup powdered sugar).

Note – Puddings can be made 2 or 3 days in advance. Reheat at time of serving.
   – Can be frozen for several months.
   – If you own 2 pudding molds (1 quart capacity, each), use them. They are lovely.

A chocolate souffle is a divine dessert. Serving it to family or friends is usually ignored because the classic recipe requires separating eggs, making a white sauce, beating the egg whites at the very last minute and timing the baking so that it can be served immediately. Well, this chocolate souffle is no temperamental primadonna and is assembled and put together in minutes. It can be assembled several hours before baking and merely popped into the oven 1 hour before serving. As if that weren't enough, it is also incredibly delicious and even "purists" will be impressed.

Soufflé Au Chocolat

1-1/2 cups semi-sweet chocolate chips
1 cup heavy cream

5 eggs
8 ounces cream cheese, cut into 4 pieces
pinch of salt
1 teaspoon vanilla or 1 tablespoon Rum

Place chocolate chips in blender container. Heat cream to boiling point and pour into the blender. Blend for about 1 minute. Add eggs, one at a time, while the blender continues running. Continue blending, adding the remaining ingredients until the mixture is thoroughly blended, about 1 minute.

Pour the mixture into a buttered 1-1/2-quart souffle dish and bake in a preheated 375° oven for 1 hour. Top will be slightly cracked. Serve with Creme de Vanilla spooned over the top. Serves 6 very lucky people.

Note— If you prefer using the individual souffle dishes, divide the mixture between six ramekins and bake for about 20 minutes.

Creme De Vanilla

1 cup cream
1 tablespoon sugar
1 teaspoon vanilla
1 cup vanilla ice cream, softened

Whip cream with sugar and vanilla until stiff. Fold whipped cream into the ice cream. Refrigerate until ready to serve. Can be made 2 hours before serving.

Instant Strudels & Danish

Frozen patty shells are really amazing. You can transform this simple pat of dough into cheese puffs, crusts for tarts, vol au vents, strudels and Danish. Best of all, you can keep them on hand in your freezer and they are ready at a moment's notice. They can be filled with jam, coconut, raisins, nuts, chocolate or cinnamon in any combination. Bake them for 25 minutes and they come out of the oven, light as air, crisp and delicious.

Technique

Allow patty shells to defrost enough to make them easy to handle. Roll each patty shell out to measure a 6-inch square. Sprinkle topping of your choice and roll the shell up 3 times, jelly roll fashion. Tuck in the ends and place little rolls on a teflon-coated baking pan, seam-side down. Brush tops with a little water and sprinkle generously with sugar.

Bake in a 400° oven for about 25 minutes or until the top is a deep golden brown. Remove from oven and cool. Sprinkle with sifted powdered sugar. Cut into slices with a sharp serrated knife. 1 package patty shells usually contains 6 patties.

FILLINGS FOR 1 PATTY SHELL

APRICOT WALNUT COCONUT: 1 tablespoon apricot jam
2 tablespoons chopped walnuts
1 teaspoon coconut flakes

CINNAMON CURRANT: 2 teaspoons cinnamon sugar
2 tablespoons chopped walnuts
1 tablespoon black currants

CHOCOLATE CHIP: 3 tablespoons chocolate chips
2 teaspoons Nestle's Chocolate Quik

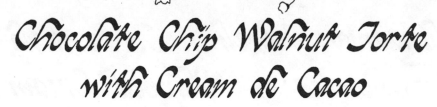

Chocolate Chip Walnut Torte with Cream de Cacao

3 eggs
1/2 cup sugar

2 cups graham cracker crumbs
1/2 cup sugar
1 teaspoon baking powder
1 teaspoon vanilla

1 cup coarsely chopped walnuts
1 cup semi-sweet chocolate chips
2 tablespoons grated orange peel

Beat eggs with 1/2 cup sugar until very light and fluffy, about 5 minutes at high speed. Stir in the remaining ingredients until they are blended.

Pour mixture into a 9-inch lightly greased pie plate and bake at 350° for 30 minutes. Frost torte with Cream de Cacao and refrigerate overnight. Serves 8.

Cream de Cacao

1 cup cream
1 tablespoon sugar
1 tablespoon Creme de Cacao liqueur

Beat cream with sugar and liqueur until stiff.

Note – *Do not be misled by the simplicity of this cake. While it assembles easily and with little trouble, it has a very sophisticated taste.*
– Torte freezes beautifully. Wrap in double plastic wrap and then foil. Remove wrappers and defrost in the refrigerator.

Hungarian Hazelnut Torte with Strawberries & Whipped Cream

This wonderful torte is spectacular for grand occasions, yet simple enough to be made at a moment's notice. Very elegant and very easy and, not the least of its virtues, it freezes beautifully.

(This recipe makes 1 layer)

4 extra large eggs
1 cup hazelnuts, toasted. Rub them between your palms to remove the skins.
3/4 cup sugar
1 teaspoon vanilla
3 tablespoons dry bread crumbs
2 teaspoons baking powder

Place eggs in blender container and whip for a few seconds. While the blender continues running, add the remaining ingredients in the order listed and blend for 30 seconds.

Pour the batter into a greased and floured 10-inch layer pan with a removable bottom. Repeat this for second layer. Bake the 2 layers at one time in a 350° oven for about 20 minutes or until a cake tester inserted in center comes out clean.

Remove rings and allow layers to cool on the metal bottoms. Remove layers with a sharp knife. Spread a layer of whipped cream on one layer. Top this with Strawberries Marnier, and then with second layer. Frost top and sides with whipped cream and decorate top with large plump halved strawberries. Serves 8 with majesty and pride.

Strawberries Marnier

Wash and pat very dry, 1 basket (1 pint) fresh strawberries. Cut them into thick slices and macerate them in 2 tablespoons Grand Marnier Liqueur for 2 hours. Drain strawberries before placing on cake.

Whipped Cream Grand Marnier

1 pint cream
4 tablespoons sugar
2 tablespoons Grand Marnier Liqueur

Beat cream until foamy. Add sugar and liqueur and continue beating until cream is stiff. Will fill and frost 1 10-inch layer cake.

ADDITIONAL COPIES OF THE LOVE OF EATING *CAN BE PURCHASED AT YOUR LOCAL BOOKSTORE OR DIRECTLY FROM:*

Recipes-of-the-month-club
P.O. BOX 5027   BEVERLY HILLS, CALIF. 90210